Adrian Brunel and British Cinema of the 1920s

Adrian Brunel and British Cinema of the 1920s

The Artist versus the Moneybags

Josephine Botting

For the other Drs Botting, Jack and Renia

Edinburgh University Press is one of the leading university presses in the UK. We publish academic books and journals in our selected subject areas across the humanities and social sciences, combining cutting-edge scholarship with high editorial and production values to produce academic works of lasting importance. For more information visit our website: edinburghuniversitypress.com

First published in hardback by Edinburgh University Press 2023

© Josephine Botting, 2023, 2025

Edinburgh University Press Ltd
13 Infirmary Street
Edinburgh EH1 1LT

Typeset in Monotype Ehrhardt by
Cheshire Typesetting Ltd, Cuddington, Cheshire

A CIP record for this book is available from the British Library

ISBN 978 1 3995 0135 4 (hardback)
ISBN 978 1 3995 0136 1 (paperback)
ISBN 978 1 3995 0137 8 (webready PDF)
ISBN 978 1 3995 0138 5 (epub)

The right of Josephine Botting to be identified as author of this work has been asserted in accordance with the Copyright, Designs and Patents Act 1988 and the Copyright and Related Rights Regulations 2003 (SI No. 2498).

Contents

List of Figures	vi
Acknowledgements	viii
List of Abbreviations	ix

Introduction: 'Might repay serious excavation . . .': Adrian Brunel as a Subject for Study   1

1. Contextualised Biography of Adrian Brunel, Part I   16
2. A Syndicate of Beggars: Minerva Films Ltd and Independent Short Film Production   42
3. Art, the Trade and *The Man Without Desire*   67
4. Making Dull Films Jolly: Brunel's Burlesques   91
5. 'A war film with a difference': *Blighty* and Brunel's Negotiation of the British Studio System   115
6. Adaptation and Screen Censorship: *The Vortex*   138
7. Adaptation and the Power of the Author: *The Constant Nymph*   156
8. Contextualised Biography of Adrian Brunel, Part II   177

Conclusion: Brunel's Legacy   200

Bibliography   211
Index   217

Figures

I.1	Adrian Brunel c. 1915	2
1.1	Adrian Brunel as a child	17
1.2	Programme for recital given in Cairo by Adey and Adrian Brunel, 3 March 1914	18
1.3	Publicity photo for Irene 'Babs' Brunel	19
1.4	Scene still from *The Cost of a Kiss*, Irene Brunel and Bertram Wallis in the foreground	20
1.5	Brunel & Montagu film can label	37
1.6	A 'hate party' gripe	37
2.1	C. Aubrey Smith and Faith Celli in *The Bump*	54
2.2	Leslie Howard and Barbara Hoffe in *£5 Reward*	55
2.3	Pressbook for the Milne comedies	58
2.4	Pressbook for *A Temporary Lady*	63
3.1	Miles Mander	71
3.2	Pressbook for *The Man Without Desire*	78
3.3	Henry Harris lines up a shot of Ivor Novello in *The Man Without Desire*	80
3.4	A lavish Venice scene from *The Man Without Desire*	81
3.5	Pressbook for *The Man Without Desire*	84
3.6	The men gather at the lawyer's office for the opening of Simon Mawdesley's letter, *The Man Without Desire*	85
4.1	Promotional postcard for *Crossing the Great Sagrada*	101
4.2	Trade promotion for Brunel's Gainsborough burlesques	111
5.1	Cartoon of C. M. Woolf	116
5.2	Nadia Sibirskaïa as 'The Girl' in *Blighty*	125
5.3	Robin meets soldiers from all walks of life at the recruitment office in *Blighty*	134
5.4	Robin's son plays with toy soldiers in a scene missing from surviving prints of *Blighty*	135
6.1	Scene still from *Easy Virtue*	147
6.2	Noël Coward visits the set of *The Vortex*	153
6.3	Advertisement for the cancelled trade show of *The Vortex*	154
7.1	*The Constant Nymph*: Trigorin and Linda, with pigs	163

7.2	*The Constant Nymph*: the Sanger family around the dinner table at Karindehütte	165
7.3	Cover of *Kinematograph Weekly* promoting *The Constant Nymph*, 2 February 1928	171
8.1	Irene and Christopher Brunel in Spain with Benita Hume during the filming of *A Light Woman*	179
8.2	Brunel with Benita Hume and the cast and crew of *A Light Woman* on location	180
8.3	Brunel & Montagu business card	183
8.4	Brunel with Donald Calthrop on the set of *Elstree Calling*	184
8.5	David Horne, Frank Moore and Sebastian Smith in a scene from *Badger's Green*	189
8.6	Mexican lobby card for *Menace*	191
8.7	Adrian Brunel awards the Brunel Cup to an amateur filmmaker	195
C.1	Adrian Brunel towards the end of his life	201
C.2	Adrian and Irene Brunel	205

Acknowledgements

Thanks to Gillian Leslie and Sam Johnson at Edinburgh University Press for making this book happen and for patiently guiding me through the process.

Many thanks also to Royal Holloway, University of London for financially supporting my doctorate, and to Professor John Hill for his expert supervision through the long years of my PhD, on which this book is based.

Many British film experts and enthusiasts have generously shared information and ideas with me. Thanks are due to: Sergio Angelini, Professor Charles Barr, Neil Brand, Geoff Brown, Kevin Brownlow, Dr Jon Burrows, Russell Campbell, Bryony Dixon, Lucie Dutton, Professor John Ellis, Tony Fletcher, David Francis, Mark Fuller, Bob Geoghegan, Alex Gleason, Professor Christine Gledhill, Julian Grainger, Ronald Grant and Martin Humphries at the Cinema Museum, Janice Headland, Dr Paul Moody, Professor Robert Murphy, Mark Newell, Jonathan Rigby and David Wyatt. Special thanks to Dr Lucy Bolton for introducing me to EUP.

The BFI Special Collections team assisted greatly with access to Brunel's papers, in particular Carolyne Bevan, Nigel Good and Nathalie Morris; thanks also to Nigel Algar for allowing me time to research, despite resistance from above. The staff at the BFI Reuben Library have been very helpful, especially Ian O'Sullivan, whose assistance was invaluable. Dr Jon Burrows and Sarah Easen kindly provided me with a haven for periods of writing; my mother, Dr Regina Botting, also greatly encouraged my work.

It has been a real pleasure getting to know Adrian Brunel's heir, Annie Kentfield, and her partner Jamie, who have been incredibly supportive.

Lastly, love and apologies to Conor and Alec, who have had much less of my attention than they deserve.

Abbreviations

ABSC   Adrian Brunel Special Collection. Material from this collection is referenced by item and box number, i.e. ABSC 5/112 refers to item 5 in Box 112
BFIRL   BFI Reuben Library
IMSC   Ivor Montagu Special Collection
KW   *Kinematograph Weekly*
MPS   *Motion Picture Studio*
n.d.   no date

INTRODUCTION

'Might repay serious excavation . . .': Adrian Brunel as a Subject for Study

On 4 May 1929, Adrian Brunel attended a gala evening at London's Marble Arch Pavilion. In front of a packed auditorium, he was presented with a Certificate of Merit for directing *The Constant Nymph*, which had been voted Best British Film of 1928 by the readers of *Film Weekly* magazine. On the surface, this was the most triumphant moment of his career: the feature had not only been hailed as a fine example of British film art but had also been a massive box office success for Gainsborough Pictures. Yet behind the gloss of the occasion lay deep divisions between the main players in the film's production. Studio head Michael Balcon refused to go on stage, so the film's star, Mabel Poulton, accepted the award on his behalf. Balcon and Brunel were not on speaking terms since Brunel had launched a legal battle against the studio over its apparent breach of his contract, and was suing them for unpaid fees. Brunel's 'supervisory director' on the film, Basil Dean, did not attend the ceremony; their working relationship had been extremely strained and, as an experienced filmmaker, Brunel's pride had been dented at having to deputise for a novice.

This event serves to highlight some of the contradictions in Brunel's turbulent film career. Each success emerged from a challenging production history and tells a story of conflict and compromise. Each also preceded a period of intense frustration and unemployment. The acclaim he received for *The Constant Nymph* from both the press and audiences appeared to vindicate his long-held conviction that art and popularity in the cinema were not mutually exclusive. But, by 1929, silent film was effectively dead, his methods seemed outdated and his career as a director of 'A' pictures was over.

This book sets out to examine and assess Adrian Brunel's film career during the 1920s through a consideration of his films and the industrial context in which they were produced, supported by detailed research into his personal papers and other contemporary sources. The intention is to bring new insights into his films by anatomising their production context

Figure I.1 Adrian Brunel c. 1915. Source: author's own collection.

and history. Each film, or group of films, is examined in relation to a particular issue or debate preoccupying the industry at the time, taking account of the difficulties posed by the unstable environment in which Brunel was at work.

Brunel is a worthy and rewarding subject for study due to the varied and unusual nature of his silent oeuvre and the contrasting production set-ups within which he worked, as well as the comprehensive record of his life and work that he left behind. His attempts to inject a level of 'art' into British filmmaking brought him into conflict with the industry powers and he was thus compelled to engage in complex negotiations in order to try and protect his artistic integrity. Mapping out the journey from inception to completion of his works reveals the obstacles he encountered during the process and the ways in which he navigated them. Brunel was a key figure in the tussle between the industry's commercial interests and the creative aspirations of many of those who worked under or alongside them; an exploration of his working practice can thus illuminate the impediments to such expression that were inherent in the British film industry of the 1920s.

The Context of British Silent Cinema

When Brunel first entered the British film industry towards the end of the First World War, it was going through an extremely difficult time. Having experienced its vagaries first-hand, Brunel felt well placed to provide a personal view of it and, in 1929, some months after winning the *Film Weekly* award, he wrote a lengthy summary of the situation as he saw it. He acknowledged the toll that the war had taken on the country's prospects; during the conflict, audience numbers rose but could not be catered for by an industry badly affected, both financially and in creative terms, by the loss of key practitioners through conscription. America lost no time and stepped in to put films on British screens, so by the end of the war its domination of world markets was well underway. Brunel's description of the postwar British film industry as 'depleted, impoverished, old fashioned and out-of-practice . . . impeded at every step by officialdom' (1929: 2) differs little from the narrative related by more recent historians (for example, Burrows 2003: 5).

Brunel regarded the government's failure to combat American domination as largely to blame for the British industry's difficulties, which were worsened by a lack of funding. This not only affected the quality of the films but also the ability of firms to sustain production while waiting to recoup profits, since films often took months to reach the screen. Cinemas were committed to showing American product due to the block- and blind-booking practices employed by US companies. While several Hollywood studios had become vast vertically integrated concerns profiting directly from their own films, as Rachael Low observed, 'much British production was conducted on a hand-to-mouth basis with an advance here and an advance there until the film was completed somehow' (1971: 278). This certainly reflects the way Brunel worked for the first half of the 1920s, and the lack of finance going into the film industry meant that production facilities were barely adequate.

The German government had instigated protective measures for its own film industry in 1922, stipulating that distributors had to match foreign product with national on an equal basis. This, according to Brunel, increased investment and saw the country's annual output rise to 240 films by 1927 (Britain produced 40); more importantly, Brunel observed, 'German picture-goers had learned to prefer their home made films' (1929: 2). In Britain, however, production continued to slow and exhibition figures for British films shown at home gradually fell, partly due to the slowdown but also because British firms simply could not combat the highly organised and aggressive distribution methods of American companies. In 1926, domestic production reached its nadir; Tom Ryall describes it as a 'calamitous year' in which only 5 per cent of trade shows were for British films (1996: 39).

This is a well-researched and much-debated period in British cinema as historians have tried to explain the reasons for the slump. The failure of many of the film companies operating in Britain partly explains the contraction, and some went out of business after one or two productions, unable to sustain themselves. But the issues facing the industry were not purely to do with quantity, and questions were also raised about the quality of British films. The popularity of American productions caused concern about the effect such films were having on British culture and society. Articles with titles like 'Do the Public Hate Our Pictures?' and 'What is Wrong with British Films?' appeared regularly in the trade papers and indicated the sense of inferiority from which the industry was suffering. Inroads have been made into dispelling the notion that British films were not popular with audiences (see Burrows 2003 and Morris 2009) and Christine Gledhill actually regards 1926 as a good year for production due to the quality of the output (2008: 163). However, it is clear that many were convinced that British films were generally of an inferior standard and two main reasons came to the fore: a failure of creative leadership and a lack of investment.

Brunel himself openly blamed 'the vulgar, uneducated film boss' (*MPS*, 26 August 1922: 6) for holding back the development of British filmmaking; actor Hugh Miller, three years later his co-founder of the Film Society, echoed this view, attributing the inadequacy of British films to a 'lack of imagination' on the part of financiers, who failed to recognise film as an art (*MPS*, 9 September 1922: 6). Liberal MP J. M. Kenworthy lamented that 'the production of . . . beautiful British films appears to be a dying industry', noting that the number of producers had dropped from twenty to just four or five in two years (1925: 16). He regarded the poor reputation of film production among financiers and the superior business acumen of American producers as major culprits. Bemoaning the damaging effect that transatlantic domination had not only on the nation's industry but also on 'our national culture and the imperial aspect generally', he called for the government to stimulate 'combination, organisation and capital' (ibid.: 17).

Two years later, the government announced the introduction of legislation in support of the British film industry. The Cinematograph Film Act (or Quota Act) came into force on 1 April 1928 and set a quota for the proportion of British films that were to be exhibited in British cinemas. It was similar in principle to the German Kontingent but with much lower quotas: distributors had to ensure that 7.5 per cent of the films they offered were UK productions, while exhibitors had to devote 5 per cent of their programme to British films. These quotas were due to be raised in stages till they reached 20 per cent by 1936, and measures were also put in place to prevent block- and blind-booking.

While most in the industry welcomed the move, producer T. A. Welsh (business partner of British director George Pearson) regarded it as misguided, asserting that there were insufficient studios in operation to meet the level of production needed to fill the quota. At first the Act proved very effective in stimulating the production of British films, Low recording that from the low point of 37 films made in 1926, the figure rose to 72 in 1928 (1971: 156). However, Welsh's assessment turned out to be correct; while the number of films increased, quality did not improve, since British studios, ill-equipped to cope with a surge in production, struggled to keep up with demand. The introduction of sound later that year set the industry back even further, as the expensive recording equipment was beyond the means of most producers.

For Brunel, the development of talking pictures armed America with a weapon to 'crush the British Film Industry at a time when it was really in the process of getting on its feet' (1929: 3). The high cost of equipping studios for sound recording and the shelving of many silent films further affected already struggling firms. Meanwhile, American studios, initially affected by the quota, soon found a way to combat its effects; the British market was extremely valuable to them, especially when the arrival of sound established a strong link in the form of the common language. Therefore some US studios established British operations to produce cheap films to fulfil the quota while others contracted small local producers to do the work for them. It was this practice that led to the production of what are referred to as 'quota quickies': British films made on a tiny budget and a tight schedule to meet regulations regarding the exhibition of domestic films.

Revisiting British Silent Film

As this summary shows, the British film industry of the 1920s was beset with problems and for many years historians did not consider the films it produced worthy of serious research. The first in-depth study of the postwar years was the fourth volume of Rachael Low's *The History of the British Film*, published in 1971. Low's work is immensely valuable for bringing together information from a large variety of contemporary written sources into a comprehensive history. However, academics have noted her general dismissiveness of British films; indeed, her views must be considered at least partly responsible for the negative reputation that British silent cinema had for many years. This lack of esteem was cemented by film historian Kevin Brownlow, who wrote: 'English films, with few exceptions, were crudely photographed; the direction and acting were on the level of cheap revue, they exploited so-called stars, who generally had little more than a glimmer of histrionic talent, and they were exceedingly boring' (1973: 591). Kenton Bamford expanded on Low's groundwork in his well-researched *Distorted Images: British National Identity and Film* (1999), but failed to reach more positive conclusions about the films.

More recent studies have countered the generally negative views of the period expressed by Low, Brownlow and Bamford. The British Silent Film Festival, which began in 1998, has generated more sympathetic research into the subject and encouraged a rethink of the criteria by which the films have been judged. For example, Gledhill's study of the 1920s takes an intermedial approach, examining how cinema incorporated other popular forms, with the aim of dispelling the perception that British filmmakers failed to develop original strategies to differentiate their product from that of other film-producing nations.

Brunel in Revisionist Studies

The varied nature of Brunel's contributions to British cinema has meant that commentators have struggled to define him. Low described him as 'something of an enigma' who was 'in the forefront of the movement towards film art . . . [b]ut despite a light wit and keen critical judgement, as a director he only made what Balcon later described as good little pictures' (1971: 170). Bob Baker ventured: '[i]t's hard to say whether we're speaking here of a great talent crushed by the moguls, but I think probably not . . . for further investigation but without, perhaps, expecting too much' (1974).

More recently, in line with the general reappraisal of the period, there has been a more generous consideration of him. Brian McFarlane makes the tentative suggestion that '[h]is work might repay serious excavation' (2003: 93), while Geoff Brown characterises him as 'one of the liveliest new directing talents working in Britain' (2005). Robert Murphy's entry on Brunel in the *Dictionary of National Biography* comes to the following conclusion:

> Undoubtedly Brunel could have achieved a great deal more in the right environment, and he suffered painful disappointment at the continual setbacks to his career.

> But his autobiography is testimony to his resilience and resourcefulness in carving out an interesting career . . . enjoying the 'nice work' of film-making when he could get it and employing his energies productively elsewhere when he couldn't. (2016)

Jamie Sexton uses Brunel's burlesques as evidence of alternative film-making practices during the 1920s, while Lawrence Napper's work on cinema's engagement with middlebrow culture identifies him as a figure who attempted to bridge the highbrow/lowbrow divide in British cinema. Kerzoncuf and Barr describe him as 'a bright young man' (30) who made a significant contribution to the Gainsborough titles he worked on in the mid-1920s. These include the early films of Alfred Hitchcock, who, they assert, benefited from his association with Brunel, then moved on when there was 'nothing more to learn' (97).

These views of Brunel and his work will be explored in the course of this study, and the contention that he was a significant player in the development of British film art is one of the major threads running through it. As part of the ongoing rehabilitation of 1920s British cinema, this book is intended to complement and extend the work undertaken thus far, providing a more detailed look at the attempts to develop a British cinema that could succeed on both artistic and popular lines.

Brunel's Biographical Legend

Brunel's memoir of his career, *Nice Work*, is entertaining, at times self-deprecating and sprinkled with anecdotes, yet gives only a partial account, with many omissions. It is a key element of the 'biographical legend' he created, the mythology that 'mediates between the empirical life history of an artist or film maker and the artistic texts themselves' (Ryall 1996: 6), created by self-promotion through interviews, articles, books and press material. Brunel was an avid writer and commentator who left behind a wealth of such material, using it to create his own mythology through the constant retelling of what he regarded as important moments in his career.

An example of this myth-making is Brunel's accounts of his 1923 burlesque film *Crossing the Great Sagrada*. Regularly returning to it over the next twenty-five years, he clearly regarded it as a highlight of his career, and with each telling, its meagre budget went up or down, while his recollections of the proportions of its constituent parts (off-cuts, titles and new footage) vary considerably. He recounted the story of its making frequently, elevating its significance as part of his own history and the history of British cinema. He claimed that it made a tidy profit (Brunel 1949: 108) and led to an offer from a Hollywood studio (Brunel 1928: 44), neither of which can be substantiated by documentation in his collection. Conversely, though he stated that his burlesques were never shown abroad (ibid.), his collection contains a credit note for their sale to South Africa, Burma, India and Ceylon (memos, ABSC 3/112). Brunel also omits the fact that two burlesques were made by another director, Harry Hughes, and he made no effort to preserve these, as he did so assiduously with his own. Thus Brunel was selective in his choice of facts and with what he physically preserved, and this book aims to temper some of the perceptions of him and his work that he had a hand in shaping.

The most striking contrast that Brunel's papers bring to his legend is that between his public and private personas. While his industry writings are marked by a light-hearted humour, the tone of his letters to friends and colleagues ranges from pleading and desperate to indignant and outraged. His mode of address was influenced by his relationship to the recipient; he was polite to the point of obsequiousness to C. M. Woolf and Graham Cutts, who wielded considerable power at Gainsborough, while his correspondence with studio manager George Hopton, and occasionally to studio head and friend Michael Balcon, could be self-important and lacking in respect.

An arrogant tone also surfaced in Brunel's early trade articles and may at least partly account for the negative reputation he had among some industry figures. The majority of his former colleagues regarded him with fondness, at least when writing their autobiographies from the safe distance of several decades. But one description of him is in marked contrast to this, although its author had his own axe to grind. In 1923, Brunel's first business partner, Harry Fowler Mear, wrote an article for *Motion Picture Studio* about his negative experiences in the film business. Though not mentioning Brunel by name, he recounted being approached by an 'individual tastefully attired in an American suit and sombrero hat, complete with shoulders, side-whiskers, and cigar' who was 'a trifle too glib to be absolutely convincing'. Mear paints Brunel as a confidence trickster, suggesting that he got Mear drunk and persuaded him to invest his money in producing a film. Clearly still bitter about the episode, Mear's intention in writing the article seems to have been to smear Brunel in a journal read by many of his peers and associates. Brunel was undoubtedly wounded and his copy of the article has several phrases carefully underlined, presumably those he felt were most unjust. He took criticism very personally and his papers contain many letters that testify to his sensitivity to perceived or actual slights, particularly those questioning his skill and integrity as a filmmaker.

Why Study Adrian Brunel?

Several British directors had careers that followed a similar trajectory to Brunel's and are worthy of investigation: George Pearson, Manning Haynes, Graham Cutts and Walter Summers were all hailed as promising, even great, directors during the silent era, only to find themselves relegated to making low-budget pictures in the 1930s. What makes Brunel a particularly good subject is the fact that he has bequeathed a remarkably comprehensive written record of his career in the form of the Adrian Brunel Special Collection (ABSC), which consists of 262 boxes of papers housed at the BFI National Archive, part of the British Film Institute. This offers an unparalleled insight into his life and work and forms a key component of this study.

Among the papers are notes for a radio talk entitled 'The Systematic Jackdaw'; it appears that it was never broadcast but Brunel probably pitched it to the BBC in the 1950s. Subtitled 'The fun and value of collecting things', it reveals that Brunel found it 'difficult to throw away anything that comes into my possession that interests me . . . as a result, I have a fascinating . . . treasure trove of interesting odds and ends.' Since this trove came to the BFI, it has become one of the most frequently accessed paper collections, consulted by researchers piecing together the early careers of Alfred Hitchcock or Ivor Montagu, or building a complete catalogue of Bonzo the Dog cartoons, of which Brunel scripted several in the mid-1920s. Many more 'odds and ends' still remain to be fully unearthed from his archive, such as the details of an airship design that William Friese-Greene apparently sold to the Germans, insights into the business dealings between Brunel's father and Bram Stoker, and Brunel's encounters with realist filmmaker-to-be Karel Reisz in the early 1950s. Discovering unknown documents such as these can provide researchers with revelatory moments, but it is only by surveying the whole collection to assemble the jigsaw of a long and troubled career that Brunel's 'jackdaw' habits really prove their value.

As well as keeping his papers, Brunel also preserved most of his silent films, donating them to the BFI in the 1930s, and his prominence in recent work on British cinema of the 1920s is at least partly attributable to the foresight he showed in ensuring their survival. The only other British directors whose silent films have been subjected to sustained reappraisal are those whose oeuvre is similarly intact, although the films have endured for different reasons; nine of Hitchcock's ten silent productions and all four of Anthony Asquith's exist. However, these survival rates are unusual for films of the period; in fact, one of the major hindrances to a satisfactory re-evaluation of silent cinema is the paucity of extant titles. It is estimated that 75–80 per cent of all silent films produced are lost (Houston: 15) and it is therefore likely that many interesting directors will never have their silent careers reassessed.

Examining the 1920s through the work of a single figure has never been undertaken in this way; in fact, director-focused analyses of the British silent period are all but non-existent.[1] Ryall's contextualised history *Alfred Hitchcock and the British Cinema* situates the director's films in relation to other cultural and industrial developments but does not offer a detailed account of their production or his interaction with the structures and practices within which he worked. This book aims to delve deeper into the work of Brunel, looking at it in relation to debates within the trade and beyond, while the richness of the supplementary material reveals the characters involved with the production process, the choices and decisions they were responsible for and how those shaped the final product. The aim is to assess the degree to which Brunel was able to exercise creative freedom in his work and what this tells us about the industry and British film culture.

David Bordwell has defined four working situations that were available to European filmmakers during the silent era: to be employed by a studio or production company, to be contracted to the 'artistic' wing of such a firm, to form an independent company or to 'join a group making films outside the industry for specific artistic or political ends' (1981: 10). Of these, three existed in the British film industry and Brunel worked across them all at various points in his career. British studios had neither the resources nor the disposition to develop 'artistic' wings, though such an enterprise may have provided the 'right environment' that Murphy suggests could have seen Brunel's career flourish.

The traditional *auteurist* approach to film studies has evolved over recent years. The analysis of the work of a director in isolation from its production context has its limitations, since it fails to acknowledge film as a text influenced and affected by many different agents. It is also problematic when applied to British cinema, since the instability and fragmented nature of the national industry has meant that few directors have been able to develop the kind of consistent and lengthy careers that permit them *auteur* status. However, new ways of employing *auteurism* can assist

---

[1] There are two academic works on early pioneers of the silent period in Britain: Simon Brown's *Cecil Hepworth and the Rise of the British Film Industry 1899–1911* and Luke McKernan's *Charles Urban: Pioneering the Non-Fiction Film in Britain and America, 1897–1925*, both published by University of Exeter Press.

with an evaluation of Brunel's career. Peter Hutchings rightly observes that '[b]agging another *auteur* for Britain is not necessarily the best way of developing our understanding of British cinema' (2000: 179) and instead offers a template for applying notions of authorship to directors within the British commercial sphere who, like Brunel, worked across diverse genres and production set-ups. Hutchings observes that Britain has produced many directors whose careers were 'truncated, interrupted or subject to sometimes bewildering transformations' (ibid.: 182), and thus Brunel's trajectory is less unusual than it may at first appear. Hutchings highlights the difficulty in establishing a 'cohesive authorial voice' in these careers but maintains that this need not invalidate the exercise of studying British cinema through the work of such directors, since it can provide insight into the industry itself and the changing role of the director.

If we accept that Brunel's authorial voice can be heard more clearly in the films over which he exerted greater control, it becomes necessary to define what is meant by 'control' and how it is secured. Kristin Thompson (2004) has usefully compared the Hollywood production process to that in France, Germany and Russia, where a more 'avant-garde' approach to filmmaking developed. She notes that a fairly rigid division of labour was established in Hollywood much earlier than in Europe, where directors continued to have an involvement in writing and editing their films until the late 1920s. She suggests that experimentation was therefore almost impossible in American studios, while European directors may have had more scope to expand narrative and aesthetic boundaries. Although similar opportunities for experimentation were not readily available in Britain, establishing the roles that Brunel undertook on each of his films is important in order to try and evaluate in what areas he was able to exert influence over the work.

As late as 1927, there was a feeling within the British industry that film directors were overstretched. *The Bioscope* reported that 'in many cases a director has had to find his story, write his scenario, do his own costing and casting, cut and title the film when completed, and on occasion play a leading part, in addition to carrying out several other odd jobs' (18 June 1927: 99). While it seems unlikely that this level of activity was still the norm by the late 1920s, Brunel's paper collection and other records bear testament to the many tasks he undertook on his productions. For his first major project, directing the A. A. Milne comedies in 1920, he claimed to have 'written the scripts, cast the pictures, designed some of the sets and dressed all of them' (1949: 58), and even while working at Gainsborough, memos show that he was often involved in writing, casting, costing and editing his films. Although performing several tasks within the production process appears to offer greater control, the pressure of this workload may also have hampered a director's ability to give full attention to the job of directing.

In Brunel's case, his level of involvement in a production was generally, though not always, in inverse proportion to the film's budget. During the 1920s, the role of the director was changing, and figures such as Brunel, who had mastered the techniques of screenwriting and editing and were keen to have an input into all three aspects of production, were becoming less common. While the skills he developed across these different roles allowed him to participate more fully in a production and therefore gave him greater scope to engage in experimentation, they also led to conflicts with the other creative and commercial forces at work.

Art versus Commerce

The chief source of these disagreements was Brunel's unwillingness to compromise his creative aspirations. He has been portrayed as both 'the odd-job man of British movies' (Baker 1974: 41) and a free-spirited highbrow, and this dichotomy is one of the central tensions that needs exploring. He sought to bring originality and innovation to British films and to dispense with what he regarded as some of the bad habits that the national cinema had developed. Yet working within the confines of commercial production restricted how far he could fulfil this aim and often saw him relegated to non-directorial roles.

At this time, the potential for cinema as an art form was beginning to be appreciated and, although Britain did not participate to any great extent in the early stages of avant-garde filmmaking, there was much debate on the subject among intellectuals. Brunel was an enthusiastic participant in these debates and a founding member of The Film Society, one of the aims of which was to encourage British directors to adopt some of the stylistic techniques of European films. As mentioned, some European nations had begun to challenge America's cultural hegemony by cultivating ways to distinguish their product from the classical narrative form. The Russians regarded film as a political tool, employing montage techniques to create association and opposition of ideas, while the German response to Hollywood dominance was to apply an aesthetic from the art world, using Expressionism to create an unsettling feel to the films. The perception has been, however, that Britain failed either to successfully compete with America in the entertainment stakes or to develop its own style of cinema which would allow representation of its national values on the screen. 'British cinema was never a popular cinema in any true sense of the word,' opined Roy Armes (1978: 61).

Gledhill has asserted that Brunel was part of a new coterie of creatives who 'saw in cinema . . . a means of negotiating the highbrow/lowbrow distinction which emerged in English cultural consciousness at the turn of the century' (2000: 86–7). However, there was little tolerance within commercial cinema for such experiments. Ryall takes the view that '[t]he radical separation of "art" cinema from its commercial counterpart prevented any interaction between the two that might have helped to create a more aesthetically interesting entertainment cinema in Britain during the interwar years' (1996: 21). This distinction between commerce and minority culture is common to most views of the period; the British film industry is portrayed as unsupportive, even suspicious, of artiness, and obsessed with turning a profit for as little investment as possible. This perception remains largely unchallenged and where glimmers of creativity can be identified in commercial cinema, they are relatively isolated and run counter to the general trend. Michael Balcon later reflected that '[w]e were in the business of giving the public what it seemed to want in entertainment. We did not talk about art or social significance' (1969: 27).

This tension emerges through detailed reference to the exchanges between Brunel and his employers, and will hopefully contribute to an understanding of why Brunel's career ultimately failed, despite his work being lauded. His first feature, *The Man Without Desire*, prompted one reviewer to predict that 'the name of Adrian Brunel is going to be big – a coming master' (typed reviews, ABSC 176), while, after seeing *The Constant Nymph*, another critic declared him 'among the leading picture directors of this country' (typed reviews, ABSC 8/56). Was this pattern of extreme highs and barren periods in between solely attributable to the precariousness of the film industry, or did Brunel's inability to successfully navigate it contribute to his erratic career path?

Structure

Chapter 1 and Chapter 8 provide a contextualised historical overview of Adrian Brunel's life and career. The biography is divided into two sections: Chapter 1 outlines the period up to 1928 and the production of *The Constant Nymph*, where the book's main focus ends, and Chapter 8 covers his subsequent career. Working from a detailed chronology constructed from my paper-based original research, it pieces together Brunel's career and identifies recurrent themes and subjects within it, laying the foundation for the chapters examining his key productions of the 1920s. This breakdown of Brunel's activities across all areas of his life gives context to his filmmaking pursuits, highlights continuities across his work and interests, and illustrates how problems affecting the industry in the 1920s persisted into later decades. The biography is key to the establishment of Brunel's 'biographical legend' and demonstrates how the trajectories of his contemporaries and associates both mirrored and contrasted with his own, recording when and how these figures resurfaced in different situations.

What emerges most strikingly from this career overview is the sheer volume of activity Brunel engaged in and that, throughout his working life, he juggled a number of projects at the same time. While this testifies to his energy and diligence, it also points up the insecurity of the structures he operated in, which forced him to seek extra sources of income in order to support himself. This intense and varied activity forms a complex timeline, where jobs overlap or run concurrently and enterprises evolve and change. Plotting such a multifaceted career and tracing all the threads within it adds valuable context to the production of his films.

Chapters 2 to 7 provide a detailed analysis of the production and reception of each of Brunel's silent works. Each chapter focuses on a film or group of films and explores them within the context of one aspect of the industry that affected their production, outlining the issues he had bringing them to the screen. This charts his attempts to prove that films with an original and creative approach could find commercial success and help to establish a sustainable British film industry. Detailing the production histories in this way contributes to a greater understanding of the different filmmaking environments in which he worked.

Chapter 2 looks at the role of the short film within the context of 1920s British cinema, a subject on which very little has been written. It evaluates the attempts by the British trade to sustain the form as a viable commercial product and examines Brunel's efforts to develop the short comedy along new lines, through the films made during his time with Minerva Films between 1920 and 1921, where he gained his first real directorial experience.

In Chapter 3, the relationship between filmmakers and the film trade is explored via a study of Brunel's first feature, *The Man Without Desire*. It examines the discussions taking place in the British press regarding the consideration of film as an art form and how these debates influenced and affected the form and reception of Brunel's film.

Chapter 4 looks at the production of Brunel's burlesque films and the various ways they have been positioned as examples of experimental filmmaking in Britain in the 1920s. Through a detailed exploration of their production history, this chapter examines some of the assertions made about the burlesques by focusing on Brunel's intentions and techniques.

In the years following the First World War there was a rash of films that took the conflict as their theme. Chapter 5 looks at Brunel's war film, *Blighty*, also his first studio feature, and considers how successfully he managed to adapt this problematic genre to represent his own political and aesthetic concerns.

Chapters 6 and 7 explore the lack of original screenwriting in British cinema, the issues created by producers' reliance on existing literary works, and the role of the censor and the author in the filmmaking process. Brunel's own desire to encourage greater originality in British cinema was thwarted by his employers' insistence on assigning him to the direction of adaptations. The study in these two chapters of the making of his next two films, *The Vortex* (1927) and *The Constant Nymph*, gives an insight into the way he negotiated the many tensions inherent in this process.

Finally, the Conclusion reflects on Brunel's legacy and the reasons why his career failed, as did the careers of many of the most successful figures of the silent period.

Conclusion

Adrian Brunel is a figure whose history can bring new perspectives to the British film industry of the 1920s. The wealth of unique documentation in the Brunel collection reveals much about the relationships and dynamics between industry players as well as their views and attitudes towards filmmaking. An increased understanding of this period of British film history can help identify the roots of some of the difficulties the industry has experienced in subsequent decades.

Through his relatively modest, yet eclectic and unusual filmography, Brunel attempted to extend the boundaries of British cinema and, although his ambitions often failed, even his unsuccessful projects reveal much about his aspirations and the industry. Various tensions emerge from this exploration of Brunel's filmmaking: between art and commerce, freedom and control, and distinctiveness and conformity. The nature of these competing imperatives and how Brunel negotiated them in the course of his filmmaking will go towards a better understanding of the obstacles to the development of a viable domestic industry that existed in Britain.

CHAPTER 1

Contextualised Biography of Adrian Brunel, Part I

Early Life and Schooling

Adrian Brunel was born at 58 Claverton Street, Pimlico, London on 4 September 1889.[1] His mother, Frances Lucy Adelaide Brunel Norman (known as Adey Brunel), earned a living giving elocution lessons and delivering poetry recitals, in her 'rich, soft and musical' voice (press notices, ABSC 161), as well as writing poems and short stories under the pen name Dale Laurence. Brunel's father also went by different names; born Reginald Brunel Harris, he ran 'The Concorde Concert Control' as Reginald Norman-Concorde, promoting his wife's recitals and arranging musical performances of various kinds. His headed notepaper is adorned with commendations of his services but, while he may have been a reliable agent, it seems he was less so as a husband, since Adey divorced him in 1903 over an affair with his secretary. Composer Frederick Delius, one of her ex-husband's clients, subsequently wrote to congratulate her on getting rid of 'that awful man' (4 November 1904, ABSC 2/158). From the age of fourteen, Adrian did not see his father and rarely, if ever, mentioned him.

His close relationship with his mother was very important to his formative years and she remained a key influence throughout his life, her love of the arts and circle of literary and musical friends shaping Brunel's sensibilities. He took a great interest in women's issues and campaigned with the suffragettes, submitted plays to the Women's Theatre Company and, in 1931, addressed one of the first gatherings of the Gateway Club, London's famous lesbian haunt. Although Adey was not able to afford the formal education she would have liked for him, she ensured that he engaged in a wide range of artistic pursuits and developed a love of travel.

---

[1] Several sources quote his year of birth as 1892 but census information confirms he was born three years earlier.

Figure 1.1 Adrian Brunel as a child. Source: author's own collection.

Brunel attended Harrow only briefly, between 1903 and January 1905,[2] but found the 'old school tie' invaluable in later life. He then had an eight-month stint at Lloyd's Bank, against the advice of Harrow's headmaster Joseph Wood, who wrote: 'He is a promising boy ... but to send him out at ... fifteen would be very hard for him, and would spoil his future career' (15 June 1905, ABSC 5/163).

War Intervenes

The 1911 census records Brunel as unemployed and living with his mother in Portslade, part of Brighton and Hove. He was training to be an opera singer and, in 1913, he and his mother performed in Egypt, *The Egyptian Gazette* remarking on his 'tenor voice of rare quality' (n.d., ABSC 176). He also tried his hand at writing and acting, the reviewer of the *Sussex Daily News* complimenting his 'remarkable little character portraits' (25 July 1913), which he would capture on film ten years later in his burlesques. He began submitting plot outlines to film companies, titles such as *His Leading Lady* and *The New Star* suggesting that even then he was keen on cinema itself as a subject for films. Croydon-based Clarendon Film Company expressed interest in his ideas but would not accede to his request to have his name on screen (28 July 1913, ABSC 'C'/170). The outbreak of war in August 1914 cut off many of the avenues he had been pursuing and, despite being a pacifist, he tried to join up to avoid accusations of cowardice; however, a foot injury barred him from active service.

[2] Email to the author from the Harrow School archivist, 10 May 2014.

Figure 1.2 Programme for recital given in Cairo by Adey and Adrian Brunel, 3 March 1914. Source: author's own collection.

Brunel's upbringing was to have a profound influence on his career. He was always to feel an inferiority due to his lack of education and wealth but the cultural stimulation he received gave him a wide range of creative ideas to draw on when he turned to the cinema.

Moss Empire

Brunel's first job in the industry was not on the creative side; in August 1915 he started working for Moss Empire's Bioscope, the film-renting department of the successful theatre and cinema chain. For an annual salary of £130 he was employed to sell the 'exclusive' films on their books; these were films renters charged extra for because they had the greatest box office potential. Years later, Brunel reminisced about his time with the company:

> I lived, breathed, ate and dreamt pictures ... I sat in my outer office arranging the transit cross-overs of such masterpieces as 'The Colonel's Wife', 'A Study in Scarlet' ... and the many other productions of the Samuelson and Clarendon film companies. I followed their success from St. Annes to Wigan; I studied the reactions of Liverpool and Dublin; I speculated on their reception at Plymouth and Ilfracombe. (*The Era*, 1 January 1936: 25)

Figure 1.3 Publicity photo for Irene 'Babs' Brunel. Source: author's own collection.

On 6 May 1916, Brunel married Irene Raphael, known to friends as 'Babs', and they moved in with Adey at 19 Randolph Crescent in London's Maida Vale. Also from a cultured family, Irene proved an ideal companion for Brunel and they entertained a wide range of society and industry figures.

Mirror Films

Late in 1916, Brunel left Moss to form Mirror Films with Harrow acquaintance Harry Fowler Mear, and they began production of a five-reel subject. Despite their tiny budget of around £700 (Mear's inheritance), the pair secured the acting services of musical star Bertram Wallis for what was to be his first film appearance. The trend for casting well-known stage actors in British silent films during the 1910s has been studied by Jon Burrows, who describes how several companies adopted a policy of filming theatre productions starring the actors who had made them famous (Burrows 2003). Brunel and Mear were thus employing a popular marketing tactic, but their approach differed in that they wrote an original screenplay, perhaps due to the high cost of purchasing an existing play. The title, 'In Old Madrid', was from a popular song (presumably in Wallis's repertoire) but it was later renamed *The Cost of a Kiss*.

Figure 1.4 Scene still from *The Cost of a Kiss*, Irene Brunel and Bertram Wallis in the foreground. Source: author's own collection.

The film synopsis registered on 24 November 1916 with the Incorporated Society of Authors, Playwrights and Composers reveals how far Brunel and Mear overreached themselves in their ambitions ('In Old Madrid', ABSC 2/158). The settings are listed as Madrid, Paris, London, Devonshire and the Sierra, while the action spans twenty years in its tale of an unfaithful wife, a husband killed defending her honour and a daughter who vows to avenge her father's death. Locations include a lavish villa, a Spanish hunting lodge and a bandit's lair over a ravine, a combination that would have stretched the resources of a major studio, let alone a pair of novices with minimal finances.

Brunel does not reveal how they recreated these exotic locales at the tiny Ebury Studios in Pimlico, London but later confessed to his ignorance of another aspect of filmmaking. 'It was to be a 4,000 foot film,' he wrote, 'and so we ordered 4,000 feet of negative . . . there was one department of production we had not studied, nor even thought of as an important creative process . . . and that was editing' (1949: 34–5). The trade show for *The Cost of a Kiss* was held on 20 February 1917 at the West End Cinema in Coventry Street. *The Cinema* had already promoted the film as 'an interesting production' in which Bertram Wallis gave 'a remarkable and finished performance' (8 February 1917, ABSC 2/107). No further reviews have surfaced and no sales were made, Mear concluding that the film was 'junk'. His attempts to recoup something from the project came to nothing, mainly because the negative had been damaged by the processors, Kine Industries, and in July 1918 he conceded 'I have to face the fact that I have an absolutely unsaleable article on my hands' (3 July 1918, ABSC 107).[3]

Brunel's experience on *The Cost of a Kiss* taught him several valuable lessons, above all the importance of editing. He also became very protective of his celluloid assets, having seen how easily a film could be ruined. In addition he realised that, while it was possible to make a film with a small amount of capital, the inadequacies of film handling and distribution services in Britain at the time meant that getting a decent copy in front of a paying audience was extremely difficult. The problems of distribution facing smaller producers continued well into the 1920s and were to be a major frustration for Brunel.

---

[3] Brunel attempted to release the film in 1921 but failed. He was still receiving correspondence from Mear about it in 1924.

War Work

Brunel was still attempting to secure the release of *The Cost of a Kiss* when he accepted a job producing propaganda films for the Ministry of Information (MoI), which had been set up in early 1918 to make promotional material for the Board of Trade, the Board of Agriculture and Fisheries and the National War Savings Committee, among others. Brunel's major contributions to the campaigns were the two-minute propaganda shorts named 'Film Tags', which were shown as part of newsreels and proved to be a highly effective way of communicating government messages.

Brunel was well regarded by his superiors and on his departure from the Ministry, Colonel W. Arthur Northam wrote: 'I am convinced your originality, creative ability and systematic methods, will get you very far – you will be a very valuable person to some lucky firm' (1 January 1919, ABSC 4/107).

Brunel remained with the MoI until the end of the war, requesting release on 18 November 1918. He, Babs and Adey had been forced from the family home by a German bomb that fell on Maida Vale on 7 March 1918, returning in October.

British Actors' Film Company

On 6 January 1919, Brunel took up a post as head of the scenario department at the British Actors' Film Company (BAFC), on the invitation of actor and producer A. E. Matthews. The company had been established in 1916 by a group of West End actors and their strategy was to populate their films with theatrical names, which, it was hoped, would be a draw for audiences. Here, Brunel was to work with some key figures in the industry including Kenelm Foss, a writer, actor, director and producer who had moved from theatre into film in 1915, and Wilfred Noy. Noy had started his career at Clarendon Film Company in 1910, where he directed well over a hundred films and may even have cast an eye over the early screenwriting efforts Brunel submitted to the company before the war.

In his new post, Brunel was to select properties and write and edit scripts. BAFC had offices in Soho's Golden Square, but filming took place at the tiny Bushey Studio at Lululaund, the impressive Romanesque mansion built by German-born artist and filmmaker Hubert von Herkomer. Herkomer had become interested in film around 1910 and converted his theatre to a studio. On his death in 1914, Lululaund was requisitioned by the British government and the studio was hired to BAFC from about 1917.

The space proved inadequate for the company's needs and it acquired the Harrow Weald Park Estate in north-west London for studio use, although it is unclear whether any filming took place there. On behalf of BAFC, Brunel petitioned Winston Churchill, Secretary of State for War, and his undersecretary Reginald Brade, to try and secure the demobilisation of the estate's chief electrician so that work on the studio could proceed. His letter to Brade grandly proclaimed:

> We are engaged in a big struggle to free ourselves from the domination of the Americans. It's a tough job. One of the most important agents in the fight is the BAFC, which is extending the sphere of its operations and raising its capital to half a million sterling. (29 July 1919, ABSC 2/107)

Brunel's framing of the company's business pursuits as part of a patriotic imperative vital to the rebuilding of the nation's industrial power may well have been inspired by his propaganda training at the MoI. However, he regarded the film industry as key not only in terms of the country's economic sovereignty but also in terms of protecting its cultural influence on the world stage. He campaigned for the release from the army of several men who had worked in the cinema before the war in his efforts to rejuvenate the industry.

Brunel was taken on at BAFC for a trial period of three months at a salary of £15 a week and was desperate to remain. He confessed to his friend John Payne:

> I have my wife telling me I am a soft hearted fool to play about with these people when I could do so much better elsewhere! But . . . it is not only money that counts. Being with decent people with reasonable prospects of an influential position is a big factor in my view of things. (30 March 1919, ABSC 2/107)

Throughout his career, Brunel sought to work with like-minded people and valued intellectual stimulation and a cultured environment above remuneration.

BAFC extended his contract and in August 1919 Brunel was attempting to secure a job for a recently demobbed acquaintance, writer Bernard Merivale. This desire to get employment for friends is another recurring theme throughout his career and undoubtedly hindered his own progression. Many of those he helped to boost had careers that eclipsed his own, while his reputation was damaged when people he recommended turned out to be unsuitable. His family also benefited from his loyalty and, in 1919, Wilfred Noy directed *The Lady Clare* from a screenplay by Brunel's mother based on Alfred Lord Tennyson's poem.

Brunel's troubles at BAFC began with his first production, *The Usurper* (Duncan McRae, 1919). He had adapted the source novel by W. J. Locke but was outraged when he attended the trade show at the Alhambra on 12 September 1919 and found that the film had been heavily re-edited by Phillips Film Company, distributor of BAFC's productions. Brunel felt compelled to write to his guests at the screening, stating:

> The film exhibited at the Alhambra yesterday was not the British Actors' copy, which the producer, photographer, and myself consented to having our names upon, but a mutilated and inferiorly printed copy which was submitted by the Phillips Film Co at the eleventh hour, against the wishes of the Directors of the British A FC and in spite of their protests. (13 September 1919, ABSC 4/107)

When Phillips found out about the letter, they complained to BAFC, who demanded an explanation. Brunel claimed that his reputation had been damaged by the trade show but he had clearly put BAFC in an awkward position as they depended on Phillips to distribute their films. Thus began the deterioration of the relationship between Brunel and Phillips, particularly its Managing Director, H. J. Boam.

Three months later, a similar conflict arose over *The Auction Mart* (1920), another McRae/Brunel collaboration. Brunel rounded on Boam in a letter to BAFC director Gerald Malvern: 'The Auction Mart also suffered through haste in editing ... Mr Boam or his representatives should in no way be allowed to alter the film' (n.d., ABSC 2/107). In the same letter, Brunel claimed that the editor at Phillips 'rode rough-shod over everything ... [and] was unable to retain the most elementary facts of the story'. Later he lamented that Boam had said that 'his customers want "cruder stuff than The Auction Mart" ... [he] attacks the titles on the ground that they are "high-brow"' (14 January 1920, ABSC 2/107).

This seems to be the first time the term 'highbrow' was applied to Brunel's work, a label that haunted him throughout the 1920s and which he came to regard as a barrier to his progression within the industry. What is interesting about this particular myth is that most of the references to him being a highbrow appear in his *own* writings or utterances. Boam may have regarded Brunel's films as too intellectual for audiences but Brunel repeated the slur many times over the following years, as an explanation for his lack of acceptance by the trade. His actions during his time at BAFC and the tone of the communications quoted above suggest that it was at least partly his behaviour that alienated industry figures.

Yet the fact that figures like Boam had such control over the output of a production company was clearly holding back the development of British filmmaking and compromising artistic integrity. Boam was a successful businessman and felt he was the best judge of what audiences wanted to see; in fact, *Kinematograph Monthly Record* regarded *The Usurper* as 'superior to more than 90 per cent of American films in "photography, production and casting"' (quoted in Bamford: 71). Phillips was still a going concern when BAFC went bankrupt in April 1921 and, the following month, Boam addressed the company's spring convention. *The Bioscope* reported that 'Mr Boam said that the company made a special effort to cut all films as short as possible. As soon as any picture had been definitely acquired it was gone over carefully and every foot of "padding" removed' (*The Bioscope*, 12 May 1921: 18). This presumably accounted for the company's advertising slogan: 'Phillips Films are 100 per cent entertainment', implying that shots or other elements deemed to be 'highbrow' or 'arty' were at odds with, or even obstructed, 'entertainment'.

This was the first time Brunel had his creativity interfered with by the business interests of the film industry but it was a pattern that was to be repeated throughout his career. His experiences with Boam no doubt fed into views he later expounded:

> The vulgar, uneducated, inartistic film boss of to-day has got to go. While he is controlling things the right talent will never get a change [sic] . . . In Germany . . . their much-advertised kultur was apparent, not only in their best films, but in their best film offices. (*MPS*, 26 August 1922: 6)

Brunel's obvious disdain for those running the industry could not have endeared him to them or inspired their trust, and his lack of diplomacy led to strained relationships throughout the decade. Later in the same interview he aired his favourite grievance: 'I am dismissed as a "highbrow". They are afraid my work will be as dull as Ibsen, as highflown as Shakespeare, and that my sub-titles will be written in Greek.'

Brunel resigned from BAFC over the two incidents, realising that the company was being held to ransom by Phillips. 'I have come to the conclusion that certain conditions are not likely to be changed, and that I should be doing myself harm by remaining,' he wrote to Malvern (9 March 1920, ABSC 2/107). Expressing regret at his departure, Malvern warned him: 'in this business one has to have a skin like a rhinocerous [sic] as one has to meet and deal with so many uncouth and impossible people' (11 March 1920, ABSC 2/107).

A New Kind of Film Agency

While at BAFC, Brunel had been planning his next enterprise via correspondence with John Meredith ('Jack') Payne, former director of

Sidney Morgan's Renaissance Films, who was in France with the British Expeditionary Force. They decided to set up an agency and on Payne's demobilisation in February 1920 formed Bramlins with Bertram Jacobs, a screenwriter who had worked for the Ideal Film Company under the name Benedict James.

The agency aimed to provide 'a comprehensive service to producers, not only in casting, but finding suitable locations for productions, or advising and researching on costumes and so forth' (Gliddon: 40). Offices were taken at 241 Shaftesbury Avenue and they began trying to recruit talent immediately, but the business got off to a slow start and Payne's letters show how his optimism rapidly faded. John Gliddon was recruited through a chance meeting with Brunel 'walking up [Shaftesbury] Avenue with Leslie Howard . . . [he] told me he and another friend . . . had just gone into partnership . . . Would I like to join them as Casting Manager?' (ibid.). Gliddon describes the enthusiasm and talent at the Bramlins offices, remarking that 'the only cloud in the sky was the pitiable state of the British Film Industry' (ibid.).

Brunel's casual manner of recruitment seems to have been common at the time and film actors seeking work would haunt this part of London, hoping to bump into a useful acquaintance. *Motion Picture Studio* summed this up in a humorous poem:

> To someone who in dulcet tone,
> Approached him for a trifling loan,
> A man in Shaftesbury Avenue,
> Said, 'I'm a movie-actor too.' (*MPS*, 18 August 1923: 7)

One commentator described the 'thousands of film actors, both male and female, thrown on the streets because the British film trade is in the doldrums' (Morton: 82); with few British films being made, agents' commissions suffered and the fact that Bramlins not only survived the decade but became a thriving agency is testament to Payne's determination. In 1930, the firm received investment from the Empire Building Corporation Ltd in a deal brokered by film director Geoffrey Malins (ABSC 3/107). Gliddon benefited from Brunel's patronage, becoming a leading agent in the 1930s, ultimately representing such stars as Vivien Leigh and Deborah Kerr.

Minerva

Brunel was now embarking on his next venture, which was to permit him more control. At BAFC Brunel had met stage actor Leslie Howard, nephew of Wilfred Noy. Howard was keen to get into films and had approached Brunel about setting up a company in August 1919 but Brunel had refused, preferring a regular income over the uncertainty of running a business. Howard established a production company with writer A. A. Milne and actors C. Aubrey Smith and Nigel Playfair and Brunel joined on a one-year contract on 24 March 1920, 'at a salary of £20 per week plus 10% royalty on the net profits of any productions you may complete during your first 3 months, and 15% for those afterwards' (3 March 1920, ABSC 2/107).

The company became Minerva Films Limited and Milne was to write short comic subjects that Brunel would adapt, produce, direct and edit, with Smith and Howard performing. Minerva was backed to the tune of around £5,000, with which Brunel began work on four two-reel films. In the midst of this activity, on 20 June 1920, Brunel's son John Christopher was born.

While reviews of the Milne films were good, the company could not sell them and struggled to continue production. Brunel became convinced that no serious attempt to make films could succeed without large investment and proper studio space. Around this time, he had a chance meeting with a man called Frederick Charles Clarke who joined the board of Minerva and offered to purchase a studio for Brunel to run. Brunel saw this as a turning point in the company's fortunes and set about finding a suitable building.

Various sites were investigated, from Ravenscourt Park in Hammersmith to Fred Karno's Island near Hampton Court, but by March 1921 Brunel had become suspicious of Clarke after several letters to him were returned. He hired a detective who tracked Clarke down to a rented room in Cheapside, East London but failed to 'obtain information as to his financial circumstance to enable us to speak for a transaction involving your figures' (28 February 1921, ABSC 4/107).

The discovery that Clarke was not the man of means he pretended to be must have been devastating but Brunel persevered with Minerva, with two further films in production: *A Temporary Lady* and *Too Many Cooks*. In March 1921, Minerva's cameraman H. M. Lomas left to join British Instructional Films, no doubt frustrated by the company's difficulties. He was an experienced cameraman who had worked for the Charles Urban Trading Company for several years and his departure must have been another blow.

By August, 'owing to the present position of the cinematograph industry', Minerva had formally dispensed with Brunel's services as Production Director, although he continued to be involved as a shareholder (20 August 1921, ABSC 6/107). This coincided with the completion of filming of

Minerva's final production, *The Beggars' Syndicate*, as announced by *Motion Picture Studio* (20 August 1921: 8). But the film never reached the screen and, apart from the Milne comedies, the only Minerva production to be shown publicly was *A Temporary Lady*, filmed some months before *The Beggars' Syndicate* but not unveiled to the trade until September 1921.

The history of Minerva is typical of many small production companies set up in the wake of the war and demonstrates the problems of sustaining film production while waiting to recoup a profit on releases. This was Brunel's first experience of having a level of creative freedom without the interference of a scissor-wielding distributor, but, as he learned, distribution was key to sustainability and without the finances to make prints and secure bookings, films were unlikely ever to be seen.

Solar Films

Bouncing back from this disappointing experience, Brunel optimistically announced to Payne that 'the doors of the Solar Services, the publicity business with which I am connected, are to be opened shortly' (30 October 1921, ABSC 3/107). At an office at 7 Suffolk Street, Pall Mall, Brunel and Miles Mander (star of *A Temporary Lady*) planned to specialise in the production of travel films, assembling a board of experts with foreign military and diplomatic experience. Brunel was to receive £10 a week while on a production and he and Mander projected an extensive series of films to be shot round the globe.

The first of these was a journey through North Africa, and Brunel set off on 28 December 1921 to Morocco and Algeria via France and Spain to film *Moors and Minarets*. With him was cameraman Crispin Hay (an actor from *The Beggars' Syndicate*) and Sir Percy Sykes, former Brigadier General of the South Persia Rifles. On completion of the travel film, Brunel and Hay were joined by Mander and Annette Benson to shoot a fiction film against the backdrop of Tangiers; the cast was limited by the small budget so Brunel made use of his acting experience and took on a role himself.

When Brunel arrived back in England, the negatives were confiscated by Customs who declared it a foreign film, and it was many months before the material was released. In the end, it proved cheaper for Brunel to arrange for the footage to be printed in Germany than to pay the import duties. Meanwhile, the board of Solar had taken on leases for two London cinemas for a minimum of three months and Brunel and Mander found themselves running the Philharmonic Hall and the Polytechnic Cinema. The former was to be primarily for the exhibition of Solar's travel films; at a lunch hosted by Sykes, he described the 'series of "personally conducted" film journeys to foreign parts' which would be shown there (*The Bioscope*, 16 March 1922: 6). Future subjects were to include cinematic tours of Andalusia, Timbuktu, Liberia, China, the Antarctic and Peru. However, the company's first release, a travelogue of Burma with an accompanying lecture, was not a success due to the poor quality of both the film and the speaker, while *Moors and Minarets* would not be ready to screen for quite some time.

To keep their cinemas in operation, Brunel and Mander booked second-run titles that were cheaper to acquire than new releases. While acknowledging that the main objective of the pair was to 'raise money quickly' (no doubt to fund their ambitious foreign filming plans), Henry K. Miller asserts that their 'eye-catching programmes', which included *The Mark of Zorro* and John Barrymore's *Dr Jekyll and Mr Hyde* (both 1920), were part of a 'grand scheme for a national repertory circuit' (Miller 2013: 50). Although Mander made a similar announcement to the press, it seems unlikely Solar would have pursued further venues considering the number of other projects with which they were involved. Brunel was still determined to pursue a career as a film director and the burden of programming a cinema while still trying to rescue the negatives he had spent months shooting may have been an unwelcome distraction. However, he took advantage of having access to a cinema to promote his own work, showing *A Temporary Lady* in mid-May 1922 at the Polytechnic Regent Street as an accompaniment to *Dr Jekyll and Mr Hyde* and giving two of the Milne comedies further exposure.

Brunel was still trying to sell the Minerva productions to any distributor or cinema that might take them. Solar was already heavily in debt and Brunel wrote in desperation to John Payne: 'After months of working for nothing – and now no hope of anything, I'm afraid for I don't expect to ever get much out of Solar . . . I now really and truly find myself with only three pounds in the world' (23 July 1922, ABSC 3/107). He was also doing small jobs for International Artists at the time and was asked to write a series of films featuring Herbert Jenkins' popular Cockney character Bindle, to be played by music-hall star Billy Merson, but the project was abandoned.

Although the North African films were still awaiting completion, Mander and Brunel headed to Germany in August 1922 in search of a suitable studio to film their next project. The pair were in the vanguard of British producers in using German studios and Brunel was one of the first directors to work there. At that time, the exchange rate with Germany was very favourable and facilities were excellent; Brunel and Mander were impressed with what they saw of the equipment and technical skills and reported that Germany was 'an earnest aspirant to the chief place in the film sun' (*MPS*, 9 September 1922: 5). They were to avail themselves of these facilities for what was to be their most elaborate project so far.

It Happened in Venice

Leaving behind the financial mess of Solar, Brunel and Mander formed the Atlas-Biocraft Company (perhaps inspired by the Atlas mountains which Brunel had admired in North Africa). Despite the problems thus far, Brunel may have been buoyed by Mander's boundless optimism or perhaps stymied by a lack of other opportunities, but he could not refuse this directing opportunity, to be funded by wealthy businessman James White. White had made his fortune in the building trade and made the move into cinema when he acquired the site of the Tivoli in London and decided to run it himself. According to Brunel, the financier was presented with two proposals: the first was the best commercial proposition, the second added merely to make the first seem more appealing. White decided to back the second and Brunel found himself embarking on *The Man Without Desire* with a budget of £5,000, a very small sum for a feature even in 1922. Ivor Novello was to star in the tale of an eighteenth-century count put to sleep for two hundred years, adapted from an original story by Irish playwright Monckton Hoffe.

By October, Brunel and his crew were in Venice, where they filmed until the beginning of December before decamping to Germany to shoot the interiors. Novello finished his scenes in early December and departed for New York to take up a seven-film contract with D. W. Griffith. Brunel returned to Britain early in 1923 but completion of *The Man Without Desire* was long delayed; while Brunel was paid for filming, editing was presumably to be done in his own time and he had to take on other work to supplement his income. Mander was pursuing further projects and Brunel was sent to France in August to scout for locations for 'The Rat', an original screenplay written by Ivor Novello. Unsurprisingly, with no return from their unreleased films, the company failed to raise enough to get this production off the ground.[4]

The Man Without Desire was finally completed at the end of 1923. It was distributed by yet another company set up by Mander, this time with E. T. Bass (who had worked for Stoll) and part-funded by Ivor Novello. Novello-Atlas Renters was to be 'directly concerned with films in which

---

[4] Novello adapted his screenplay for the stage and it became a huge hit, allowing him to sell the film rights to Gainsborough for a large sum. It was filmed in 1925 by Graham Cutts.

Ivor Novello is starred' (*The Bioscope*, 6 December 1923: 38). Novello had returned to England after making only one film for Griffith, *The White Rose* (1923), and was clearly trying to establish himself as a film star. As Leslie Howard had with Minerva, he felt that involvement on a business level was the best way to ensure self-promotion. *The Bioscope* announced that the trade show of *The Man Without Desire* would take place on 14 December and listed other titles to be handled by the new firm: the long-languishing North African films *Lovers in Araby* and *Moors and Minarets* along with 'three half-reels of silhouette' commissioned by Mander from an animation company in Munich (ibid.). This package of releases testifies to the intense year of editing work undertaken by Brunel in 1923 to get all these films ready. In addition, he had been given the mammoth task of editing down 33,000 feet of film shot by Sir Rupert Clarke in New Guinea, which was released the following year as *Cannibals of the South Seas*.

The Man Without Desire was released in late February 1924, by which time Brunel was planning a much-needed holiday. Babs' mother had died and left them several hundred pounds, so in early March the family set off for Algiers. The strain of his work schedule over the previous eighteen months had taken its toll on Brunel and his doctor had recommended a long holiday, but he did not waste the opportunity to make another film and *The Boy Goes to Biskra* depicted the exotic locations through the eyes of his three-year-old son. During Brunel's absence, *Lovers in Araby* had its trade showing, Mander reporting that it got an excellent reception and expressing confidently that 'we shall certainly make money out of it' (17 March 1924, ABSC D/170). Despite this optimism, the company's releases failed to make a significant profit and it appears there were few bookings beyond the Tivoli Theatre. When Brunel returned from his trip he again had to look for work.

The failure of *The Man Without Desire* to establish him as a major director must have been a tremendous blow to Brunel and more or less spelled the end of his filmmaking partnership with Mander. They could not raise further funds for production, hardly surprising given that their financiers had seen no return on their investment. Yet, despite the frustrations and lack of financial reward, this collaboration was perhaps the most promising that Brunel had within small producing firms. The partnership lasted three years, quite a feat considering the myriad difficulties they faced, and this seems largely due to Mander's incredible drive, sound business ideas and excellent sales skills. He understood that controlling all three aspects of the business – production, distribution and exhibition – was the only way to guarantee that films would reach an audience, but the company was never sufficiently well-staffed or funded to sustain the necessary levels of activity. Mander also recognised the appeal of bringing exotic locations to the screen, whether in the form of documentaries or feature films, yet was not able to support the enormous costs associated with this. Unsurprisingly, Mander's talent and energy served him well and he went on to write, direct and star in his own films, eventually going to Hollywood and forging a career as a character actor.

Having spent his wife's inheritance on a family holiday rather than paying off his debts, Brunel returned from Algiers to find bankruptcy looming. He had by now set up a cutting room at Dansey Yard off Wardour Street where he undertook work for Atlas-Biocraft as well as any other jobs he could get. He had become a very adept editor and was fascinated by the potential of the process to affect the way audiences reacted to images. He had communicated some of these through humorous writings in the trade press but now began to put into practice the theories he had been developing by dabbling in creative cutting.

The Burlesques

Brunel was obviously pleased with the results of his editing experiments and, on 31 July 1924, he organised a screening of the resulting film, *Crossing the Great Sagrada*, at a private Wardour Street theatre. It was a burlesque on the popular travelogue *Crossing the Great Sahara*, which was still on British screens six months after its initial release, a success which may well have rankled given the failure of his own travel film. The following week *Kine Weekly* reported that Brunel's parody had 'set a small audience rocking' and suggested he 'should do more of this sort of thing' (7 August 1924: 40). Brunel was delighted with the response to the film and took their advice, trade-showing a spoof newsreel, *The Pathetic Gazette*, in October. Both films were distributed by Novello-Atlas and, according to Brunel, took a small fortune; *Sagrada* was certainly picked up by several regional distributors, as shown by the promotional postcards produced for the film (ABSC 1/164).

That autumn, Brunel was approached by Abel Gance to make a film on the life of William Shakespeare. Gance recorded having watched one of Brunel's films (presumably *The Man Without Desire*) on 15 September and later spending an afternoon with Brunel (Napoleon Dossier, quoted by Kevin Brownlow in email to author, 23 November 2010). Cameraman Henry Harris accompanied Brunel to the meeting at Gance's Paris flat and reported that the two men had 'clicked' (Harris audio interview by Kevin Brownlow, 21 May 1969, private collection). Gaining the attention of one of the world's foremost artistic film directors must have strengthened

Brunel's belief in his own creative ideas and he was no doubt also relieved at the prospect of a lengthy spell of paid work on a prestigious production. Unfortunately, the death of the German financier put paid to the project and the encounter, which Brunel strangely omitted from his autobiography, joins the long list of 'what ifs' that haunt his career.

A Start at Gainsborough

Brunel's burlesques had caught the eye of producer Michael Balcon, Director of Production at Gainsborough Pictures, whom he had met socially earlier that year. Balcon persuaded the studio's distributor, C. M. Woolf, to back another five burlesques with a £150 advance for each. Brunel and Balcon were to be joint producers, with profits split equally between them after Woolf had been repaid. To become involved with a major producer, albeit on a freelance basis, must have felt like a significant step towards gaining a foothold in a more stable part of the film industry.

Almost immediately, Brunel was given some quite responsible tasks at the studio, including negotiating international co-productions. Higson observes that 'the problem for European companies such as Gainsborough and Gaumont was that domestic markets were too small to support high-budget films that might reasonably compete with American pictures' and the answer seemed to be 'to collaborate with companies elsewhere in Europe' (1997: 61). This meant larger budgets could be assembled by pooling production resources, and films gained much wider distribution, assisting national industries to increase profits. Presumably due to his experience of working at German studios, Brunel was sent to meet some German producers on Balcon's behalf, as he outlined in a letter:

> But to continue about Alfred. I saw his friends this afternoon. They come from Munich. Emelca [sic]. They've already fixed up a picture for Woolf with a £3,000 guarantee . . . They want to fix up everything at once, if they care for the story . . . they particularly want me to give them an estimate of the cost of production.[5] (14 November 1924, ABSC 2/112)

Hitchcock shot his first feature, *The Pleasure Garden*, at Emelka's Munich studio in 1925. However, Balcon had already embarked on a co-production and distribution arrangement with Emelka's rival Ufa and correspondence shows that Brunel was involved in this collaboration on

---

[5] According to Henry K. Miller, 'F. Alfred was an import/export man responsible for bringing over some of the German films . . . Alfred's address at 29a Charing Cross Road was as of early 1925 used by Emelka' (email to author, 29 April 2016).

various levels. In early 1925, he was working on the German titles for the co-production *The Blackguard* (Graham Cutts, 1925), the first film made under the agreement with Ufa. It had been shot at their studios in Germany, with Hitchcock as production designer and later collaborating with Brunel on the titles. Brunel also re-edited and titled *The Woman Who Did* (*Die Frau mit dem schlechten Ruf*, Benjamin Christensen 1925) for the English market.

Although Brunel clearly had a flair for titling, he was not pleased that this, along with other editing and salvage jobs, seemed to have become his main occupation at Gainsborough. Balcon acknowledged the anomaly in a letter to the head of Ufa, Erich Pommer: 'Mr Brunel is not a title writer in the ordinary sense of the word (although he is the best man in England at this work) – he is a film director with an excellent reputation and is doing this work as a personal favour to me' (28 February 1925, ABSC 3/112).

Brunel had barely completed the first Gainsborough burlesques when he was asked to make a special short for the premiere of the Harold Lloyd film *Hot Water* (Sam Taylor, 1924) on 31 December 1924. Woolf had made his name and fortune through promoting Lloyd in Britain and Brunel's short was a 'happily inspired and audaciously contrived little "spoof" film' about film distribution, wryly entitled *Money for Nothing* and featuring Woolf himself (*KW*, 8 January 1925: 45–6).[6] These varied tasks indicate the amount of trust Balcon placed in Brunel, yet the level of activity took him away from making the burlesques, which were not completed until October 1925.

According to Ivor Montagu, the burlesques were responsible for Brunel's negative reputation within the industry: 'he was accounted a dangerous intellectual, because he specialised in satirical one-reelers . . . it was axiomatic in the trade that audiences would not accept satire and that anyone intelligent enough to be satirical was dangerous' (1970: 274–5). Yet Brunel had long been aware of the opinions of him and his work held by certain members of the trade, which had started when he first clashed with Phillips Film Co. in 1919 and had probably not been helped by the views on the industry he had expressed in the trade press. Five years earlier he had complained to Leslie Howard: 'I am no more popular than I was. I should awfully like some of the anti-Brunellites to have a week in my shoes' (28 December 1920, ABSC 4/107).

Brunel had earned Balcon's gratitude for his 'very loyal co-operation and services' (3 July 1925, 3/111) in reshooting, re-editing and titling two

---

[6] This film has not survived. Brunel asserted that Woolf 'projected it until it was worn out' (1949: 110).

Graham Cutts films, *The Blackguard* and *The Prude's Fall* (both 1925). Alfred Hitchcock had worked with Cutts on both films and was also appreciative of Brunel's remedial work. In a letter to Brunel from Munich, where he was directing *The Pleasure Garden*, Hitchcock wrote, 'I'm very pleased to hear that the Prude's Fall has come out of your "film hospital" a new being' (n.d., ABSC 1/112). Although he was not under contract to either Gainsborough or W. & F., Brunel was paid reasonably well for his work; however, he was by now supporting two associates, Lionel Rich (known as Tod) and J. O. C. Orton (known as Jock). He had taken them on to help in his cutting rooms and the three were kept busy with the work coming from Gainsborough, which was too much for Brunel alone.

The influx of young graduates such as Rich, Orton and Montagu to the film business during the interwar years was to change the complexion of British cinema, and Brunel's recruitment and training of some of them contributed to the advancement of the industry in subsequent decades. Balcon had long been keen to bring more intellectuals into Gainsborough and several of Brunel's trainees went on to work for him both there and, later, at Ealing Studios. In fact, in the 1930s, Ealing became known as 'Mr Balcon's Academy for Young Gentlemen' due to the social status and educational attainment of its creative staff. The film industry was not the only area that was undergoing this kind of 'intellectualisation' between the wars; as Graves and Hodge observed, 'The recruits that newspapers needed were no longer drudges trained from the age of fourteen in a newspaper office, but university men with a superficial knowledge of many things, full of "ideas" and with a snappy way of expressing them' (1971: 58).

The Film Society

If Brunel was suspected of being a 'dangerous intellectual' for his burlesques, his association with the Film Society must have brought confirmation of the fact. Approached in early February 1925 by Montagu and actor Hugh Miller, he agreed to help set up the Society and became a key figure within it. The group's aim was to screen films that would not otherwise get a showing in Britain and its formation was announced in *The Bioscope* on 7 May 1925. The Society immediately found itself branded 'highbrow' by the press, a label that stuck despite strenuous denials by its members. The first screening took place on 25 October and their monthly gatherings on a Sunday evening soon became popular with the bohemian crowd. The work and legacy of the Film Society has been examined in detail elsewhere (see Sexton 2008 and Miller 2013) and its importance in establishing curated repertory programmes is generally accepted. Brunel's involvement led to more editing work and, more importantly, established a friendship with Montagu that was to endure throughout his life.

Gainsborough took a dim view of Brunel's participation in the Film Society, feeling it 'would damage the prestige of the films [he] made for them' (Brunel 1949: 114), and on 11 December 1925 Brunel resigned from the board. But he maintained links with both the Society and Montagu, who later joined the board of his editing firm, which was registered as Brunel & Montagu Ltd in 1927. At their Dansey Yard cutting rooms, the company retitled the foreign films imported for the Society's screenings. Brunel continued to edit a great many films for W. & F., both Ufa titles and others, including a series of horse-racing features starring champion jockey Steve Donoghue.

Brunel, Montagu and Friends

Brunel & Montagu Ltd barely provided sufficient income to support Brunel and his family. But he thrived on the camaraderie that his informal training school engendered and from a personal perspective this was probably the most fulfilling period of his working life. The coincidence of this enterprise and his association with both the Film Society and Gainsborough led to Brunel becoming a key member of a vibrant scene whose participants were involved in the practical, commercial side of the business while pursuing and encouraging a more varied diet of film viewing. This group of industry aspirants and participants, referred to by Miller as 'the Brewer Street Pack', gathered daily at the Legrain coffee shop and other Soho meeting places (Miller 2013: 119).[7] Balcon recalled that members included cameraman Henry Harris, directors Graham Cutts, Alfred Hitchcock, Victor Saville and Edwin Greenwood, screenwriter Eliot Stannard and, of course, Brunel and Montagu.

Brunel and Babs also entertained regularly at home and her obituary described her as 'a well-known hostess of the film world' and 'a woman of legendary hospitality' (*Daily Telegraph*, 31 March 1987, BFIRL cuttings). The pair hosted 'hate parties' at their flat, where guests were encouraged to air their dislikes about films and cinemagoing. Invitees included 'Hitch and Alma, Mich and Aileen [Balcon], Victor Saville, [Herbert] Wilcox, Vivian

---

[7] Balcon recalled that the Legrain was in Brewer Street but Brunel suggests their rendezvous was in Gerrard Street, much closer to his Dansey Yard office. Legrain was certainly at 22 Gerrard Street in the 1950s, so Balcon's memory of its location was presumably at fault.

Figure 1.5 Brunel & Montagu film can label. Source: author's own collection.

Van Damm, Sidney Bernstein, Iris Barry and [Walter] Mycroft' (Montagu 1958: 230). An article in *Picturegoer* entitled 'Our Hate Party' revealed that among the gripes of those present at the gatherings were 'close-ups of hands knocking at doors . . . the person who reads subtitles aloud . . . hurriedly made films . . . and lingering screen kisses' (Mannock 1927).

The rather loose arrangement under which Brunel was working for Gainsborough during this period meant he was paid separately for each job he undertook, sometimes even accepting a share in a production's profit in lieu of payment. He clearly felt a sense of loyalty to Balcon that appears to have been reciprocated, given Balcon's considerable involvement with the burlesque production and distribution. However, by mid-1926 Brunel was becoming increasingly impatient and claimed to have

Figure 1.6 A 'hate party' gripe. Source: *Picturegoer*, October 1927, p. 18.

turned down several offers of employment on the understanding that he was to be given a directing commission at Gainsborough. His patience finally ran out when he learned that George Cooper and Hitchcock had been handed directing jobs ahead of him and he laid out his discontent in a letter to the board (18 May 1926, ABSC 1/111).

This promotion of others before him became a particular bugbear, references to it littering his correspondence with the company. His assessment that 'my prospects of obtaining employment as a director are now a negligible quantity after such a long period of inactivity' (ibid.) indicates the level of anxiety he felt about his future. The tone of this correspondence undoubtedly put a strain on his relationship with Balcon, his main supporter at Gainsborough. Montagu later described how 'intrigues kept [Brunel] ever from the floor' (1970: 274), the main culprit apparently being the company's star director Graham Cutts, whose last two films Brunel had prepared for release. The correspondence between Brunel and Cutts is civil, but it is easy to imagine that Cutts did not take kindly to having his films 'improved' by someone whose career he sought to stifle.

Brunel's demands to the board of Gainsborough would have alienated them further and this may explain why his first feature was made under the auspices of Piccadilly Pictures, formed by Balcon and Reginald Baker in February 1926. The company offered him a one-off contract, drawn up on 3 November 1926, to direct *Blighty*, a film depicting life on the Home Front during the First World War based on an idea by Montagu. It was to cost no more than £8,000 and Brunel edited as well as directed, presumably to keep costs down.

Piccadilly Pictures' advertisement for its upcoming releases foregrounded *The Rat*, *The Lodger*, *The Triumph of the Rat* and *The Rolling Road* and prominently featured Cutts and Hitchcock. Relegated to the second page, *Blighty* was promoted by a list of its stars, with no mention of Brunel (*The Bioscope*, 6 January 1927: 4–5). Elsewhere appeared the news that Brunel was to shoot a film in France for low-budget producer and distributor Butcher's Film Service; it was never made but the announcement indicates that Brunel's insecurity drove him to continue to pursue opportunities elsewhere. This would have been further fuelled by an observation in *The Bioscope* that Brunel had 'not made a full-length film for a considerable time', while elsewhere Alfred Hitchcock was described as a 'brilliant young director' (17 March 1927: 39 and 34). Brunel had little time to brood though, since he was now busy writing a scenario for producer Sam W. Smith. Entitled *Land of Hope and Glory* (Harley Knoles 1927), it was based on the patriotic song and starred Ellaline Terriss (also in *Blighty*) as a mother whose sons set off to explore the far-flung corners of the British Empire following the First World War. Brunel's script includes some imaginative opening shots, at first fading in on a newly made wheel, crafted by the patriarch of the family and symbolising Britain as the hub of the Empire. The wheel begins to revolve and the image cuts to shots of Piccadilly Circus and Leicester Square, their electric lights coloured red, followed by a shot of a globe with the countries of the Empire similarly coloured and with clouds superimposed round the edges. The Empire fades until England remains centre screen, still coloured red, then gradually diminishes until it dissolves into the centre of the wheel hub and disappears. This introductory sequence demonstrates Brunel's belief that a film should creatively and succinctly summarise its themes and his dramatic use of colour was an unusual touch.

The editing of *Blighty* was delayed by Brunel's arthritis and problems with obtaining actuality shots but it was finally trade-shown on 22 March 1927 at the London Hippodrome. Reviews were positive and Low asserts that the film's success established Brunel as 'one of the most talented young British film makers' (1971: 149), although he was by now approaching forty. Both Cutts and Hitchcock had announced they were leaving Gainsborough at the end of their contracts, Cutts to direct for First National, Hitchcock for British National Pictures, and Brunel may have felt more optimistic about his future with the company. In the event, the departure of the two figures Brunel felt were blocking his progress did not improve his situation and he began to feel that his willingness to undertake any job thrown his way, often for little pay, had contributed to a perceived lack of respect from the studio. In one particularly candid letter to Balcon he wrote: 'I . . . saw how Cutts' propaganda about my being "high-brow" had so undermined me and my own restraint had made me seem so unimportant, that I could be treated anyhow' (n.d., ABSC 1/112).

The Vortex

Brunel's next Gainsborough commission was to be a film version of the controversial Noël Coward play *The Vortex*. He knew that the story would have to be drastically cut for the screen to get past the censor, but what really soured his experience of making the film was the fact that he was not allowed to edit it himself, instead being sent immediately to Europe on his next project. He attributed the financial failure of *The Vortex* to the fact that he had not been permitted to see his vision for the film through to its completion but, despite his attempts to distance himself from the production, its poor reception further damaged his standing at the studio.

Before shooting began on *The Vortex*, *The Bioscope* had revealed that Brunel's next film was likely to be an adaptation of an original story by Roland Pertwee called 'A South Sea Bubble' (19 May 1927: 30). News that Gainsborough was to produce a film version of Margaret Kennedy's best-selling novel *The Constant Nymph* had also reached the trade, along with the report that it was to be brought to the screen by Basil Dean, theatrical director and co-author of the stage version, with 'the aid of a very expert assistant director whose name I shall be able to announce very shortly' (*The Bioscope*, 28 April 1927: 27). Brunel was working on the scenario and casting for *The Vortex* at the time and began filming in June. At the end of that month, Balcon was preparing Brunel's contract to direct *A South Sea Bubble* but by July an agreement had been drawn up outlining the terms of Dean's working relationship with Brunel on *The Constant Nymph*.

The Constant Nymph

The Constant Nymph is generally considered to be Brunel's most accomplished feature, even though he did not receive sole credit for its direction and his input is thus not easy to quantify. Dean was a well-established theatre director keen to break into the cinema and saw this as his opportunity. As co-author of a highly sought-after property, he was in a strong position to dictate his own terms. Balcon asked Brunel to direct under Dean's 'supervision', an arrangement which Brunel was aware would further damage his battered reputation, but which he agreed to. Despite the difficulty of this arrangement, Brunel found himself able to influence the production more than he had hoped, winning the trust of the cast and crew who quickly became aware of Dean's lack of film experience, a limitation Dean himself later acknowledged.

The Constant Nymph was greatly anticipated by the press and public alike, so much so that a sneak preview of some scenes took place at the Marble Arch Pavilion several months before its completion 'by request of the Prince of Wales' (*The Bioscope*, 17 November 1927: 47). The trade show was held in February 1928; reviews were almost exclusively excellent and, as already mentioned, it went on to be named Best British Film of 1928 by readers of *Film Weekly*.

Conclusion

This biography gives a sense of the roller coaster nature of Brunel's career in the 1920s: the discrepancy between critical and financial success and the myriad frustrations endemic in the industry that hampered filmmakers during the decade. As the second half of this biography, in Chapter 8, will show, from this point on, the peaks were much more widely spaced and considerably less lofty than during the silent period. In Chapters 2 to 7, I will examine in more detail the major film projects outlined here, the conflicts Brunel encountered while making them and how he navigated those with greater or lesser degrees of success.

CHAPTER 2

A Syndicate of Beggars: Minerva Films Ltd and Independent Short Film Production

In the summer of 1921 the following report appeared in *Film Renter and Moving Picture News*:

> Certain scenes in 'The Beggars' Syndicate,' which Adrian Brunel is producing for Minerva Films, are laid in the famous Caledonian Market . . . A few days ago the Company . . . assembled in the market, while Adrian Brunel and Frank Hoffman, the camera-man, climbed the central tower for some high 'shots' . . . When Brunel returned to earth, looking like a tramp on account of the dirt from the tower, a stall-holder, looking at Mary Patterson and Bert Darley, who were dressed very shabbily, asked what the film was called. On being told 'The Beggars' Syndicate,' he replied 'No, I asked what was the name of the film and not the name of the company!'
> (16 July 1921: 34)

This anecdote made an entertaining piece of publicity for what was to be Brunel's final production for Minerva Films Ltd but the stallholder's quip is a telling one. Given the meagre funds then available to them, the film's title was indeed equally applicable to the company itself. While the first six films made under the auspices of Minerva had been two-reel shorts, *The Beggars' Syndicate* was a five-reeler, a considerable risk given the company's already precarious finances. The shorts had been produced on minimal budgets but it was impossible to make enough profit from their sales to sustain further production, leading the company to pursue less reputable sources for ever-dwindling amounts of investment.

But back in March 1920, Brunel had embarked on the venture with high hopes, anticipating his first proper chance to direct and put into practice his creative ideas without the interference he had endured at BAFC. Minerva's first project was a series of four short films based on stories by playwright and humorist A. A. Milne. Short- and medium-length productions were a key element of the cinema programme at this time, yet, as with features, British films faced tough competition for screen time from America, particularly as shorts often formed part of the packages sold by studios through their practices of block booking. While it may appear obvious now that the feature film was always destined to become the primary commercial cinematic form, there were those in the early 1920s who championed the short film. During the decade, it developed both as a commercial object and as a cinematic form capable of offering opportunities for British cinema to develop along more creative lines. This is how Brunel regarded it when he joined Minerva Films, but his ambitions were hampered by the insecure financial conditions of the small production outfit.

Brunel and the Short Film

Most writing on the short film is interested in it as a medium for experimental and underground productions but some of the theory that has emerged can be applied to the form in a more general sense. Myles P. Breen observes: 'The short film can legitimately be considered as a showcase for technique. What might distract and detract from the narrative in a feature, may be legitimate in a short' (1978: 4). During periods of unemployment, Brunel turned to the short film as a way to keep his hand in, maintain his profile and 'sell himself' as a director, and it is not too much of a stretch to compare him to artist filmmakers, who '*have* to make their films as a poet *has* to write a poem. The main satisfaction is in the realization of the creative impulse' (David A. Sohn, quoted in Raskin 2002: 3, his italics). While Brunel's 'creative impulse' should not be overemphasised, neither should it be entirely ignored; his short films are perhaps the clearest expression of his style and humour and offer some of the best examples of his ability to harness his imagination within various generic forms.

From his time at the Ministry of Information during the First World War, where he developed the 'Film Tag', until the Second World War, when he was again working on propaganda, the short film is woven throughout Brunel's career. Without the resources to work on feature films, he would turn his hand to short subjects to experiment with ideas and keep himself occupied. Yet while Brunel did experiment with film form and was sufficiently dedicated to the medium to work independently when no other option was available, it is possible to overstate the originality of the works. As described, the period between 1920 and 1925 was an extremely tough one for British film. The domestic industry was going through great changes and by the middle of the decade the kind of inadequately financed productions undertaken by short-lived and precarious companies such as Minerva came to an end. Yet at this moment in Brunel's career, Minerva offered him a way out of the difficult and demoralising situation he found himself in at BAFC. He was caught between his desire for artistic control and a need for financial stability, and hoped to achieve both through Minerva. He also regarded it as a chance to raise the intellectual tone of the cinema and contribute to the development of an identifiably British filmmaking style.

The Minerva Set-up

Brunel's experiences in the industry prior to joining Minerva had given him valuable insights into the business. The making of his first film, *The Cost of a Kiss*, had been particularly educational, not only about the practicalities of production but also the importance of protecting the negative of a film as a valuable asset which could easily be ruined. His run-ins with the distributor while at BAFC had made him aware of an anti-intellectual streak among trade figures who, in turn, regarded Brunel's approach as 'highbrow'. Observations on the industry that Brunel made in his correspondence reveal the way that his thinking about the business was developing. He understood the economics of film production well enough to know the difficulty of profiting from it without having sufficient funds up front, not only to ensure the quality of the product but also maintain control of distribution. Writing to his friend John Payne, Brunel asserted that a film company needed initial investment of £100,000, saying, 'It is only doing business on such a scale that big money can be made. One must have enough to rent one's own pictures' (30 March 1919, ABSC 2/107).

Yet when Brunel joined Minerva Films Ltd he was allocated only £5,000 with which to produce four short comedies. The firm was set up by actor Leslie Howard to boost his own film career, an aim presumably shared by co-founder and actor C. Aubrey Smith. Also involved was actor-manager Nigel Playfair, while financial backing for the enterprise came from Richard Fitz Power and Harry F. Towler, both recently demobilised. Towler appears to have been new to the film business but Power had 'spent a very considerable portion of his time in investigations into the technical side of kinematography' (*Kinematograph Year Book*, 1921: 547), although it is doubtful that he had much experience of production. Both may well have invested their army pay-outs in the new company, as did many former soldiers eager to get into the film business.

Brunel immediately took charge of production, eager to put his ideas into practice. However, with this creative freedom came considerable frustration caused by the limited financial resources and a company board with little understanding of how films were made, pressures which led to a stressful working situation. On the positive side, he found himself at the centre of a creative group of like-minded men and thrived on their companionship and support. Milne's humour and style were a good fit with Brunel's own, while Howard and Aubrey Smith also contributed considerable talent. Experienced cameraman H. M. Lomas and writer and assistant Bernard Carrodus, a Cambridge graduate also recently demobbed, completed the team. These largely university-educated men set to work to create four comedy shorts, aiming to raise the form above the usual slapstick offered by supporting programmes.

Minerva as Experiment

In her article 'Play as Experiment in 1920s British Cinema', Christine Gledhill identifies Minerva's project as part of a strand of peculiarly British cinematic experimentation located within what she terms the 'midstream' of filmmaking, i.e. somewhere between mainstream and amateur, which existed immediately after the war. She describes an environment that allowed filmmakers to 'expand, or "play" upon, the boundaries of what cinema might do' (2008: 16) and links this to the penchant for entertainment and game-playing which developed in postwar British society. Gledhill's case for this very British form of experimentation relies heavily on Brunel's work to illustrate the argument, referencing all of his extant pre-1927 works. While Gledhill refers to the 'Minerva comedies', she focuses on the Milne films rather than the company's other three titles. While these illustrate nicely the kind of child's play that marks such experimentation, the later Minerva films, although lost, are equally worthy examples; the pressbook for *A Temporary Lady* (1921) sums up the film's plot thus: 'It is all nonsense of course, but the best fun is always that'.

Gledhill's description of Brunel's filmmaking activities suggests that entertainment was a key element of both the films and the production process, referring to the 'spontaneous invention and "fun"' only occasionally dampened by the 'frustration' of having to find funding (2008: 17–18). This conjures up a picture of a happy-go-lucky group engaged in filmmaking largely for their own amusement, but reference to Brunel's paper collection reveals the reality of his experiences during his time at Minerva. Under intense scrutiny by producers and financiers, struggling to get his films made and shown and constantly on the edge of bankruptcy, Brunel is unlikely to have regarded it as 'cinematic Bohemia' (2008: 18). Although his humour was irrepressible and he never lost his enthusiasm for filmmaking, his experiences with Minerva were another harsh lesson in the realities of the British industry. While Brunel had definite ideas about developing British cinema along more artistic lines, he had to make a living and was aware of the need for commercial success. His pursuit of these twin aims through the short film shows his faith in it as the ideal form for the type of intelligent yet accessible humour he was keen to perfect.

The Problem of the Short Film

The lack of academic attention given to the short film has led one commentator to describe it as 'the neglected stepchild of cinema studies' (Hjort: 81). While writing on the short narrative film is relatively rare, works that trace its development from the earliest days of cinema, either as a form of expression or as a commercial proposition, are all but nonexistent. For the first fifteen years of the cinema, all films were short, restricted by the length of the reel inside the camera, and the history of the medium is inextricably linked to changes in cinematographic technology and developing exhibition structures. While longer 'feature' films gradually became the preferred commercial format, short films remained a key element of an exhibition strategy that emulated the theatrical variety show.

The first cinematograph films lasted a few minutes and were records of locations or events, made primarily to demonstrate the capabilities of the new technology. As the equipment and the imagination of filmmakers improved, films were no longer limited by the amount of celluloid that the cameras could hold and the art of 'cutting' together several reels into a narrative began to be explored. Until around 1914, most films were one- or two-reelers, running between 10 and 20 minutes. The length of the films dictated the exhibition practices, leading to programmes consisting of several films, or a mixture of film and theatrical variety, depending on the venue. Low records that there was resistance in the exhibition trade when this pattern was threatened by the increasing length of films: 'The Trade Press, responsible commentators, and exhibitors' meetings repeatedly and in defiance of the facts expressed the view that "there are few plays which could rivet the attention of an audience for an hour"' (1949: 48). Small showmen were fundamentally against the development for economic reasons, as Low explained:

> When films were short . . . and a programme need last only an hour, a hall with four hundred seats could hold enough shows every day to cover costs, but programmes of two or three hours reduced the turnover to such an extent that even the cheaper 'super films' were beyond their means. (1950: 27)

Into the 1920s, there was a fear that longer films would eventually drive out the shorter subjects, yet there were still those who believed that some audience members preferred shorts. F. Rupert Crew expressed the view that 'long films do not appeal to everyone' and that 'rather than sit through two long features, many people . . . stop away . . .' (1922). But films continued to get longer and the feature film, as its name suggests, was driven by commercial imperatives as much as artistic ones. However, the feature film's gradual takeover of the exhibition market, far from spelling the end of the short film, encouraged its development in different directions. Bryony Dixon observes that while 'the 90-minute feature began to dominate the cinema programmes . . . [s]hort films . . . continued to be the bread and butter of production' (2012: 5). In the late teens and early 1920s, most films released were one of three lengths: the one- or two-reel filler (each reel lasting just under 10 minutes), the five-reel feature and films of eight to ten reels, the most lavish of which were dubbed 'super-pictures'. By 1923, the mid-length five-reel feature was becoming obsolete, one observer noting that 'one of the most important British producing organisations . . . has ceased making them entirely, and is devoting its energies to the comparatively expensive "super-picture" . . . and – *the two-reel subject*' (*MPS*, 12 May 1923: 10; their italics). Production companies invested ever-larger amounts into making features and heavily promoting their stars. Meanwhile, short films, which rarely fetched the kind of rental sums commanded by features, were made on relatively small budgets and therefore could still offer filmmakers a degree of freedom to experiment.

While producers often struggled to profit from short fiction films, 'interest films' were very popular with audiences and elevated the form above its lowly and often lowbrow status. Series such as Percy Smith's *Secrets of Nature* made for British Instructional and John Betts' *Sporting Life* films produced by Stoll were lauded as intelligent programme fillers. They experimented with cinematic techniques such as time-lapse and slow-motion photography, techniques also being employed by the European avant-garde filmmakers. Brunel himself was later to play with such techniques in the pursuit of humorous effects and the Film Society programmes would screen all three genres of silent film that regularly used cinematic trickery: artistic, scientific and comedic.

Exhibiting the Short Film

Crew's belief in the short film was vindicated by a statement of faith in its commercial and artistic value near the end of 1923, when *The Bioscope* announced that producer and distributor New Era Films had taken over the Embassy Theatre in Holborn 'for the purpose of showing an all-short programme' (6 December 1923: 36). The journal reported: 'There has been a great deal of discussion recently in the trade regarding the box-office value of short features, and many people have advocated the establishment of a short feature house.' New Era was keen to emphasise that quality was key to their plans, *The Bioscope* asserting that 'the exhibition of any short film at the Embassy will become a real hall-mark of merit'. However, while newsreel cinemas had proved a popular form of exhibition specialisation, it appears that the concept of a cinema programme consisting of short films was not a draw for audiences and New Era's experiment was short-lived. By April 1924, the Embassy Theatre adopted a new programming strategy and became, according to Henry K. Miller, 'a leading claimant to the title of London's first "continental" or "art" cinema' (2013: 79). This too was a transient phase for the venue and, the following year, it was converted into a factory.

For exhibitors, the short film remained an important element of the cinema programme, with audiences expecting a combination of a long feature, accompanied by one shorter (often five-reel) feature or several fiction shorts, and the 'topicals' (news and interest films). However, by the 1920s the selling point of the programme was the main feature, meaning the short 'fillers' were of less value to the exhibitor and could not usually command high rents. With the large number of American shorts on the market, it was difficult for new British producers to get their films on the screen, especially comedies, since there were many well-established comedy franchises already on the market.

For ease of marketing and to render them more attractive, shorts were generally sold in packages of six or twelve titles, usually with a common theme or star. Larger companies were better able to fund these and could make use of available equipment, personnel and studio space in between feature productions. For smaller firms looking to produce a series of six films the investment required could be as much as the cost of a feature, or perhaps even more, since the shorts would require the writing of six scenarios and very probably different casts, costumes and locations.[1] A further problem was the long delay between the trade show of a film and its release, a gap of between six months and one year, which was an impossibly long period for a small company to wait for the profits from rentals to come in. Thus there was little incentive to spend large amounts on such films, and shorts were often criticised as cheap and inferior products, leading to demands within the trade for better-quality short and mid-length films. In fact, throughout the first half of the 1920s,

---

[1] This did not apply to the serial, an episodic storytelling mode which was screened at cinemas weekly to tempt audiences back to find out what happened next.

the role of the short film was a popular topic of discussion in the trade press.

Profiting from Short Films

Although Brunel's Minerva shorts received positive reviews, he failed to profit from them, either financially or in terms of significantly furthering his career. To some degree, his lack of progression within the film industry was exacerbated by his pursuit of a filmmaking form that was particularly difficult to make money from in the short term. For most of this period, the financing his companies received was very much on a hand-to-mouth basis and Brunel often worked without pay for long periods, or found himself having to supplement production costs from his own pocket. Together with the failure to establish a relationship with a reliable distribution set-up, these problems meant that Brunel and his associates spent a disproportionate amount of their time and energy managing the business side of Minerva rather than concentrating on their creative output. Without the infrastructure of a more firmly established production company, it was almost impossible for a filmmaker to forge a stable career and produce a body of work upon which to build a reputation. As the landscape in Britain changed from small-scale concerns and independent film production to a more secure studio system, directors like Brunel found it increasingly difficult to make an impression on the market through short films, especially as the 'feature' presentation became the commercial norm.

The key to the successful distribution of the short film was a well-packaged series with an obvious selling point. One British firm that managed to establish a reputation in this area was Ideal, a company that started out in production but soon realised that controlling the sales of American comedy shorts was a more secure basis for a business. Under the directorship of Simon Rowson, Ideal was the most high-profile provider of such films, the company's adverts promising to add 'pep' to programmes and assuring exhibitors that their shorts, far from being mere 'fillers', were 'fillers of seats, fillers of theatres, fillers of pay-boxes!!' (*The Bioscope*, 19 March 1925: 21).

The idea that shorts were as valuable to exhibitors as features was eagerly promoted by those involved in their production. Screenwriter Eliot Stannard, who went on to collaborate with Brunel and, more notably, Alfred Hitchcock, penned many short film scenarios for British and Colonial Kinematograph Company (B&C) in the early to mid-1920s. These included the six-part series *Wonder Women of the World* (1923), depicting scenes in the lives of female historical figures, and *Gems of*

Literature (1923), twelve two-reel films which offered audiences potted versions of works by the likes of Shakespeare and Dickens. Speaking to *The Bioscope* on behalf of B&C, Stannard described the company's shorts as 'pictures from which all the padding has been eliminated and only punch left, and in which a subject that could well fill eight reels has been compressed' (18 January 1923: 50). As such, he expressed the view that the company's two-reelers deserved to earn much higher rental fees than they currently commanded and should be put at the top of the bill. Stannard was already one of British cinema's most experienced and accomplished screenwriters and wrote many articles about his craft and its importance to the creative process of filmmaking. A writer of his experience must have realised that, while reducing great literary works to bite-size programme fillers may have been a successful sales tactic, it was unlikely to contribute to the development of the art of film.

Despite Stannard's apparent belief that shorts could be a substantial draw for audiences, the continued supremacy of the feature film as the main selling point of a cinema programme was inevitable and, if it was to improve, the short film required an approach more suited to the form. Some felt that the obsession with film length was a distraction from, or even a hindrance to, the development of quality products. 'Is it not just this fetish of length worship that is throttling the free development of picture making?' asked one observer: 'You meet many five-reel "stories" sawn and chipped in order to fit into one spool of film, and a depressingly large number of pale, thin, anaemic themes stretched and strained over five pain-packed reels' (*The Bioscope*, 9 March 1922: 5). Clearly, some in the trade were beginning to realise that the form should fit the subject, rather than the other way round.

Art and the Short Film: Cooper's Quality Film Plays

One of the most successful series of short subjects drew on literary sources less highbrow than those adapted by Stannard, but which were almost certainly more suitable for screen adaptation. Director George A. Cooper garnered considerable attention for his 'Quality Film Plays', two-reelers made between 1922 and 1924 based chiefly on short stories from popular magazines such as *Pan*. Cooper's films had screened at the Embassy in Holborn and were singled out for praise by Crew, who believed a successful cinema programme had to include good-quality fiction shorts. Writing off the typical cinema programme as 'boring', he advised exhibitors to seek out better-quality shorts to complement their feature presentations. Earlier, Crew had bemoaned the fact that one particular short film, which he regarded as a 'brilliant little effort at originality', had received no bookings at all (Crew 1922). The reason for this, according to his neighbour at the trade screening, was that the film was 'Too good for 'em! Won't understand it!' (ibid.). Crew, who went on to become a leading literary agent, was one of a growing number of educated cinemagoers who felt that exhibitors were failing to provide thoughtful fare, instead lazily pandering to the less demanding audience members. He called for a more 'highbrow' approach to the medium, which should aim to bring to the screen 'the world's masterpieces in short fiction pictured in one or two reels' and comedies that 'break away from the American slap-stick, of which the kinema-going public is so tired' (ibid.).

Cooper could not afford 'masterpieces' but found other ways to raise the standard of his films above the majority of those on the market. Crew hailed him as 'a man . . . [who] has truly grasped the vital need for producing short stuff on super lines. He has given his little pictures not only artistic and conscientious direction, but has utilised star casts, proper sets, lighting and fine photography' (*MPS*, 23 September 1922: 6). Cooper's training had consisted of several years running the editing department of London Independent Film Trading Company, a rental firm that imported European films for distribution in Britain. Here, Cooper 'probably viewed and edited more Continental pictures than anybody in the industry and his experience . . . certainly afforded him unique opportunities to acquire an intimate knowledge of film construction' (*The Bioscope*, 16 February 1922: 20–1). Brunel was to have a similar education through his own editing work.

Unfortunately, none of Cooper's Quality Film Plays have survived and records are scant. They received good coverage in the trade press, not least for their casting of star performers. Although Miller claims they were 'well received but poorly distributed' (2013: 77), Cooper managed to produce three series and even sold some to America. *Motion Picture Studio* asserted that his objective was 'to give to the public little dramatic or humorous stories in which the subtlety of detail finds expression . . . None of the plots . . . are conventional or banal . . . the subtitle is always subordinate to pictorial expression' (*MPS*, 10 February 1923: 6), aims that chimed with those of Brunel. The films certainly earned Cooper considerable respect within the trade and in 1924 *Kinematograph Weekly* was eager to know 'What George Cooper thinks', printing an article in which he expounded his views on the art of filmmaking (10 January 1924: 71). The previous month, *Motion Picture Studio* had also sought his opinion, this time on the conditions of British film production. His response was to call for film financiers to have a belief in the purpose of the British film, its ability not only to give entertainment value but also to express England! If you are only interested in British films for the money that may lie in them, then YOU do not help their progress. (1923)

Cooper clearly shared Brunel's faith in the creative potential of the medium and saw the need for the development of an indigenous form of filmmaking. The trajectories of the two directors ran parallel: like Brunel, Cooper was taken on by Gainsborough in the mid-1920s but found himself underemployed and in May 1926 was released from his contract. His career did not live up to the promise of his Quality Film Plays and he too spent the 1930s engaged in quota quickie production.

Minerva: The Genesis

Cooper's Quality Film Plays may well have developed and improved upon Brunel's earlier efforts at Minerva to raise the standard of the short film. While both series featured actors with a theatrical pedigree, the Minerva films had the unusual advantage of being based on Milne's original screen stories, essentially British in tone, which Brunel adapted into neat modern playlets. Brunel's idea of commissioning original screen stories from popular writers made sound business sense, since the producer could benefit from the author's name yet not pay the high prices commanded by a published work.

Despite a desire to create a new and very British departure in short filmmaking, Minerva looked across the Atlantic for its model, taking inspiration from the work of American variety star Sidney Drew. His hugely popular films were made between 1911 and 1919 and paired him with his wife in comedies that focused on the pitfalls of married life. While most screen comedians traded on a named alter ego, Drew's films were situational and he often portrayed the hen-pecked husband trying to appease a domineering wife. Production values were high; promotional material for the 1919 film *Romance and Rings* claimed that the films were

> produced with all the care and skill that Mr and Mrs Sidney Drew can possibly put into them . . . [i]t takes them a month to make one of these new comedies – a month but it's worth that to give your people a half hour of hearty laughs.[2]

Brunel had much less time and considerably less money to make his films. Budgetary restrictions found him back at the cramped and

---

[2] Accessed at http://en.wikipedia.org/wiki/File:Romance_and_Rings.jpg on 27 June 2021.

inadequate Bushey Studios filming the interiors between 17 and 29 May 1920. The following weeks were spent on location and the films include a great deal of exterior shooting, in line with Howard's original idea that the company should bring to native comedy the 'joie de vivre that only the sunlight, and nature's own surroundings can infuse into a production' (n.d., ABSC 1/107).

Like the Drew comedies, Milne's stories turned to the foibles of middle-class contemporary society for their subject matter. However, rather than the dynamics between husband and wife, he focused on modern youth and intergenerational relationships, in particular the obstacles the older generation put in the way of young love. The Milne films stand up well in comparison to the Sidney Drew shorts. While the American films had intricate plots that required frequent and lengthy intertitles to guide audiences through them, Milne and Brunel aimed at narrative simplicity, employing titles more creatively, often to embellish the action or address the audience directly. Four Milne comedies were made and while they all pursue a romantic outcome, the target of the humour varies.

The Bump

In *The Bump*,[3] C. Aubrey Smith plays famous explorer John Brice, who is idolised by bright young thing Lillian Montrevor. Brice is like a hero of *Boys' Own* stories who explores uncharted territory in the name of King and Empire. He has recorded his adventures in several books, which Lillian devours eagerly and, although he appears old enough to be her father, she is thrilled when she meets him at a party. Her beau, Freddy Fane, is devastated to be thrown over but cannot compete with the manly exploits of Brice, since his only talent is an aptitude for modern dance steps. Brice accepts Lilian's invitation to tea but since 'He has never been on an expedition by himself before' it takes him six months to find her house. Meanwhile, she has settled for Fane and their wedding is underway as the explorer finally arrives at Stuccoway Terrace.

While this points up the fickleness of modern youth, the real target of Milne's humour is British imperialism, as embodied by the explorer. The first view of Brice is in close-up, his facial attributes described using arrows and handwritten luggage labels which appear on screen. The image

[3] The title refers to Brice's 'Bump of Locality', a dig at phrenology, the study of the significance of bumps on different parts of the head which was popular in the early nineteenth century. Although long discredited by the scientific community, it experienced a renewal of interest in the twentieth century. The bump of locality indicated a good sense of direction.

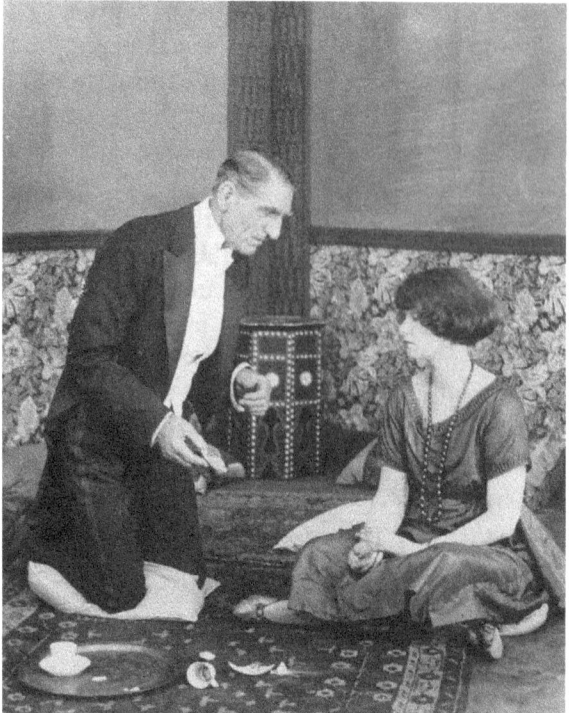

Figure 2.1 C. Aubrey Smith and Faith Celli in *The Bump*.
Source: BFI National Archive.

draws attention to the scars from, variously, 'argument with leopard', 'dual [sic] with scorpeon [sic] in Africa', 'shark bite in Red Sea' and 'legacy from angry bison (N. America)'.[4] Smith was well cast as Brice; his middle-aged upper-class bluster perfectly suits the character of a pompous celebrity. Brice embodies Lillian's ideal; as she tells Freddie: 'If I ever marry, it must be a <u>man</u> who has <u>done</u> things.' But it becomes apparent that without his native guide and carriers, the accoutrements of an outdated colonialism, Brice is incapable of functioning – an anachronism more useless than the apparently fatuous 'jazzer' Freddie Fane.

£5 *Reward*

Leslie Howard secured himself roles in two of the Milne films, in the hope of establishing himself as a comic film actor. In *£5 Reward* he plays a young

---

[4] The spelling mistakes may have been deliberate, perhaps implying the explorer's ignorance, or may be the fault of the title designer, Carlo Norway.

Figure 2.2 Leslie Howard and Barbara Hoffe in £5 *Reward*.
Source: BFI National Archive.

aristocrat in love with a farmer's daughter. The plot turns on its head the more usual convention in British films, that of lower-class characters achieving upward mobility via inheritance or marriage. In Milne's story, it is the aristocrat (Tony Marchmont, 'son of a hundred earls') who must prove himself worthy of Audrey, the daughter of a farmer (clearly a landowner rather than a labourer). The discrepancy in their status, according to the intertitles, 'is no reason why he should not kiss her again'. Unimpressed with Tony's private income, the farmer insists that any suitor for his daughter must be able to earn money 'by the sweat of his brow' and gives Tony a month to earn £5. Audrey expresses doubts that an indolent member of the upper classes such as Tony could possess any talents by which he could earn a living but he sets out to prove her wrong. His first assignment is cleaning out a pigsty for a shilling and the realisation of the scale of the task before him gradually dawns ('If a man earns one shilling in one day, how many months will it take him to earn five pounds?'). The incomplete copy of the film held in the BFI National Archive ends here but the conclusion of the tale can be found in the script in Brunel's collection (ABSC 2/121). The farmer loses Tony's pocketbook, having taken charge of it when he set the challenge, and Audrey finds it. She persuades her father to offer a reward for its safe return and engineers it so that Tony finds the pocketbook and can claim his £5 reward along with Audrey's hand.

Like Brice, the aristocratic Tony is painted as an anachronism in the postwar world. With no discernible skills, he is only able to win the hand of his love with her help and, by outwitting her father, she proves herself smarter than both men. Howard has some quite effective comedy 'business', demonstrating how lost the young aristocrat is away from his home comforts. Forced to wash in the farmyard, Tony rubs his face with water from a barrel, then, eyes closed, holds out his hands to receive a towel from a non-existent valet. Later, he contemplates a ploughman's lunch with confusion before attempting to construct a sandwich from the huge wedges of bread and cheese.

Bookworms

In *Bookworms* Howard plays Richard, another young man in love, but this time the object of his affection is closely guarded by her uncle and aunt, forcing him to invent clever ruses to get close to her. By inserting a note into a library book intended for his amour, Miranda, he inadvertently reawakens the passion between the girl's stern guardians as well as matchmaking the housekeeper with a stranger. With these characters out of the way, the path is clear for Richard to declare his love to Miranda. Howard's character is another rather feckless youth who lays in bed till all hours and contemplates suicide or emigration when his romantic plans are foiled.

The story is presented as a fairy tale, with Miranda as the fair maid imprisoned in a castle and guarded by a dragon in the form of the elderly housekeeper-cum-chaperone. The titles are decorated with appropriate imagery and set up oppositions with the shots that follow, in a foreshadowing of Brunel's more extreme juxtaposition of text and image in his burlesques. Thus a card announcing that Miranda 'lived in a lovely Castle' is followed by a shot of an ivy-covered suburban house. Richard is cast as the 'Young Knight' who must defeat the dragon and the Wicked Uncle who protect Miranda, yet he is far from the ideal storybook hero. This construction of the plot around fairy-tale tropes is an element of the film's thematic link with books, the title card announcing it as *A Comedy in Two Volumes*. The plot itself revolves around visits to the library, and books are the means by which the romantic outcome is engineered. Characters are marked out by their reading material: Miranda is shown buried in Adam Smith's *The Wealth of Nations*, while her uncle and aunt read more sensational fare such as the biographical *Life in Mormon Bondage* and *Shadow of a Crime* by middlebrow author Hall Caine.

Twice Two

The last of the four films, *Twice Two*, again features matchmaking, as a young couple attempt to unite their widowed parents so they can marry each other without leaving them alone. Jack and Jill meet when both decide to paint a picture of the same thatched cottage by a river. They gradually fall in love but neither wants to abandon their solitary parent, so they hatch a plan to bring them together by arranging a rendezvous with them that they fail to attend. The plan works and the film ends with them forming two couples. Here again, the generation gap is a key element of the film and both young people, despite being devoted to their parents, find their lives and interests dull. Thus, in their respective homes we see 'the Colonel telling Jill how he went round the course that morning in 82 – or 182 we forget which' and 'Mrs Romer telling Jack how the vicar bored her'.

The Reception of the Milne Comedies

The trade show for the Milne comedies at the West End Cinema in September 1920 featured only three of the films: *The Bump*, *Bookworms* and *£5 Reward*, with *Twice Two* still being edited. The pressbook contains humorous synopses written by Milne, and comic observations on the productions. For example, it announces that for the production of *Bookworms* 'it is estimated that 18973524 books are employed in the library scenes. We wish, however to contradict the rumour that these are unsold copies of Mr Milne's latest novel', while the credits for *£5 Reward* include the note that 'pigs, cows, farm-hands, geese, donkeys and other wild fowl [were] trained with inexhaustible patience by Bernard Carrodus and photographed at great personal risk by H. M. Lomas'.

The newspapers greeted the films with general enthusiasm but some reservations. The *Daily Express* felt that '[t]he technical qualities displayed in these clever two-reelers are good without being brilliant' while the view of the *Morning Post* was that '[i]t is all slight but there is a vivacity, a gaiety and a humour' (ABSC 176). However, some in the trade appeared to understand what Brunel and Milne were aiming to achieve and *Film Renter and Moving Picture News* declared that 'Mr Milne has raised the standard of film art on its lighter side and shown that it is possible to be humorous without pails of whitewash' (ABSC 4/107). There was also an appreciation that the films were attempting to produce something original and British: 'It can be truly said that, prior to this show, British film humour did not exist' claimed the *Daily Express*, while the *Morning Post* declared, 'The new venture of Minerva Films Limited gives us great hope that we have at last evolved a true native type of "the movie"' (ibid.). *Picture Show* devoted a two-page spread to the films in which columnist Edith Nepean's interview with Brunel confirmed his heightened sensitivity regarding his standing in the film community. He stated that due to his enthusiasm for film writing 'my highbrow literary friends . . . dropped me as a crank' yet asserted, 'I was also regarded as one by my new associates in the film world, since I looked upon picture-making from another standpoint than that of mere money-making' (20 November 1920: 15).

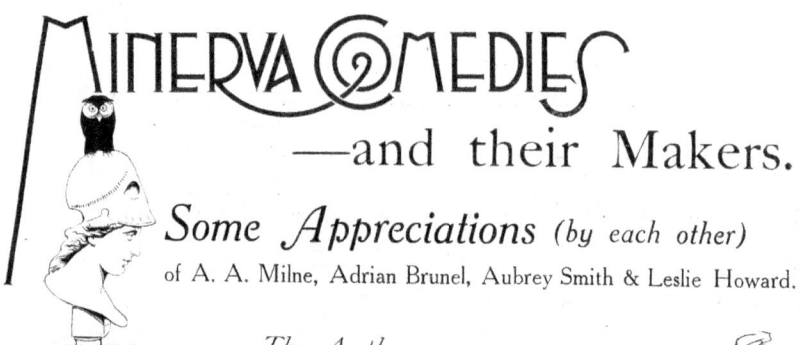

The Author.

A. A. MILNE. His famous contribution to "Punch" and his successful Stage Comedies have placed Mr. Milne high in the ranks of our wittiest writers. I am sure that you will agree that his clever Film Comedies with their true British humour will further enhance this reputation.

By L.H.

The Producer.

ADRIAN BRUNEL is that *rara avis*—a producer with a sense of humour.

L.H.

The Stars.

AUBREY SMITH is a man of colossal ability and keen insight and has often admired my acting. True, he has never said so, but you know what these strong, silent men are.

L.H.

LESLIE HOWARD. I *could* say something strong about this young fellow—but I prefer to say something silent.

A.S.

Figure 2.3 Pressbook for the Milne comedies. Source: author's own collection.

The company board members seemed less than happy with the finished films. Playfair found fault with the performances and the sets and Brunel responded defensively: 'I did my best under the circumstances' (ABSC 5/107). The trade show had failed to attract many film renters and the subsequent delay in securing a sale meant the positive press reaction counted for little and distributors were wary. *Kinematograph Weekly* announced that the films were to be handled by the Cinematograph Intelligence Bureau, a small cinema chain, but this came to nothing. Brunel eventually sold the films to Moss Empires for £200 each, a significant loss, negotiating an additional 25 per cent of the profits on bookings over £750 per picture.

Early in 1921, Moss advertised the films rather half-heartedly at the bottom of their bill of new releases, as 'Minerva Comedies', dubbed 'A new departure' (*The Bioscope*, 6 January 1921: 58–9). Meanwhile, Brunel continued to try and sell the films abroad, but his hopes of earning a profit to finance further productions soon faded and, despite the apparently marketable combination of a popular writer and a relatively well-known theatrical cast, the Milne comedies disappeared from view.

Re-evaluating the Milne Comedies

George Perry pinned the failure of the films on the fact that 'there was as yet in British film comedies no place for West End theatrical humour' (1975: 49). However, Milne's film stories rise above this label: peppered with wry intertitles and shot largely outdoors they eschew the staginess it suggests. In fact, they are highly cinematic and contain some original and genuinely amusing devices. The Milne comedy of which Brunel was most proud was *The Bump*, referring to it as Minerva's '*chef-d'oeuvre*' (1949: 61), and Gledhill regards it as an 'exemplary' comedy of the period (2003: 159). She identifies what she terms a 'literateness' in the film, by which the images possess an 'articulacy', effectively purveying narrative or characterisation (ibid.). Thus in *The Bump*, a shot of Freddie's feet, dancing 'divinely', pans up to his smile, the two images illustrating his personality. Elsewhere, verbal and visual messages mix so that the film images contain text (such as the labelling of Brice's face), while the decorated titles are illustrative as well as informative. The illustrated intertitles are a key element in the films' comic effect; considerably more detailed and complex than those used in most films, they alternately complement or undermine the text, a technique Brunel was to use four years later in *Crossing the Great Sagrada*. These titles were designed by Brunel's friend Carlo Norway, founder of the Decorative Arts Society and a member of a group of bohemians centred around Augustus John's Crab Tree Club. Brunel's connection to this group was to come to the fore when he directed his first feature, but commissioning a modernist artist to illustrate the titles was clearly part of the strategy to raise the films above the usual standard of British productions. In his future plans for the company, Brunel proposed the artists Edmund Dulac and Claud Lovat Fraser as potential collaborators (ABSC 6/107).

The innovative approach of Brunel and Milne is also apparent from the sophisticated comic devices used in the films, such as the subversion of traditional storytelling modes and cinematic convention. The films play with the notion of the 'omnipotent author', chiefly through intertitles written as if the authorial voice they represent is as ignorant of the outcome of the narrative as the audience. As *The Bump* begins, we are shown images of each of the main characters but the titles express doubt over the importance of the male leads: 'It's just possible he may be the hero. We are not sure yet. Have another look at him just in case'. The titles thus call into question the films as works of fiction; the first title of *£5 Reward* states, 'It is convenient to begin with that Tuesday ...', as if events are picked at random rather than plotted in advance. According to Brunel, *Twice Two* opened with a 'burlesque of the popular Wild West film' which ended abruptly to be followed by a title reading 'Sorry – wrong film' before beginning the story in earnest (1949: 61).[5]

This type of self-reflexivity was not new to British comedy and the series of shorts featuring Fred Paul's popular character Pimple, which ran from 1912 to 1922, flaunted cheapness and ineptitude to humorous effect. Brunel relied on it less for the Minerva films (more so in his later burlesques), although it is glimpsed in the use of cartoon representations of Brice's adventures at the Pole and the Equator in *The Bump*, which stand in for location shots. Brunel and Milne chose to use the technique in a more complex way, foregrounding not the artificiality of the set and props but the very nature of the short film, laying bare its intrinsic narrational devices and drawing humour from the exposure of the usually omniscient storyteller as powerless to predict the outcome of their own tale.

The Minerva project was a valuable exercise in exploring new sources for the cinema. Having experienced the difficulties of adapting existing literature for the screen while at BAFC, Brunel turned to specially

---

[5] Brunel attributes this joke to Milne and states that it was at the start of *£5 Reward*. However, while the Wild West sequence itself has not survived (perhaps discarded by an overzealous archivist, or maybe even reused elsewhere by Brunel himself), the title relating to it can be found in the BFI National Archive's print of *Twice Two*. I therefore assume it belongs in that film.

written film stories, and the collaboration with Milne seemed a perfect arrangement. His plan was to continue commissioning original stories by other popular authors and playwrights. Others were thinking along the same lines; Bamford notes that Jesse Lasky, of Famous Players-Lasky, came to Britain in 1920 seeking deals with authors such as J. M. Barrie, H. G. Wells and Arnold Bennett for 'original stories written specifically for the screen, with special consideration for [its] requirements' (*Cinema Chat*, quoted in Bamford: 73). Brunel had his sights set on similar targets and his notes record that, after working with Milne, he hoped to obtain the 'co-operation of distinguished authors at minimum cost', contenders also including Wells and Bennett along with W. W. Jacobs, George Bernard Shaw and F. Anstey (ABSC 6/107). Brunel's idea of commissioning film stories from authors was a canny one as it lent the production the kudos of a popular name but avoided the high cost and the considerable pressure of adapting a popular work. Brunel's plan was a step towards a more constructive and economical use of the talents of writers interested in the medium and could have marked a genuinely innovative approach to British cinema.

Before the Minerva films were sold, Howard had set off for New York to pursue his stage career. Brunel wrote to him there, complaining about the state of the industry and asking for a cheque as he was 'terribly hard up' (28 December 1920, ABSC 4/107). Despite the interest the trade press showed in his work, Brunel struggled to win support within the industry. While his attempt to bring intelligent humour to British screens was appreciated by commentators such as Crew, Minerva did not have the business experience to secure proper distribution for the Milne-authored comedies.

A Temporary Lady

Despite the financial failure of their first four titles, Minerva embarked on two further films early in 1921. The announcement of these productions in the trade papers suggested that the collaboration with popular authors was at an end; one was based on a short story while the other, entitled *A Temporary Lady*, was co-written by Brunel and an apparent unknown called Mill Wadham. *A Temporary Lady* was a two-reel comedy and, although it has not survived, *Kinematograph Weekly*'s review provides this plot summary:

> A 'slavey' who works in a boarding house falls in love with a man who drives up each week in a Rolls-Royce. She gets a legacy of 50 pounds. She leaves 'service' and

dresses as a man and follows the man to a hotel. They become acquainted. She then changes and introduces herself as the sister. The man falls in love with her. She confesses her deception, and he tells her that he is not rich and only a salesman. (11 May 1922, ABSC 4/107)

The film starred Annette Benson and Miles Mander. In keeping with Brunel's interest in cinema as a source of humour, Benson's character was a movie obsessive:

> Her whole outlook on life was affected by 'the pictures'. If she had a tiresome job to do in the kitchen, she thought how Charlie or Tommy Meighan or Sessue Hayakawa would do it, and the drudgery of the task would disappear as if by magic. (Pressbook for *A Temporary Lady*, author's own collection)

The long delay between the shooting of the film in spring 1921 and its release in May 1922 indicates the company's continued distribution problems. In fact, the film had been trade shown in September 1921 and Brunel claimed 'it got splendid notices' (1949: 62) but, by the time of its release, Minerva had ceased production and Brunel had gone into business with the film's star, Miles Mander. The pressbook produced to promote it, in an example of optimistic self-promotion, sported a portrait of Brunel on the cover, presumably seeking to trade on his reputation within the industry. The reviews it contains are indeed positive and recognise its combination of humour and intelligence; *The Cinema* found it 'clean, crisp, amusing and clever' while *Film Renter* described it as 'A piece of delicious fooling', singling out Benson as a 'comedienne of genuine power and ability'. The reviewer in *Kinematograph Weekly* describes an intriguing 'original touch' in the form of 'the frequent introduction of a cat and two beetles whose actions illustrate some point of the story'; whether this was in the form of animated sequences, live action or titles is not recorded but it may have been a comedic reference to the natural history films of Percy Smith. The other Minerva film in production at the same time as *A Temporary Lady* was *Too Many Cooks* but although *The Bioscope* announced its completion in June, it was never released.

After the company's first six films failed to make a profit, Brunel sought advice from others in the business, collating the results into one document. T. A. Welsh and George Pearson advised him to abandon the two-reel film and invest in a five-reeler because 'like this one can spend much more per reel and get a bigger return' (ABSC 4/107). The editor and chief reviewer of *The Bioscope* also felt that expanding into production of five-reel films was the next step, but recommended continuing with two-reelers as well. They came up with the suggestion that the company 'should link three

Figure 2.4 Pressbook for *A Temporary Lady*. Source: author's own collection.

two-reel films together as the Fox Film co did at a recent trade show . . . We might put three films together dealing with suburban life' (ibid.), a canny way to extend the life of a series of shorts and a ploy used in the 1950s to bring television productions to the cinema.

Brunel clearly took these ideas on board, as *The Bioscope* announced in June 1921 that Minerva was working on a five-reeler entitled *The Beggars' Syndicate*. The original story by Brunel and Mill Wadham tells of an aristocrat fallen on hard times who joins forces with a coffee-stall owner and a woman called Maggie to set up a business. Comedy ensues as they try their hands at decorating, portering, pavement artistry and selling quack medicine. As in *A Temporary Lady*, the action is commented on by an animal, this time an anthropomorphised dog named Caesar, who has his own intertitles. He was even going to have his dreams visualised via an image superimposed alongside a shot of himself asleep, but this sequence proved too difficult to film. Shooting took place in various London locations, including Selfridge's roof garden and Victoria Station, as well as the crew's expedition to the Caledonian Market described at the beginning of this chapter.

The film starred comic actor Bert Darley alongside 'Minerva discovery' Mary Patterson, who was described by *The Bioscope* as having 'a quaint method of portrayal which is peculiar to herself' (23 June 1921: 19). This was presumably a polite way to say that Patterson had no acting experience; the film was being financed by businessman Arthur T. Locan in an attempt to launch her as a film star. In an undated document Brunel records that 'I shall use my best endeavours to train this gentleman's wife as a cinema-artist with the view to her starring in our productions' (ABSC 6/107). Patterson (whose real name was Mildred Baker) was in fact Locan's mistress and he had ploughed a large amount of money into trying to establish her on both stage and screen. As early as December 1920, a script for *The Beggars' Syndicate* had been submitted to him for approval and by July 1921 shooting was well underway, but Brunel was struggling with Patterson's lack of experience. A frantic letter to Locan indicates that the businessman had expressed discontent with the material shot thus far, in particular the amount of screen time Patterson had been allocated; Brunel assured him that 'everything was done to build up Miss Patterson's part' (18 July 1921, ABSC 4/107).

Locan had made a fortune out of the mass production of cheap housing for the working classes after the First World War, winning valuable contracts from local authorities for his concrete constructions. However, he could not fulfil them and was exposed for devious practices and eventually bankrupted in August 1921 (see Marriner 1990: 74–7), an event which coincided with the completion of filming as well as the termination of Brunel's employment as Production Director for Minerva. With Locan's bankruptcy, the film went unedited but Brunel remained on the company board to deal with the financial fallout of its demise. Despite Minerva having suffered 'a great legal disaster', details of which remain obscure, as late as November 1922 financial backer Richard Fitz Power was still attempting to raise funds for the company, which was then pursuing the idea of making 'business development films' to promote products and corporations (ABSC 6/107).

By this time Brunel had been in business with Mander for over a year and was heavily involved in various new projects. He had spent less than eighteen months with Minerva and could justifiably look back on his work there with some pride, having completed five films which had approached the short form with genuine creativity and originality. However, the pride was undoubtedly overshadowed by the bitterness of the struggle he had had to get the films seen, keep the company afloat, wrangle with difficult and even corrupt funders, and support his wife and child. When *A Temporary Lady* was eventually released in May 1922, Brunel instructed his associate at Solar Films to promote it under the name of the distributor, Globe Film Company, rather than Minerva, acknowledging that the name had lost what little publicity value it briefly had.

Conclusion

This chapter demonstrates that the makeshift and insecure nature of the British film industry after the war was a major hindrance to a sustainable production set-up, and thus discouraged attempts to develop new modes of cinematic expression. While it did provide a space where Gledhill's 'artistic "amateur"' (2008: 16) could experiment with filmmaking relatively free from interference and thus develop British cinema in new directions, this approach to filmmaking was disastrous for the industry. John Payne at Bramlins observed how 'firm after firm has started to produce comedies and then closed down, having no more money' (n.d., ABSC 6/107) and, despite the support of industry figures, Minerva became another casualty. The trade papers emphasised the need for the British film industry to develop along more sustainable lines with pleas for an end to the 'pottering at production' which had characterised it thus far. Throughout the decade, commentators pressed for a co-ordinated approach to film production backed with large-scale funding: 'What is lacking is men with a combination of finance and courage', wrote the editor of *The Bioscope* (1 January 1925: 34); certainly there was a good deal of mistrust among financiers, who did not regard filmmaking as a viable form of speculation and preferred more traditional forms of investment. Thus, much of the finance that went into film production, as Brunel discovered, came from businesses that were as tenuous as the film companies themselves.

The importance of Brunel's collaborative working practices began to become apparent, a theme that developed throughout his career. While at Minerva his key partnership was with A. A. Milne, and Brunel clearly learned a great deal from him, expanding the subversive use of intertitles when he made his burlesques. Also important were the connections to the theatre via Howard and Smith, and the way he used their performance styles to enhance characterisation contributes to the humorous effect of the films. Balancing the contributions and expectations of author and actor was a key skill for a director, especially where those collaborators also had a financial stake in the production. As will be seen in subsequent chapters, each of Brunel's ventures threw up benefits and challenges in terms of the forces and personalities he came into contact with. The negotiations he engaged in to preserve his own artistic vision are key to his attempts to strike a balance between a desire to innovate and a need to satisfy commercial imperatives.

By describing the development of the short film during the early 1920s, this chapter highlights the pitfalls of the form for a small company such as Minerva. While their films were well-received by the critics, selling them proved almost impossible in an overcrowded market, a problem Brunel faced frequently during his independent producing career. The fact that British producers clung on to the hope that short films could be viable despite the domination of big-budget American 'super-films' was perhaps a form of patriotic resistance to Hollywood's dictation of the rules by which cinema operated. Directors like George Pearson understood that the feature film was becoming the principal commercial form and had shown that British productions could promote a national approach to cinematic artistry. Brunel's next venture was to give him a chance to do the same.

CHAPTER 3

Art, the Trade and *The Man Without Desire*

> The aim of the men who make motion pictures is to line their pocket books . . . the only way in which the financial backer . . . can obtain a return of the funds . . . to say nothing of a profit, is to appeal to the great masses. And the thing which satisfies millions cannot be good. (Tourneur 1924)

French film director Maurice Tourneur wrote this in *Kinematograph Weekly* in January 1924. It is one of many articles published in the British trade and daily papers in the early 1920s that addressed the question of whether cinema could be considered an art form or would only ever be an entertainment medium. In its earliest days the moving picture was primarily a working-class diversion usually exhibited in insalubrious surroundings, but by the First World War it had begun to attract a better class of patron as films became more sophisticated and cinemas and theatres took over as the principal venues to watch them in. This gradual movement upmarket was accompanied by calls for British cinema to develop along more artistic lines, though there were differing views about what that actually meant.

Voices were heard both from within the industry and from outside but the trade press took particular interest in the opinions of those who worked in the American film industry, presumably believing that they held the key to box office success. As a top-rung director in Hollywood since 1914, Tourneur's contribution to the debate was of particular interest to *Kinematograph Weekly*'s readers, which almost certainly included Adrian Brunel.

Tourneur's views appeared just weeks before the release of Brunel's first feature but were in sharp contrast to his own. 'Ours is an art before it is a business,' Brunel had told *Motion Picture Studio* in 1922, adding, 'look after the art and the pounds will look after themselves, for in the kinema, art pays' (26 August 1922: 6). But while Brunel's theory was as yet untested, Tourneur's realisation that commercial imperatives excluded film from the arts had emerged through bitter experience. He had set up his own production company in 1918 to take his directing into a more artistic realm than the studios would permit. Under its auspices he made some lyrical features, among which *The Blue Bird* and *Prunella* (both 1918) stand out as heavily stylised, fairy-tale-like theatrical adaptations. Both films were regarded by critics as 'an artistic achievement' but failed financially, which he put down to the fact that 'the managers of the smaller houses throughout the country considered [them] "too high brow" for their patrons' (Tourneur 1920). Tourneur could not sustain production independently; he claimed he 'would rather starve and make good pictures' (ibid.), yet resented the fact that he was making films no one would see. He abandoned this personal, poetic mode of filmmaking and returned to a more mainstream approach.

Tourneur's discouraging words are unlikely to have swayed Brunel from his own belief that film could raise itself to an art form. At that moment he was experiencing the same pleasure that Tourneur must had felt when he read the effusive reviews of *The Blue Bird*, since his debut feature *The Man Without Desire* was receiving excellent critiques. He was full of optimism about his artistic vision for British cinema but, like Tourneur, would soon endure bitter experiences of his own, which must have shaken his belief that 'art pays'.

Enter the Intellectuals

For some years, British cinema had been pursuing a greater degree of respectability in order to attract a better class of patron to the purpose-built cinemas which began to appear in the early 1910s. The middle of that decade saw an influx of creative figures who began to 'think seriously about the relationship between films, scenarios and the fields of literature, drama and painting; . . . intellectual domains on which they were able to draw' (Turvey 2003: 85). Gerry Turvey identifies screenwriter Harold Weston as one such figure, who suggested that to rise above the level of a hack, a screenwriter should 'study the techniques of the drama, and when he has satisfied himself that he is fully cognisant of the dramatic values, he should turn his attention to the art of picturisation – that is, he must study the work of great painters' (1916; quoted in Turvey: 87). Fellow scenarist Eliot Stannard endorsed this approach some years later, offering the view that great works of art could provide 'immobile subjects which might well have formed episodes in a screen play' (1920; quoted in Turvey: 90).

A 1924 article in *Pictures and Picturegoer* posited the notion that, in contrast, the cinema itself could be a source of artistic images to rival the world's great paintings. Its author, Marjorie Mayne, claimed, 'The Motion Picture is just finding itself as an art, and the directors use the megaphone and the camera much as the painters use their palette and brushes' (1924: 41). Taking the comparison further, she wrote:

> as the artist paints rather that which his soul sees than the actual lineaments of the model before him, so the camera, in the hands of a skilled photographer who sees eye to eye with the director can idealise and even etherealise scenes and faces. (ibid.: 43)

She regarded British directors as excellent proponents of this new art, claiming that Maurice Elvey and George Pearson could hold their own among the Europeans and detecting, for example, 'a distinctly Hogarthian atmosphere' in Pearson's *Love, Life and Laughter* (1923) (ibid.).

As Christine Gledhill (2003) has described, British filmmakers had for some years been employing techniques of framing and composition familiar from works of art, a device much admired by contemporary critics. Yet Mayne insisted that the pursuit of visual beauty on the screen did not mark out film as a highbrow pursuit, regarding it rather as a democratic medium that could have an educative role. 'The film reaches the poor as well as the rich, the ignorant as well as the cultured, and sooner or later, all must benefit by the artistic lessons it teaches,' she declared (1924: 42).[1] The evocation of fine art compositions on screen advocated by Mayne formed a key part of Brunel's visual strategy for his first feature. He modelled the mise en scène and framing of *The Man Without Desire* on the paintings of Pietro Longhi, an eighteenth-century artist who specialised in scenes of Venetian life. In this sense, he was employing an established visual approach in British cinema; his choice of artist, however, was in pursuit of a more exotic effect than Mayne's examples.

Educating the Public

In the spring of 1923, not long after he had completed filming on *The Man Without Desire*, Brunel attended a reception held by the recently formed Faculty of Arts, a group which aimed to 'develop the arts and crafts of the country as a national asset' (Low 1971: 35). At the meeting, its representatives encouragingly reported that they had 'been considering the film as an art for the past year' (*MPS*, 17 March 1923: 10). One exhibitor addressed the gathering to request that the 'Faculty of Arts . . . endeavour to educate

---

[1] A similar view pertained to the filming of theatrical works in the 1910s, which Jon Burrows suggests led to 'a considerable expansion of the nature and breadth of the social constituencies that would be exposed to them' (2003: 17).

the public to appreciate the best stuff and so assist the Trade as a whole', but the Faculty rejected the need for such schooling, asserting that 'the "gallery" was as well educated as the "stalls"' (ibid.). This was a view Brunel had long supported and he pointed the finger back at the trade: 'the intellectual standard of audiences [is] so much higher than that of those film men who are ruining our business' (*MPS*, 26 August 1922: 6). Brunel's faith in British audiences encouraged him to believe that it was possible to bring original ideas to filmmaking to create something with popular appeal.

Two Audiences

While Brunel publicly credited ordinary cinemagoers with intelligence, the creation of the Film Society in 1925 was seized on by the trade press as evidence that its founders, of which he was one, held them in contempt. The Society's aim was to cultivate an alternative, less commercial programming strategy in Britain to accommodate films its committee felt were worthy of exhibition or re-release, but which mainstream distributors were not picking up. The group rapidly found itself labelled 'highbrow' by the press, compelling co-founder Ivor Montagu to defend the venture and clarify his definition of cinematic art. Taking care to praise the merits of commercial films, he suggested that the 'factors that make a picture interesting . . . are often quite independent of the factors that make for a popular success' (*KW*, 15 October 1925: 69). He identified these factors as 'ingenious technique of acting, of production, of lighting, of design' and pointed out that 'a picture important from this point of view is quite rightly, in most instances, judged unsuitable for public exhibition by the Trade, owing to its morbidity, or that obscurity which we agree in labelling highbrow' (ibid.). Thus his attempts to clear the Film Society of charges of exclusivity seemed rather to reinforce the impression that the group regarded its tastes as separate from and superior to the majority of the filmgoing public. Yet perhaps his real target was the film trade; his explanation implies that by failing to book such films, distributors and exhibitors were responsible for creating and sustaining the division.

Indeed, the perception by the trade that most of the viewing public were incapable of appreciating more 'difficult' or 'artistic' cinematic fare appears to have been fairly common. Some commentators have taken the view that, to those running the film industry, 'the word "arty" was the ultimate in invective' (Brownlow 1973: 591) and, as Montagu pointed out and Tourneur had discovered, distributors had the power to decide what they deemed suitable for audiences. As already described, some distributors even took it upon themselves to re-edit films to remove elements they felt detracted from their entertainment value. Although Tourneur was adamant that cinema could never be an art form, he accepted that there was room for artistic intervention into it, conceding that it offers 'a great field for expression' and that all audiences could appreciate 'beauty on the screen' whether in a performance, visual composition or screenplay (1924). In other words, a director could inject a degree of 'artiness' in order to make a narrative film with visual expressiveness and originality that was not too 'highbrow' to reach a general public.

Atlas-Biocraft

Brunel and Miles Mander appeared to be well aware of this need to balance art with business when they set up their new production company, Atlas-Biocraft, in September 1922. The establishment of the firm was heralded by *Motion Picture Studio* with a full-page article and, demonstrating that

Figure 3.1 Miles Mander. Source: author's own collection.

they had put some thought into articulating their ambitions, Brunel and Mander stated their aim to produce 'pictures with the maximum amount of artistry compatible with commercial enterprise' (28 October 1922: 16). By the time the article appeared, Brunel was in Venice shooting *The Man Without Desire*, with which the new firm hoped to demonstrate 'the craftsmanship of picture making' (ibid.). Indeed, the positive response to the film's eventual release suggests that, had it come out a few weeks earlier, Mayne may well have listed Brunel among Britain's 'New Masters'. Made on a very small budget, the film represents a unique experiment by a group of creative individuals from a range of cultural spheres each contributing their ideas around film as art to produce something genuinely original. As well as a testament to Brunel's ability to use limited resources to considerable effect, *The Man Without Desire* shows his skill at drawing on the talents around him and combining their ideas in a coherent way. But how well did this experiment manage to navigate a path between art and commerce?

Brunel and Mander

'The state of the English market is simply awful. Firms are going broke or are trying to avoid catastrophe the whole time,' wrote Brunel to Leslie Howard after the failure of the Milne comedies (28 December 1920, ABSC 4/107). Brunel's correspondence from the period paints an increasingly gloomy picture of the British film industry and he was soon to give up on Minerva to join forces with Miles Mander. A year older than Brunel, Mander had spent his twenties fighting in the First World War and farming sheep in New Zealand. After trying his hand at acting, he developed much bigger ideas and decided to turn to production. His drive and dynamism meant their three-year association was probably the most promising period of Brunel's career in terms of the creative opportunities and wide experience it brought him. Mander and Brunel operated with limited resources but high ambitions and had connections with an impressive array of businessmen, military and diplomatic figures, politicians and bohemians. Between 1921 and 1924, they developed a series of ideas for film projects and managed to secure investment from a variety of sources, from aristocrats to 'a fellow . . . in the motor trade' (14 January 1922, ABSC 207). While Brunel occupied himself writing, directing and editing the films, Mander appears to have been tirelessly engaged in raising funds, although Brunel also proved adept at this, possessing, according to Mander, an 'unostentatiously persuasive' manner (21 February 1922, ABSC 207).

Mander's correspondence with Brunel during their association reveals him to be someone who worked unstintingly to recruit funders and eminent board members and was constantly cultivating new ideas. Their first enterprise, Solar Films, was, in Mander's words, a 'sprat to catch a whale', the strategy being that when they had made 'a decent profit on our small capital . . . the whales are waiting to be caught' (19 January 1922, ABSC 207). Mander's business plan appeared promising and he confidently stated: 'I shouldn't be surprised if in three months' time the capital of our company wasn't £50,000 as we have one or two really rich men in tow' (ibid.). The production and exhibition of travel films seemed a sound proposition at the time, as audiences appeared to have an appetite for them. Mander noted that 'Ponting took £42000 in 35 weeks' at one cinema (21 February 1922, ABSC 207) (referring to the lectures Herbert Ponting gave in 1919 accompanying his film of Captain Scott's Antarctic expeditions) and, later, that *Crossing the Great Sahara* was still attracting audiences several months after its release. However, the level of investment needed to maintain a roster of productions shot in far-flung regions of the world was beyond the means of Solar Films, and without a famous name such as Scott to draw in audiences, the kind of profits Ponting apparently made remained out of their reach. But Mander's optimism was not dented and, although the two films Brunel had shot in North Africa were still waiting to be edited, he was determined to push on with their production plans.

A First Feature

As they neared the end of their first year in business together, Mander and Brunel approached wealthy businessman James White to fund a major feature. White was a property investor who had become involved with the cinema when he bought the Tivoli Theatre in the Strand, but he apparently 'had little faith in the kinema as a financial proposition' (*KW*, 7 July 1927: 26) and was much more interested in the stage, with a controlling interest in Daly's Theatre, off Leicester Square. However, Brunel and Mander persuaded him to put up £5,000 for the production of a feature film, a very small amount for such a venture, even in 1923.

The challenge posed by the limited budget was intensified by the decision to shoot on location in Venice. However, Brunel was enthusiastic about the prospect of taking exteriors in Italy and interiors in Germany. The decision to use a German studio was at least partly a pragmatic one; during the immediate postwar period, the German economy had been weak and the exchange rate was very favourable to British producers. Brunel and Mander spent time there in August 1922, visiting studios and production companies, and were very impressed with what they saw. Brunel was one of the first British directors to make a film in Germany and he and Mander reported back positively to the British trade press about conditions. The kind of British studio that a small company like Atlas-Biocraft could afford was barely adequate and the superior facilities Brunel and his crew enjoyed in Germany, as well as the technical and creative support from the staff there, proved vital to the project. In this sense, Atlas-Biocraft showed itself to be in the vanguard of a move towards internationalism in the British film industry, with German co-operation becoming common by the middle of the decade.

The Man Without Desire

The skilled German technicians were just one of a range of talents brought together for the making of *The Man Without Desire*. The film starred actor and composer Ivor Novello, who was developing a reputation as a screen idol, while opposite him appeared Russian actress Nina Vanna. In order to save money, Brunel and Babs (under her stage name Jane Dryden) took on the roles of a newspaper editor and his fiancée. Flamboyant theatre designer Hugo Rumbold took charge of the art direction as well as playing the villainous Count Almoro. Rumbold's participation in the project had begun long before filming got underway; in fact, it was he who engineered the firm's introduction to White. As Brunel later acknowledged, Rumbold was a key creative collaborator who contributed to the screen story, proposed filming in Venice and suggested taking visual inspiration from the paintings of Pietro Longhi.

Rumbold was, by all accounts, an extraordinary character and the lavishness of *The Man Without Desire* is undoubtedly largely attributable to his flair and imagination. From a traditional diplomatic family, he was a decorated military hero of the First World War but was best known for his theatrical designs and as a bohemian at the centre of London's beau monde. His penchant for play-acting was famous, Cecil Beaton describing him as 'the prize dresser-upper of our day' (1937: 116); renowned for his female impersonations, legend has it that he once spent several weeks dressed as a maid in order to pursue an affair with an Italian princess (Grantley 1954). *The Man Without Desire* was Rumbold's only excursion into the cinema and his influence on the production was significant, from its elements of sexual intrigue to the meticulous period detail, created by a man who 'apparently carries the 18th century atmosphere about in his pocket' (*Times*, 13 January 1916: 11).

With Rumbold on board and decisions about locations and period made, Brunel and Mander needed a story. Though they liked the idea of Longhi's Venice as a backdrop, they felt that period films had limited audience appeal and sought a device that would allow them to switch to a contemporary setting midway through the film. As with the Milne comedies, an established writer was approached to come up with an original storyline, Brunel inviting Irish playwright Monckton Hoffe to contribute an idea.[2] Hoffe had developed an interest in suspended animation and proposed a tale in which an eighteenth-century Count was put to sleep for two hundred years, then woken up in the present day, thus allowing for the time transition the filmmakers desired. From the few lines penned by Hoffe, Brunel wrote a treatment entitled 'It Happened in Venice', which was registered with the Incorporated Society of Authors, Playwrights and Composers on 5 September 1922. He then commissioned Frank Fowell, a former colleague at the Department of Information, to write the scenario, a task he must have completed in record time since Brunel set off for Venice on 11 October 1922 accompanied by his cast and crew and armed with a script entitled *The Man Without Desire*.

Unseasonably wet weather in the Italian city held up filming but, unsurprisingly, the combination of personalities on set also threatened the proceedings. Brunel was working under the watchful eye of Tommy Dawe, General Manager of the Tivoli, who had been despatched by White to protect his investment. White was a canny businessman but was apparently vain and arrogant; Vivian Van Damm, who managed the Tivoli, found him 'repulsive' (1952: 63). Dawe must have reported back to his employer that there were problems on the shoot and, less than two weeks after they arrived in Venice, Brunel was instructed that Hugo Rumbold 'must not take any further action in the production' (23 October 1922, ABSC D/170). This necessitated recasting the role of Count Almoro with Italian actor Sergio Mari, and Dawe stipulated that actress Dorothy Warren should take over the art direction.[3] Following Rumbold's despatch, filming went reasonably smoothly, although the poor weather prevented Brunel from taking all the shots of Venice he wanted before they moved on to Germany for the interiors.

[2] Hoffe's play *The Little Damozel* had been filmed by Wilfred Noy in 1916, so Brunel may have met him via this mutual contact.
[3] Warren was apparently 'an actress of some note, who possesses a literary and artistic knowledge unrivalled by her sex' (*MPS*, 28 October 1922: 16). She may be the same Dorothy Cecil Wynter Warren who ran a London art gallery later in the decade.

A Long Gestation

By early January 1923, Brunel was back in England after two and a half months abroad. The year ahead was to be a particularly trying one which he spent on the verge of a breakdown due to mounting debts from Minerva Pictures and Bramlins Agency, as well as the lack of cash flow at Atlas-Biocraft which meant he had to edit *The Man Without Desire* without pay. By November that year he was desperate and wrote to former MoI colleague Colonel Bromhead at Gaumont announcing that he had resigned from Atlas and would be grateful for any freelance work available. Despite his gloomy prospects, the following month finally saw the trade show of *The Man Without Desire* and it must have brought Brunel renewed hope. In his collection at the BFI is a large scrapbook into which someone, perhaps Brunel himself, meticulously pasted hundreds of cuttings, creating a collection of enthusiastic write-ups for the film. Buoyed by the reviews, Novello-Atlas Renters, the distribution company Brunel and Mander had set up, took out full-page adverts in the trade press, crammed with examples of the hyperbole lavished on it.

It Happened in Venice

The film's plot received much praise for its original and thought-provoking nature, *Motion Picture Studio* enthusing that it was 'so unhackneyed and in every way a departure from the stock plots of current pictures that the promoters, author and producer are to be heartily congratulated on breaking away from the traditional ingredients of the modern screen' (22 December 1923: 5). It begins with a scene in contemporary London, where Robert Mawdesley has been summoned to his lawyer's office for the opening of a letter deposited there two hundred years previously by one of his ancestors. He left instructions that it was to be read at midnight on 4 September 1923 in the presence of a lawyer, a bank representative and a doctor familiar with Indian occultism. As the lawyer begins to read the letter, the film returns to 1736 to recount the tragic story of Count Vittorio Dandolo.

Dandolo is in love with Leonora, who is trapped in an unhappy marriage to Count Almoro who is having an affair with La Foscolina. Leonora is reluctant to enter into an extramarital relationship despite her feelings for Dandolo, partly due to her devotion to her young son. Angered by a newspaper report about him and La Foscolina, Almoro crushes the hands of the editor who wrote it. The editor determines to take revenge and charges his fiancée, who is maidservant to Leonora, with poisoning Almoro. But the Count discovers a letter from Dandolo to Leonora and forces Leonora to drink the glass of poisoned wine destined for him. Dandolo arrives just in time for Leonora to die in his arms; furious, he strangles Almoro then seeks refuge in the home of English scientist Simon Mawdesley. Mawdesley has been conducting experiments in suspended animation and offers to put Dandolo to sleep so he can escape the law.

The film then returns to the present, where the gathered group have finished reading the letter. Robert Mawdesley and the lawyer travel to Venice and find Dandolo inside a bricked-up grotto. After opening the casket in which he has lain for two hundred years, they leave the Count to wake up alone, fearing that the sight of them in their modern clothes might be too great a shock for him. He gradually comes round but, with no memory of why he is there, goes to Leonora's house where he finds her descendant, Genevra, and assumes she is his lost love. He also meets the twin of Almoro, in fact Genevra's cousin, Count Gardi-Almoro. The lawyer gives Dandolo a letter left for him by Simon Mawdesley which warns that, once reawakened, he may find life 'so different as to be almost colourless. You may even awake to find yourself utterly without desire of any kind.' Dandolo falls in love with Genevra and they marry but, as the letter predicted, he is devoid of passion and the relationship falls apart, propelling him to suicide. Retrieving his eighteenth-century clothes he finds a poisonous pill bequeathed him by Simon Mawdesley and writes a farewell note to Genevra. She goes to his room and, finding him dying, experiences a reawakening of her love for him. After a passionate embrace, he dies in her arms.

Although the film is a melodrama with fantastic elements, Brunel could not resist inserting some humorous touches and exploits the comic possibilities of Dandolo's reactions to twentieth-century innovations. He bows to Genevra's voice on the telephone, is baffled by matches and cigarettes, expresses disgust at the efforts of a modern barber (in a contrasting scene to an earlier one depicting an eighteenth-century hairdressers) and wrestles with a collar and tie. These elements lighten the mood of the film, *Motion Picture Studio* regarding Brunel's use of levity as a refreshing sign of Britishness: '[t]he director has ... refrained from undue heaviness, which would have been very marked had a German directed it, for instance. Several light touches are most welcome' (22 December 1923: 5).

A Departure

While critics described the plot as 'clever and ingenious' and 'a new type of film story', the themes explored in *The Man Without Desire* can be

Figure 3.2 Pressbook for *The Man Without Desire*.
Source: author's own collection.

traced to various literary sources. The notion of cheating death or ageing had been explored in fantastic fiction like *Dracula* and *Peter Pan*, but a closer analogy to Dandolo's escape from the ravages of age can be found in Oscar Wilde's 1890 novel *The Picture of Dorian Gray*. For both Gray and Dandolo, their prolonged youthful state leads to a dissatisfaction with life. Dandolo declares, 'I find life to-day so savourless' and his loss of zest for life echoes Wilde's writing: '"I wish I could love," cried Dorian Gray, with a deep note of pathos in his voice. "But I seem to have lost the passion, and forgotten the desire'" (1983: 226).

Elements of the fairy tales *Snow White* and *The Sleeping Beauty* are detectable in the story, with visual allusions to them provided by both the death of Leonora and the putting to sleep of Dandolo. The dusty sarcophagus in which Dandolo is entombed is more reminiscent of a coffin than of Snow White's bier, but Novello, an actor of considerable romantic imagination, may well have drawn the parallel in his own mind. The theme of a character who sleeps for years was familiar from Washington Irving's 1819 story *Rip Van Winkle* and more recently (and more pertinently) in H. G. Wells' science-fiction novel *The Sleeper Awakes*. First written in 1899, it tells of a man who falls into a coma for two hundred and three years, waking to find the world a very changed place. Although Wells uses the device to construct a dystopian fantasy rather than to study the effects of the experience on the sleeper, the parallels with Hoffe's hastily penned tale are striking.

While literature had long been fascinated with such fantastic tales, British cinema rarely strayed into the genre and it was the Germans who had cornered the market, with films such as *Der Golem* (Paul Wegener 1915) and *Das Cabinet des Dr Caligari* (Paul Wiene 1920). Critics welcomed the injection of 'mystery and spookiness'[4] into a British film and detected a debt to the Teutonic style, one asserting that 'the film was directly modelled on German methods of production. The hands are the hands of Brunel, but the voice is the voice of Lang.' The film's director of photography, Henry Harris, was the ideal man for the job, having worked with Abel Gance on *J'Accuse* (France, 1919), and his camerawork in *The Man Without Desire* contributes to its eerie feel. The creative use of lighting is notable at several points, such as the moment when the gloomy entrance hall of the Almoro palazzo is suddenly illuminated by a block of bright sunlight through an open door, and the shot of the dank mausoleum where Dandolo reposes, lit only by a tiny window high up, which casts a faint shaft of light onto his pale features. The shadow of Mawdesley's hand moves over Dandolo's face, recalling the claw-like fingers of Murnau's *Nosferatu* (Germany, 1922),[5] a moment that elicited rare praise from Rachael Low for the film's 'unexpected angles . . . and . . . touch of the macabre and the mysterious' (1971: 258).

---

[4] All reviews quoted in the rest of this chapter are to be found in the press cuttings book in ABSC 196, unless otherwise stated.
[5] Brunel may have seen *Nosferatu* on one of his visits to Germany since, as Miller notes, it was not shown in Britain until 1928 due to copyright difficulties (2013: 123).

Figure 3.3 Henry Harris lines up a shot of Ivor Novello in *The Man Without Desire*. Source: BFI National Archive.

These shades of German expressionism may well have prompted the critic on the *Evening News* to comment on the film's 'distinctly "highbrow" touch'. The word may have made Brunel's heart sink but he would no doubt have been reassured that the reviewer had used it to link his film with two other titles opening that week: US film *Anna Christie* (John Griffith Wray 1923) and the delayed 1921 German feature *Destiny* (aka *Die Müde Tod*, Fritz Lang). The critic described the three films as 'the welcome ray that heralds the dawn of imagination in the photo play'.

The number of effusive reviews that Brunel's debut feature received suggests general agreement that it was a striking and original contribution to British cinema. *Motion Picture Studio* noted a 'refreshing avoidance of the obvious', the *Daily Graphic* praised the 'dramatic and original story', while *The Bioscope* found it 'ingenious in conception'. Its artistry was another draw: 'As an artistic whole it can confidently be recommended as the best film of the year' said the *Times* and the *Sketch* asserted, 'No more beautiful setting, no greater accuracy of detail could be demanded.'

Putting Art on the Screen

In the light of Mayne's contemporaneous article in *Picturegoer*, it seems surprising that critics failed to remark on the film's debt to Pietro Longhi's paintings. Perhaps the reference was too obscure, although there is a scene in the contemporary section showing Dandolo looking nostalgically at prints of the artist's works. Or perhaps this was regarded as one of the less progressive devices used in the film and critics preferred to focus on its more original elements. Yet the use of Longhi's art as inspiration makes the early scenes an intriguing window onto an unfamiliar time and place, assisted by an exceptional attention to detail, with some of the costumes and props being genuine antiques. It also suggests an editing structure for these sequences, whereby the interiors are captured first in long-shot in the form of tableaux, carefully arranged but relatively static, allowing each scene to be appreciated for its artistic composition and period detail before the action begins. The figures remain in one spot, each performing some 'business' within the scene, the camera then picks out these details, focusing on individuals to give the sequence greater authenticity. It also lends it a theatrical feel, creating a backdrop of Venetian decor which is as integral to the plot as the characters.

As in the artist's representations, Brunel populates the chambers of Il Ridotto ('the fashionable gambling and meeting place of Venice') with masked figures, Africans and dwarfs, creating a suitably authentic milieu for the intrigues and infidelities of the plot. But the film's most atmospheric setting is the den of scientist Simon Mawdesley, elements of which

Figure 3.4 A lavish Venice scene in *The Man Without Desire*.
Source: BFI National Archive.

can be found in Longhi's *The Alchemist* and *The Apothecary*. A forerunner of the mad scientist's laboratory seen in the horror films of later decades, his dark chamber contains a skeleton, huge dusty leather-bound books, heavy chains, vials and a serpent-like creature suspended from the ceiling. The room is further adorned by the striking figure of Mawdesley himself in a fur-trimmed floor-length dressing gown of exotic fabric, his bushy eyebrows protruding from beneath a patterned headscarf.

As well as the carefully composed interiors, Brunel fully exploits the aesthetic potential of the Venice locations. Scenes are staged using architectural details such as balconies and staircases, while gondola rides provide a contrasting sense of perspective. As the film moves from London to Venice, Brunel uses high-angle panoramic shots of the city to establish the transition of time and place, prefaced by the description in Mawdesley's letter being read to the gathered group: 'Venice is unlike any foreign parts that I have visited. Life is entirely devoted to pleasure and the God of Love reigns supreme . . . It is typical of Venice that what I have to relate should have happened here.' The description makes the transition even more profound; not only are we going back in time two hundred years but to a place that promises a very un-British atmosphere of high living and decadence. This use of titles was something Brunel had theorised about some years before, and he regarded it as vital to ensure that a change of key was properly signalled to the audience. Such tonal shifts should be flagged by a title to provide 'a connecting link between the two parts of the story, [that] would also contain a separate idea which should be impressed on the minds of the viewers from this point onwards' (1921b).

Symmetrical Structure

The division of the action of the film across two time zones allows for the creation of a series of symmetries and parallels, which suggest both comparisons and contrasts. Each of the principal actors portrays two characters, one in the eighteenth-century section and the other the descendant of that character in the contemporary scenes. Although this was undoubtedly for budgetary as well as creative reasons, it was noted as an effective device. *The Times* observed that '[t]his calls for the most delicate acting on the part of the . . . principals, and each is so nearly alike, and yet so utterly different, in the two characters that there can be nothing but praise for their work'. Novello's Dandolo undergoes a transformation of a different kind as a figure transposed to another century whose 'life and love are of the past'. The performance styles of the actors differ markedly in each half, with a mannered theatricality in the gestures and expressions of the costumed actors giving way to a more relaxed, informal acting style in the modern-day scenes. Novello also moderates his acting, gradually abandoning the flourishes he still adopts after first emerging from suspended animation, as he becomes accustomed to modern modes and eventually appears comfortable in a dinner suit. Gledhill observes that the character must "'grow up" . . . in conformity to the new conditions of verisimilitude in the postwar 1920s' (2003: 171) and Novello/Dandolo attempts to do so, his natural flamboyance stifled by the dull suits he is forced to wear. Meanwhile, the more elaborate font used to convey his speech in the intertitles marks him out as different from the twentieth-century characters. He loses all trace of his roots in the more genteel age and it is not until he dons his original costume again that he resumes the air of melodrama befitting his final tragic scenes. The more stagey, static eighteenth-century sequences represent a more traditional style of composition and performance which Brunel symbolically abandons halfway through the film to usher in a more modern, forward-looking aesthetic.

Brunel also employs this structure to stage several sequences that are mirrored across the centuries. Leonora and Almoro are seen boarding a gondola in one scene, while a later shot shows Robert Mawdesley disembarking at the same spot; Dandolo and Genevra have their first kiss in the same bower framed by columns and climbing plants where he embraced Leonora two hundred years before. Novello's Dandolo has his own repeat performances in the form of the two love affairs, neither consummated, he 'dies' twice, both times through the intervention of Simon Mawdesley, and his final demise in the arms of Genevra is foreshadowed by Leonora's death in his own embrace.

The relationships between the four main characters take on a new complexion in the contemporary scenes, allowing the film to offer a commentary on generational differences and the decline in modern morals. In the eighteenth-century section, Nina Vanna's Leonora holds back from fully indulging her feelings for Dandolo for the sake of her son; she tells him that she needs a friend and he seems content to fulfil a chaste role. Genevra, a modern woman, is more demanding than her ancestor, regarding Dandolo's non-consummation of their marriage as an affront to her feminine appeal, and she inhibits him further by her sexual forwardness. She begins to find the advances of her cousin more appealing in the light of her husband's frigidity. So, in the modern section it is the vampish Foscolina who becomes the 'wronged woman' and complains of her lover's pursuit of his cousin's affections. Although Dandolo has had his passions dulled, he experiences jealousy inspired by Genevra's plotting and attempts to strangle Gardi-Almoro in a replay of Almoro's murder in the first act.

Novello's intense and self-absorbed acting style is ideally suited to the melodramatic role and he clearly relished the period sets and costumes. At the climax, Dandolo engineers the situation in order to die alone, but Genevra comes to him, allowing the film to close on a tender scene in which she finds her love reawakened by his suffering and self-sacrifice.

Figure 3.5 Pressbook for *The Man Without Desire*. Source: author's own collection.

Figure 3.6 The men gather for the opening of Simon Mawdesley's letter, *The Man Without Desire*. Source: author's own collection.

As he comes to the end of his life, the furniture and wallpaper behind the couple disappear and they are shown against a black background, as if the lights have dimmed on a theatrical stage and a spotlight is picking out the two figures. The final shot of the film shows Novello's pale face in profile, head lolling back and closed eyes raised heavenwards. Novello reported, 'Vittorio's death scene was generally said to be my best bit of acting' (Wilson 1975: 59) and critics at the time seemed to concur. 'Mr Novello does his best screen acting' claimed the *Evening News*, with *Kine Weekly* crediting Brunel for this: 'No other director has been able to get into the work of this actor . . . fifty per cent of the power and charm he displays under the guidance of Adrian Brunel.'

However, some cinemagoers at West End and larger venues may have been treated to a different conclusion to the tale. *The Bioscope* informed its readers that 'alternative "sad" and "happy" endings of the film have been produced for use at the choice of the individual exhibitor'. While European producers occasionally made alternative endings to their films to suit the demands of foreign markets, Brunel presumably intended this as a marketing ploy aimed at cinema owners, which appears to have been very unusual. Strangely, the publicity for the film made no mention of the gimmick, perhaps because in reality it did not live up to its promise. The 'happy ending' consisted of a coda to the film which returns to the lawyer's office, where the four men gathered at the start of the film are seen again. Apparently they were 'discussing the thing for so long that they had all fallen asleep over it and the re-awakening of "Vittorio" and this second tragedy of his life are nothing but a visualisation of their dreams' (*Pictures and Picturegoer*, January 1924: 35). The prints were presumably distributed with this coda intact and by removing it the exhibitor could end the film with Dandolo's dramatic death. It is not clear how or when this idea came about since no script for the film survives, but the likelihood is that it occurred to Brunel during the editing, perhaps because he was unsure how to end the film. While Novello unsurprisingly favoured the tragic finale, *The Bioscope* expressed a preference for the happy ending, taking the view that '[t]here is no material or psychological reason why the hero should be debarred for ever from happiness, and the picture already contains a full ration of melancholy'. However, reducing over half the film's narrative to a kind of group hallucination may have struck audience members as a rather unsatisfactory conclusion to the drama.[6]

Temporary Boycott

In response to the praise for *The Man Without Desire*, Brunel penned an article for *Motion Picture Studio* entitled 'Is Originality Popular?' In it he expressed his surprise at being labelled 'courageous' for producing a film which apparently differed so radically from typical British fare, and offered damning views of the way some critics and exhibitors regarded the cinemagoing public. He hints at the contradiction hindering progress within the film production business, writing

> When a film that is out of the ordinary is offered, it is, if any good, welcomed by the Press on behalf of the public, but is resented by a large section of the Trade . . . the old-fashioned exhibitors . . . dread progress or innovation

and suggesting that the trade believes 'the public is composed of vulgar imbeciles' (1924). His ire was no doubt directed at the author of the

---

[6] While Brunel was editing the film, George Pearson's feature *Love, Life and Laughter* (1923) was released and he may have been struck by its unusual narrative structure. That film's tragic ending turns out to be the climax of a story being told within the film and the final scene shows the heroine listening to the sad tale. Apparently, some German distributors removed Pearson's finale, preferring to end the film with the heroine abandoned by the hero.

negative review in the *Impartial Film Report*, which was, with a touch of irony, included among the fulsome commendations compiled for the film's trade advertisements. This weekly report, circulated among independent cinemas, labelled the film 'heavy … dull entertainment … weak'. Privately, Brunel accused the trade of waging a campaign against him: 'the film has been dubbed "high-brow", "too good", "above the public" etc. which is all rot and the result is a temporary boycott which I mean to fight for all I'm worth' (n.d., ABSC H/170).

The Man Without Desire began a pre-release run at White's Tivoli Theatre on 18 February 1924, directly following Rex Ingrams's *Scaramouche* (1923). By all accounts, the West End run of Brunel's film was hugely lucrative and a letter from the Tivoli's manager Vivian Van Damm, in which he claimed that in one week '23,857 people paid for admission to view it', was reproduced in press advertisements (*KW*, 28 February 1924: 20). But despite the enthusiastic reviews and encouraging opening the film failed to deliver a profit and fairly rapidly sank from view. Brunel's later assertion that this was because Novello-Atlas was 'ridiculously and unbelievably under-financed and could not keep pace with the agents' commissions on the bookings' (1949: 101) perhaps tells part of the story. However, suggestions of hostility towards the film from renters would explain Mander's summary of the situation that, while the film had gone down well in the capital, particularly at Marble Arch and Kilburn, outside London it did very badly.

The Man Without Desire appears to have suffered a similar fate to Tourneur's art films, being deemed by exhibitors as unsuitable for the average audience. Tourneur had retreated from his pursuit of artistic filmmaking in Hollywood and, in 1926, returned to his native France. Brunel, however, was not prepared to accept his fate and his article in *Motion Picture Studio* was presumably intended to hit back at his critics. The retaliation was ill-advised, as were Brunel and Mander's publicly expressed views on the ignorance of the film trade. Around this time, Mander proudly recounted that a speech he gave at a Film Week in Newcastle offered 'a golden opportunity of digs at Stolls, unenterprising exhibitors and the Impartial Report' (n.d., ABSC 207). Mander's 'digs' and Brunel's open hostility to the trade indicate a level of overconfidence, even arrogance, at odds with good business practice and it is impossible to avoid the conclusion that it turned certain of its members against them.

With so many new films being released each week, *The Man Without Desire* soon disappeared from cinemas. On 4 February, Michael Balcon's much-anticipated (and hugely budgeted) first feature, *Woman to Woman* (Graham Cutts 1923), opened in the UK to reviews that rivalled those of

Brunel's film. It had even received a Hollywood preview, after which US director Rex Ingram hailed it 'one of the best and most sincere films I ever saw in my life' (*Kine Weekly*, 1 February 1924), and Balcon's success in securing state-side distribution meant that he had ample funds for his next production, *The White Shadow* (Cutts 1924). Mander, meanwhile, had pinned his hopes on making enough money in Britain and was compelled to conduct 'a whirlwind campaign for capital all over England', optimistically hoping that the company would 'click for £20,000 or so' (n.d., ABSC 207). While the company's travel films, *Moors and Minarets* and *Cannibals of the Southern Seas*, were doing reasonably well, they did not bring in sufficient profit and the proposed production of Novello's screenplay *The Rat* had to be abandoned.

Art and the Commercial

With Atlas-Biocraft in dire financial straits, Mander enlisted all the help he could muster in his campaign to raise money. Among his supporters were director Edwin Greenwood and writer Eliot Stannard who, according to Mander, were 'untiring in their efforts to find money for the only honest film people they have ever met' (17 April 1924, ABSC 207). Perhaps Stannard's support for their cause was due to his own conviction that by adopting more artistic methods, British cinema might liberate itself from the dominance of Hollywood. Yet it appears that the fusion of artistic and commercial imperatives which Brunel had attempted with his first feature did not find favour with general audiences in search of entertainment, if it reached those audiences at all. Echoing the words of Tourneur, Arthur Wellesley L'Estrange Fawcett later summed up the dilemma thus:

> A film that is an art success and not an entertainment success can never be seen except by a small, eclectic public, and no one can afford to make pictures for an eclectic public – at least, not more than one. Many clever people have made that one good film, but no one in the world will or can afford to back him a second time.' (1927: 250)

For the time being, Brunel would have to be content with that 'one good film', as his career directing features was to stall for the next three years.

Conclusion

Brunel both contributed to and was influenced by the debates that were taking place within the British press around whether cinema should, or could, aspire to being an art form. He acknowledged film as the product of an evolutionary process, involving the creative input of many associates, and for *The Man Without Desire* he brought together a group of artistic, bohemian co-creators and skilled technicians. This made his first feature an unconventional affair with lavish sets and costumes and an exotic and indulgent atmosphere. But it would appear that the elite coterie Brunel and Mander had assembled for the production was out of touch with the tastes of ordinary cinemagoers, and this particular experiment may have confirmed the belief of some in the trade that art and commerce were not compatible.

In its review of *The Man Without Desire*, the *Sunday Herald* predicted that 'the name of Adrian Brunel . . . is going to be big'. Had Atlas-Biocraft been able to generate funds to film Novello vehicle *The Rat*, Brunel might have established himself as a major talent, but the short memory of both press and public meant that his celebrity soon faded. The appetite of cinemas for new product meant that audiences were constantly being sold the next 'super picture', each publicised with a level of hyperbole to rival that heaped on Brunel's film. However, in spite of the immense frustrations his association with Mander had caused him, with long periods without a proper wage and under challenging working conditions, he had gained valuable experience of many aspects of the business.

Brunel's first feature was an impressive achievement, especially considering its tiny budget, and testifies to the originality and ambition with which he and Mander approached filmmaking. However, *The Man Without Desire* suffered from a surfeit of ideas, and the competing visions of those involved in the project did not necessarily chime with Brunel's personal aspirations for the film. More to the point, they did not appear to be in accord with what the film renters deemed suitable for the cinemagoing public. In the end the film reinforced the perception that the audience was divided into two distinct groups, a division that was further delineated by the formation of the Film Society the following year.

As a stylised period melodrama with fantastic elements and moments of grand guignol, *The Man Without Desire* is atypical of Brunel's work. However, his personal stamp emerges in the humorous interludes and the original touches, which demonstrate his implementation of some of the ideas he had been developing about filmmaking. While he was not ready to abandon his conviction that it was possible to inject into British cinema an originality that could appeal to all audiences, the failure of his first feature compelled Brunel to strip back his ambitions both artistically and economically. His experience with *The Man Without Desire* had shown him that in order to achieve financial success he needed to win over the trade, a feat he managed to achieve with his next project.

CHAPTER 4

Making Dull Films Jolly: Brunel's Burlesques

Brunel's next venture was in complete contrast to the visual excess of *The Man Without Desire*. His short comic burlesques condensed the filmmaking process down to basics and saw him working in a semi-amateur context with much greater creative control. The results are the most personal works in his filmography, representing a direct expression of his humour and perspective on the British film industry. Made between 1923 and 1925, these eight one-reel films were born of a combination of necessity and frustration, and experimented with technique in their parody of cinematic genres.

Of all Brunel's films, the burlesques have garnered the most attention from film historians, who have varying views on their nature. Michael O'Pray describes them as 'an avant-garde attack on the conservatism of the British film industry' (2000), while Laraine Porter asserts that they demonstrate Brunel's 'creative genius' (2012: 36). Rachael Low dismissed them as 'facetious parodies' (1971: 149) and Luke McKernan was also unimpressed by Brunel's comedic output, regarding him as 'a restricted talent with a narrow frame of reference' (2000: 9). More charitably, Geoff Brown concludes that 'the burlesque comedies . . . give [Brunel] a distinctive place in British cinema history as a satirical jester and a key player in the film industry's uneasy war between art and commerce' (2005). How distinctive Brunel's work on these films actually was and whether they managed to advance the troops in Brown's 'uneasy war' will be explored in this chapter.

Brunel made two loose series of burlesques: *Sheer Trickery*, *Crossing the Great Sagrada* and *The Pathetic Gazette* in 1923 and 1924 for Atlas-Biocraft; and *So This is Jollygood*, *Battling Bruisers: Some Boxing Buffoonery*, *A Typical Budget*, *Cut it Out; A Day in the Life of a Censor* and *The Blunderland of Big Game*, produced in 1924 and 1925 under the Gainsborough umbrella.[1]

---

[1] Amy Sargeant credits the film *Whats* [sic] *Wrong With the Cinema?* (1925) to Brunel (2005: 93). However, although it has similarities to his burlesques there is nothing to connect him to it.

A British Avant-Garde?

Brunel's burlesques have been regarded as evidence of an alternative film culture in 1920s Britain, even an avant-garde tradition of a sort. In 2000, the British Film Institute released a VHS entitled *Britain in the Twenties*, as part of its series *History of the Avant-Garde*. The films included date mainly from the end of the decade, and the only link between them is that they were all made beyond the confines of the industry proper. While the films by (non-British) artists Len Lye (*Tusalava*, 1929) and Hans Richter (*Everyday*, 1929) more comfortably fit the definition of an avant-garde film offered by curator Michael O'Pray (one which aims to 'subvert commercial cinema in the name of art'), he concedes that the others are better described as 'more experimental than avant-garde' (2000). Brunel's *Crossing the Great Sagrada* (1924) is the earliest film in the collection, which also features Ivor Montagu's *Bluebottles* (1928), *COD A Mellow Drama* (1929) and $X + X = O$ (Brian Salt 1936).

O'Pray identifies 'a broader experimental film community' in Britain, grouped around the Film Society and the journal *Close Up*, which, he suggests, was in thrall to the avant-garde filmmaking coming out of Europe. Yet *Crossing the Great Sagrada* pre-dates both the Film Society and most of the key European avant-garde works and, in common with *Bluebottles* and *COD*, employs experimental techniques in pursuit of comedy.

Although Brunel's burlesques and the other films assembled by O'Pray contain some modernist elements, they were not made within the context of an avant-garde movement. While they combine features of an experimental approach with a semi-industrial structure, the diversity in their styles and the contexts in which they were made rule out any consistent categorisation of the filmmakers as belonging to a movement with similar methods or aims. This practice of artistic experimentation within the context of the industry found a more natural home in the British documentary movement of the 1930s, with Len Lye and others making films sponsored by government and industry, allowing a greater degree of freedom than British studios were willing to grant. Contemporaries of Lye, such as Oswell Blakeston and Daniel Birt, graduated into the studios, where artistic ambitions were kept very much in check.

Alternative Film Culture

Jamie Sexton's work on minority film culture between the wars takes in Brunel's burlesque films. Acknowledging that the term 'avant-garde' is problematic in relation to British films of this period, he refers to an 'alternative film culture' which, he states, constituted a 'broader alternative network . . . opening up new pathways for the progression of film as art' (2008: 5). He describes a filmmaking community beyond the mainstream exhibiting its work in non-commercial settings with the aim of expanding the artistic horizons of British filmmaking.

Sexton asserts that Brunel's burlesques exhibit a 'scathing attitude towards different aspects of the British film industry' (2008: 53) and offer an 'exposure of . . . aesthetic dead ends' (2008: 59). He also suggests that they were not made with the aim of commercial exploitation. However, while Brunel's first two burlesques were made in the spirit of experiment, he clearly had in mind their commercial potential, setting up press screenings for both. Surprised at the trade's enthusiastic reception for *Crossing the Great Sagrada*, he lost no time in cashing in on its success. *Crossing the Great Sagrada* is best regarded as an example of what David E. James terms 'calling-card films', experimental shorts made by filmmakers to get attention from the industry.

Gareth Buckell rejects the classification of the burlesques as avant-garde and feels that the attempt to claim them as such 'smacks of desperation', since they 'barely captured the imagination of Britain's avant-garde critics' (2005: 37). The Film Society members were certainly not impressed by them; however, in 1949, curator Jacques Ledoux screened *Crossing the Great Sagrada* alongside works by Germaine Dulac and Jay Leyda in a programme of avant-garde films at the 'Festival Mondial de Film et des Beaux-arts' in Belgium. While the aim of this chapter is not to make a case for Brunel as an avant-garde filmmaker, new ways of defining the cinematic avant-garde during this period can usefully feed into a reading of his burlesques.

Experiment through Play

Both Sexton and O'Pray use the term 'playfulness' to describe the gentle satire Brunel applies in his burlesques, a concept that Christine Gledhill expands on. She outlines a subgenre of the avant-garde or modernist tendency that includes the 'notion of "play" as an outlet for testing . . . the technical capabilities and formal parameters of filmmaking' (2008: 15). This notion of a more light-hearted form of film experimentation accommodates the work of Brunel and other practitioners who were intent on integrating themselves into the industry but whose approach to filmmaking was less serious or political in its aims.

The avant-garde works emanating from Europe in the 1920s assumed various guises. Experimental films which generated meaning via satire, such as *Ballet mécanique* (Fernand Léger, 1924) and *Entr'acte* (Francis Picabia/René Clair, 1924), perhaps have the most in common with British experiments of the period. However, these were also apparently too frivolous for the members of the Film Society and Ivor Montagu recalled that a riot nearly erupted during the screening of *Entr'acte* in January 1926, a reaction which perplexed him, since he regarded the film as merely 'a witty cod' (1975: 224).[2]

While the British intelligentsia took the avant-garde seriously, David E. James observes that the surrealists scorned French art cinema and found their inspiration in the films of Buster Keaton and Charlie Chaplin (2005: 22). Alex Clayton also connects the development of the cinematic avant-garde to the work of Keaton and Chaplin, along with Georges Méliès, finding parallels in their self-reflexivity and lack of narrative logic, as well as the use of formal tricks such as stop-motion and fast motion (2010).

A 'Typical' Avant-Garde

In his 2005 book, James directs his attention to filmmakers at work on the fringes of Hollywood from the 1920s onwards. He regards the avant-garde not as a form of expression with a purely artistic or political impetus, but springing from a desire to experiment and, through experimentation, produce something original which may assist its creator's entry to the industry. His earliest example is American filmmaker Dudley Murphy, who assisted Fernand Léger on *Ballet mécanique*. Prior to this, Murphy had independently produced three lyrical dance films which James describes as 'neither purely artisanal and domestic nor purely industrial but rather a cottage industry spanning both and casually using marginal industry labor' (2005: 24). Despite this marginal production context, Murphy's use of standard cinematic conventions meant the films found an audience, being bought immediately by distributor Sol Lesser who commissioned him to make more.

James focuses on Los Angeles, where filmmaking was the principal industrial activity and thus any non-studio production was physically and metaphorically on the fringes of Hollywood. He identifies several types of practitioner who turned to film for different reasons, observing that

> people outside the studios – and sometimes in them – began to make films on contrary aesthetic and political principles; some understood their activities as art rather

---

[2] According to biographer Russell Campbell, in some sources Montagu attributes this incident to the screening of *Ballet mécanique* (2016: 52).

than commerce, some were politically inspired, and some made films for recreation and the sheer pleasure of the exercise of their faculties. (2005: 3)

He is particularly interested in the way that some of those who engaged in cinematic experimentation became integrated into the industry proper and had their techniques absorbed into mainstream filmmaking, a phenomenon which also occurred in Europe.

James draws attention to the fact that many of the films produced on Hollywood's fringes take filmmaking or aspects of the film industry as their subject matter. Slavko Vorkapich shot his 1927 experimental short *The Life and Death of 9413 – A Hollywood Extra* in his own kitchen at a reported cost of $97. It combines humour and surrealism in its depiction of a man who tries to become a film extra but endures inhuman treatment by an unforgiving industry. James observes that

> despite its formal sophistication, artisanal production and critical thematics, *The Life and Death of 9413* did not place itself outside of or opposed to the industry so much as find a place in it. As well as being specifically about Hollywood, it engaged Hollywood practically in several ways. (2005: 40)

He notes that the day after the first screening of the film, Vorkapich was offered a contract by Paramount to work in special effects. It seems Hollywood studios were keen to recruit talented amateurs into the industry and that some of the films produced under the conditions James describes achieved commercial exhibition and even facilitated their creators' absorption into the industry proper.[3]

In contrast to James's examples, the films discussed by Sexton were made by figures with experience in the industry, but in a liminal space between the amateur and commercial realms. However, Brunel's burlesques have distinct parallels with the experiments emanating from Los Angeles: they were made at his own expense, took the industry as their subject matter and their exhibition helped to gain him a foothold in mainstream production. In addition, although branded as 'Adrian Brunel Burlesques', these films were collaborative works, made with a group of friends and colleagues who contributed their skills and ideas yet worked for little or no pay, thus qualifying them as 'marginal labour'. Perhaps most importantly, Brunel also engaged in experimentation to indulge his creative faculties, as he elucidated in two articles in the trade press.

---

[3] This also occurred in France and Britain. René Clair began a successful mainstream career after making *Entr'acte* and Germaine Dulac moved between the avant-garde and professional realms. As mentioned, Len Lye and Daniel Birt graduated to the British industry in the 1930s.

Film Transformation

In making *Crossing the Great Sagrada*, Brunel inadvertently pioneered a form of what is now termed the 'collage film'.[4] He had accumulated off-cuts from various completed projects and, ever averse to waste, decided to use them to test some of his theories of editing. He had first aired these ideas four years earlier in an article entitled 'How to Make a Dull Film Jolly', in which he made the light-hearted claim that 'it is possible to convert a bad drama into a good comedy. It hasn't been done yet but the process presents vast possibilities' (1920). He set about constructing his spoof using outtakes from various productions, including the travel films *Cannibals of the South Seas* and *Moors and Minarets*, as well as his first feature, *The Man Without Desire*. Using witty title cards he created a loose narrative from the disparate fragments of celluloid and some newly shot footage, mostly featuring Brunel acting various roles. The humour is largely derived from the disparity between the titles and the content of the ensuing image, which subverts expectations and undermines the authoritative voice of the narrator. This was a device used in the Milne comedies and, in fact, the article was written around the time he was making these. In it, he also advocated foregrounding the filmmaking process through formal tricks such as running film backwards and speeding it up, methods used to manipulate the images in *Crossing the Great Sagrada* and *Sheer Trickery*.

After the success of *Crossing the Great Sagrada* had vindicated his ideas on the comic potential of editing, Brunel again expounded them to the press. In an article entitled 'A Film "Transformation" Factory', trade journalist Hubert Waring describes the small cutting room belonging to one 'Sparkleton', a thinly disguised Brunel. In an alley off Wardour Street, Waring encountered Sparkleton

> standing almost knee-deep in film boxes. On some benches round about were various coils of celluloid, a large number of appliances for cutting and 'editing' and piles of dusty-looking scenarios. At one end of his shop stood a projector and at the other a screen. Sparkleton was busy alternately holding up sundry strips of films to the light and consulting a 'book of the words.'

He enlightened Waring on his novel moneymaking enterprise:

> thanks to the new 'transformation' process you needn't despair even of the stupidest drama . . . I can assure you that, after I had cut them up a bit, transposed, rejoined,

---

[4] For a definition, see Beaver 2007: 46, although rather than aiming for a 'visual and rhythmic effect', Brunel's films are deliberately disjointed for comic effect.

scrapped the sub-titles, put in some snappy ones of my own and started all over again with the fifth reel first, you wouldn't have known them.

Despite the tongue-in-cheek tone of both these articles, there is implicit criticism of mainstream filmmaking, more pointed in the second, Brunel's disillusionment with the industry undoubtedly having grown in the intervening years.

Backgarden Films

Brunel maintained that the filming of the new footage for *Sagrada* was performed in a typically unconventional manner in his back garden. However, cinema manager Vivian Van Damm claimed that the film was shot in *his* back garden, asserting in his autobiography that he himself was

> a pioneer in home-movie making ... mostly backgarden movies. About the only title I can recall now is *Crossing the Great Sagrada*, shot entirely with the natural background of a seaside beach and the adjoining garden of my house. That week-end our guests included Henry Edwards and Chrissie White, Miles Mander, Godfrey Winn ... and last but not least, Adrian Brunel, who wrote the script and directed the film. (1952: 176)

Van Damm's description of *Sagrada* as a home movie offers a different perspective on Brunel's burlesques. The fashion was growing for the rich and aristocratic to invite friends to spend weekends at their country homes where they would dress up and make silly, sometimes rather outré, films for their own amusement. At the same time that Brunel was conducting his first 'ultra-cheap experiment' in Van Damm's garden, Lord Beaverbrook's rather more impressive estate at Cherkley Court, Surrey, was the location for an amateur film entitled *They Forgot to Read the Directions* (1924). His house guests, including fellow newspaper proprietor Sir Edward Hulton and authors H. G. Wells and Rebecca West, appeared in the production, penned by West, which featured babies being drowned and punning character names similar to those Brunel concocted.

That same summer, Oxford graduate Terence Greenidge made a film using the latest technical development, the 16mm camera, which had appeared on the market the previous year and was specially designed for amateurs. While staying at the Hampstead home of his friend Evelyn Waugh, he shot *The Scarlet Woman*, written by Waugh and featuring Elsa Lanchester and future film producer John Sutro. That year also saw the formation of the Cambridge University Kinema Club, whose members were to become a driving force behind the development of amateur filmmaking.

Amy Sargeant (2005) has drawn a parallel between this 'hobbying' and Brunel's own experiments, while Gledhill's description of a wider group of 'artistic "amateurs"' (2008: 16) at work within small, loose and informal enterprises is also compelling. However, neither description acknowledges Brunel's professional experience and the commercial necessity underpinning his work that obliged him to create his own opportunities. His experimentation thus often sprang from a need to maintain his profile or find ways of working that were free from interference by the industry.

The Birth of the Burlesques: *Sheer Trickery*

Sheer Trickery was produced along precisely these lines and very much in a spirit of experimentation. Filming was completed in the summer of 1923, although the idea had been conceived two years earlier as a project to demonstrate how films are made, which Brunel maintains was vetoed by the industry. *Sheer Trickery* was first shown in February 1924 as part of the supporting programme for *The Man Without Desire* during its prestigious pre-release run at the Tivoli Theatre. The kind of tricks it employed were not new to film; as Laraine Porter notes, '[t]he early period in British cinema . . . is populated with comedians that delight in the technical possibilities of film' (2012: 19). However, these early films were more interested in manipulating the image in camera to create illusions, while Brunel primarily used editing techniques, foregrounding the technical trickery and building a narrative around seemingly unrelated shots.

Sheer Trickery opens with images that flip between positive and negative, purportedly to prove that 'black is white'. Traffic is shown leaving Piccadilly Circus backwards at high speed, making for 'a much brighter London', and slow and fast motion are used to illustrate various scenarios, including builders working in slow motion due to 'that Monday morning feeling'. Next, a man eats his lunch in reverse, wine pouring upwards from a glass into a bottle and a banana miraculously being restored to its skin. The diner, the worse for wear after his topsy-turvy meal, sees double, with shots superimposed to create the effect. Fast motion is used again as he gets into a taxi and is taken through the streets at breakneck speed, intercut with close-ups of him looking nervous and queasy. When he arrives, he refuses to pay the driver and decides to return by tube, which turns out to be a similarly alarming experience since the train hurtles along the tracks without stopping at any stations. This harrowing journey is shot from the driver's cab, mimicking the popular early cinema genre of the phantom ride. The surviving print of the film ends at this point and thus seems to be incomplete.

Sheer Trickery was made the year before René Clair's avant-garde film *Entr'acte* but the two films have some similarities. Both use slow motion, film run backwards and superimposition to create effects and both contain a long sequence of movement as the central focus, which emulates a staple form of early filmmaking. In Brunel's film it is the phantom ride, while *Entr'acte* appropriates the chase film, as a funeral cortège descends into chaos when the cart bearing the coffin breaks loose and is pursued through the streets. Ivor Montagu took the view that *Entr'acte* 'was not made with the intent . . . of the serious surrealists. It is made for a giggle' (1970: 334–5). More recent assessments of the film regard it somewhat differently, Chris Townsend recognising it as a satirical comment on the mass repatriation of the bodies of French soldiers killed during the First World War. Although Brunel's film was made before Clair's, it does appear to be, at least in part, a response to surrealism. The sequence of the man feeling nauseous contains a double-exposed shot of houses filmed using a Dutch tilt and intercut with a wind-up Charlie Chaplin toy, a dog and a shaky shot of the street, creating a disconcerting viewing experience. The Chaplin toy would appear to be a reference to *Ballet mécanique*, also made after *Sheer Trickery*, raising the possibility that Brunel added this shot at a later stage; he regularly re-edited his films to make them more topical. Brunel's humour is less confrontational than either of the French surrealist works, drawing attention to the image manipulation with titles which point up and contextualise it, and his use of cinematic conventions such as explanatory titles places him more firmly in the mainstream.

Crossing the Great Sagrada

Brunel claimed that *Crossing the Great Sagrada* was 'made as the direct result of a challenge that he was unable to infuse the leaven of humour into a production' (*KW*, 28 August 1924: 70). As outlined above, much of this humour derives from the juxtaposition of image and text, so a title announcing 'We left Blackfriars Bridge behind us on Thursday. A unique view of same crowded with mid-day traffic' is followed by a shot of a rope bridge being crossed by Africans. This dislocation between expectation and actuality continues throughout the film, as we are taken on a fictional journey with explorers 'Holmes, Sweet and Holmes'. Gledhill regards 'the precociously literary interplay of word and image in . . . Brunel's . . . burlesques' as an inheritance from 'the emerging popular arts of the nineteenth century' (2008: 22), comparing Brunel's use of text and image to an artistic trajectory within British culture which originated in the eighteenth century and William Hogarth. However, Brunel's ironic explanation for the mismatch is due to flaws in the editing process: 'The sections of this film having been joined together in a hurry, the indulgence of the audience is craved for any mistakes.' By demonstrating what can occur when editing is done inexpertly, he illustrates its importance to the filmmaking process and uses his skill at manipulating the medium to poke fun at the genres and techniques of British cinema that he regarded as formulaic.

Crossing the Great Sagrada opens with extensive punning titles that point up the pomposity of the travelogue, a genre to which Brunel was no stranger, having shot and edited *Moors and Minarets*. Although this travel film has not survived, off-cuts deposited by him at the BFI National Archive include the title cards, which announce: 'Novello-Atlas Renters present Moors and Minarets Through the heart of Morocco with the great Traveller Sir Percy Sykes K.C.M.G.', followed by the credits 'Personally Supervised by Adrian Brunel' and 'Photographed by Crispin Hay'. *Sagrada* apes and parodies these titles: 'John D. Spoof and Jess E. Lastic by arrangement with Al Donnerblitz present Holmes, Sweet and Holmes' Great Voyageogue "Crossing the Great Sagrada" A Priceless Picture'. A subsequent card records, 'All the foregoing specially supervised, carefully watched and partially controlled by Adrian Brunel assisted by Lionel Rich.' Brunel here pokes fun at the notion of the explorer as celebrity that such films perpetuated, and the shot following this title card punctures the pomposity of the genre by showing Brunel and Rich lounging on a bench in the sun.

Holmes, Sweet and Holmes then appear, all played by Brunel in different costumes. Although brothers, the three are presented as being of different nationalities. The first wears a huge fur coat and Russian hat, the second sports traditional British colonial gear including pith helmet, fly swatter and monocle, while the third is garbed in Scottish national dress consisting of kilt and tam o'shanter. Brunel's penchant for dressing up was amply indulged in the burlesques and his appearance in bizarre costumes is a constant feature. He also appears as 'Prince Olarf of Yugo-Slowa' (a regular cameo) and wealthy financier of the film Lord Pifford, another recurring character who facilitates digs at the power of the money men.

Other mismatched titles and images follow: the outskirts of London are illustrated by a view of Venice, while a painting of a sailing boat in a harbour purports to be 'Enos, a neighbouring fishing village – where Harry Tate was born'. Between the scenes of the various destinations, Brunel intercuts diagrams showing the trajectory of the travellers. Title cards bearing maps of the countries depicted were a standard device in travel films and were used by Brunel in *Moors and Minarets*, but he pokes fun at them here. An animated sequence of an arrow flying randomly across the screen is said to be a 'Diagram of the direction in which we were going' and the title 'Diagram of the direction in which we thought we were going' is followed by a map of the London Underground, indicating the explorers' continued confusion.

When they eventually reach their destination, The Great Cascara of Sagrada, a shot of a waterfall appears, followed by the same image flipped, representing the view *after* crossing it. Thus begins the journey home but, travelling back through the desert, they all perish and the final images show the various celebrations of their deaths around the world.

Crossing the Great Sagrada had a private trade show on 31 July 1924 at the American Theatre in Wardour Street; the *Evening Standard* described the film as '17 minutes of chuckles', the *Weekly News* asserted that it

Figure 4.1 Promotional postcard for *Crossing the Great Sagrada*. Source: ABSC 1/164, BFI National Archive.

'would make a misanthrope laugh' and critics reported that the audience responded to its humour enthusiastically (reviews, ABSC 1/164).

Pathetic Gazette

According to Brunel, *Sagrada* was a financial success and went on to be shown at 'hundreds of theatres throughout the United Kingdom' (1928: 44). The irony that large profits were generated by a film put together by Brunel in his spare time at a cost of around £90, while productions costing thousands failed to bring a return, was surely not lost on Brunel and Mander. They immediately tried to repeat the phenomenon and in October held a trade show for *Pathetic Gazette*, a spoof of the *Pathé Gazette* newsreels. *The Bioscope* deemed it a 'merry and original trifle which would enrich the programme of any better class or middle class house' and noted Brunel's 'marked gift of versatile characterisation and quite . . . astonishing mastery of make-up' (9 October 1924: 58). The film has not survived but the review summarised its contents as: a scene of 'Government officials at Constantinople and Sicily', the different locations being distinguished by the headgear worn; speeded-up shots showing a famous sprinter after taking drugs; 'a famous film star entering (and leaving) a convent . . . the loss of a Scotchman's sixpence . . . and a display of Paris fashions for men by a male mannequin'.

The Harry Hughes Burlesques

The review in *The Bioscope* deems *Pathetic Gazette* an 'entertaining novelty production' yet on the same page a similar-sounding short is described almost identically as 'a novel and entertaining production'. This one-reel comedy, entitled *Adam's Film Review* (a play on Pathé's popular cine magazine *Eve's Film Review*), was directed by Harry Hughes and also distributed by Novello-Atlas Renters. The review suggests Hughes' film trod the same ground as Brunel's, describing it as one 'which wittily burlesques the inconsequential jumble of subject matter and frivolity of treatment characteristic of some magazine pictures'. Hughes is credited with 'remarkable gifts as a parodist' and the film employs the devices of 'clever titling', racial stereotyping ('Margate and Southend are summarised in close-ups of a visitor of the Hebrew persuasion') and manipulation of the footage ('A scientist demonstrates his Death Ray which . . . pushes a train backwards').

Hughes also directed and scripted another burlesque for Brunel and Mander; entitled *Unnatural Life Studies*, it is described as 'A burlesque on the life of a flapper' and was apparently also trade shown in October 1924

(Gifford 2016: 07282). It would seem that Brunel and Mander were so convinced this new format was a money-spinner that they hastily invested in three more burlesques, taking on Hughes so they could rapidly assemble a marketable package of shorts. Despite its trade show, *Unnatural Life Studies* does not seem to have been reviewed.

How exactly Hughes and Brunel crossed paths is uncertain but they had had similar experiences in the industry and shared many of the same views about British film. After many years as an editor, Hughes had begun touting himself as a scenario writer. In 1921 he took out a one-page advert in *Motion Picture Studio* entitled 'Do You Want Me?', in which he lamented that British films were in a 'grievous rut' (20 August 1921: 6). This he attributed to the dependence of the industry on adaptation and the failure to appreciate the value of scenarists such as himself. At this point he seems to have had only one writing credit to his name, the 1921 feature *The Shadow of Evil* for British Art films. He, like Brunel, believed that the British industry needed to encourage more original screenwriting, expressing the view that 'the adapted novel is always a failure', and he revealed that, also like Brunel, he was on the point of bankruptcy through continued unemployment.

It is possible the two had met the previous year after Hughes wrote to Brunel in praise of *The Man Without Desire*. His letter would certainly have recommended him to Brunel as a man after his own heart. 'I came away from your Trade Show of the "Man Without Desire" with the feeling that I must write to you at once to congratulate you on a masterly piece of work,' he wrote, continuing,

> I put it off, however, because I am only a scenario-writer and film editor of fifteen years' experience and, as such, cannot be expected to know as much about the merits of a film as . . . those erudite critics who broadcast their impartial and ungrammatical opinions to a sheep-like trade. (19 December 1923, ABSC 'H'/170)

This antipathy towards the trade would no doubt have convinced Brunel that Hughes was a worthy collaborator.

The careers of the two men continued in parallel; Hughes moved from editing to direction, joining Nettlefold Studios in 1926 and then working for British International Pictures (BIP) from 1930 onwards, overlapping briefly with Brunel's period there. In the mid-1930s Hughes and Brunel were both engaged in the production of quota quickies for Argyle and Butchers, before Hughes began a stint at Welwyn Studios. Hughes maintained a directorial career into the 1940s, his final credits being on children's films after the war. Thus Hughes fits Rachael Low's definition of a 'loner': a figure searching for a place within the industry and willing to try his hand at whatever task would earn him that place, but ultimately failing to establish himself securely (1971: 146).

Screen Parody

Comedy cinema on both sides of the Atlantic had long been poking fun at the film industry. In 1903, British pioneer Cecil Hepworth parodied scientific series *The Unseen World* with his own version, *The Unclean World*; comic Fred Evans made *Pimple as a Cinema Actor* (1912) and *Pimple Writes a Cinema Plot* (1913), featuring his popular alter ego; *Mike Murphy as Picture Actor* (Dave Aylott, 1914) saw the Irish character cause havoc in a film studio. In 1923 Bertram Phillips produced and directed a series of six shorts, each burlesquing a different style of narrative film. These 'Syncopated Picture Plays' included skits on melodrama (*Stung By a Woman*), D. W. Griffith (*One Excited Orphan*) and a 'dream comedy' (*Tut-Tut and His Terrible Tomb*) (*MPS*, 16 June 1923: 12–13), though the highest praise came for *Dickens Up-to-Date*, which put American slang into the mouths of characters from *Oliver Twist*.

Brunel's burlesques can be seen as part of the tradition of such spoofs. However, what sets them apart is his aesthetic approach: the experimentation with techniques employed by European avant-garde filmmakers, the re-editing of footage to produce new meanings and interpretations, and his collaboration with a loose group of like-minded creatives on the industry's fringes who shared his desire to bring originality to British cinema. As 'calling-card' films, Brunel's first burlesques were a success, leading to his attachment to Gainsborough Studios.

The Gainsborough Burlesques

Vivian Van Damm arranged a screening of *Crossing the Great Sagrada* for distributor C. M. Woolf at his private theatre and Michael Balcon agreed that, if Woolf liked the film, Brunel could have access to studio space and equipment to produce further burlesques. The screening was a success and Brunel was commissioned to make five more with a budget of £150 each, on the understanding that he would work for nothing but get a share of the profits after Woolf had been repaid. Given the huge takings his earlier efforts had generated, he had no doubt that this venture would be financially successful.

Yet Brunel was to find that the studio set-up was not conducive to the kind of rapid production he had been used to and it was several months before the press got wind of this new series of burlesques. By July 1925, more than six months later, Gainsborough was still announcing the series as part of its upcoming programme of releases; a two-page advert in *The Bioscope* listed six new Brunel shorts, one of which, *Defective Holmes*, was never made (16 July 1925: 15).

The script for this film survives and confirms it as a spoof of the popular Sherlock Holmes serials. Why it was never made is not clear; possibly Conan Doyle was not keen to have his characters parodied, though it is more likely that Brunel simply did not have the time or the money to complete it, since it required a great deal of location shooting. It bears the hallmarks of Brunel's other burlesques: punning character names (Dr Whatson and Professor Veriarty) and visual and verbal comedy ('Holmes . . . starts to smoke three pipes at once, plays the ukelele wrapt in thought and the familiar dressing gown') (ABSC 1/172).

So This is Jollygood

Brunel's first Gainsborough burlesque was his most direct commentary on the vagaries of the film industry, highlighting the cheapness and dreariness of Britain in comparison to the glamour of Hollywood. A shot of Buckingham Palace, purporting to be the residence of 'Miss Mary Philbanks', is followed by the 'Typical Home of British Film Star', a terrace in a rundown backstreet. Brunel also turns his attention to the money-grabbing figures that producers have to deal with, showing a financier and an author demanding such huge percentages of the profits that the filmmakers end up out of pocket.

Brunel illustrates the pre-production process, beginning with the scenario department, 'where 11 stories are rejected every 29 1/3 seconds' by three men who plough through a pile of books reading a few lines before flinging them over their shoulders to be caught in a wastepaper basket by a man behind. This echoes Brunel's earlier lament that 'hunting for a good film story amongst the stuff deluging a scenario-editor's desk is like looking for a Lilliputian needle in a Brobdingnagian haystack', and his complaint that 'the undeveloped organisation of a studio . . . necessitates work being done in a hurry by men whose brains are worn out through reading other people's rubbish until their heads swim' (1921d).

The 'types' that populate American films are caricatured, from the vamp and villain to the firm-jawed hero and innocent heroine, while Hollywood melodrama is targeted in the recreation of a scene from 'Starving Hearts on Broadway'. In it, an evil landlord attempts to evict a poor widow, along with her mother and child, from their hovel; overacting and clichés abound, with glycerine being dropped into the actors' eyes to feign tears and a rotund director bellowing instructions through a megaphone. The decadent lifestyle of studio personnel is revealed in the final scene. The title 'And so, the day's work over, they betake themselves, these slaves of the public, to the haven of their own firesides, or the quiet joy of the nursery at the children's hour' is followed by a shot of men and women partying with wild abandon.

Battling Bruisers

Battling Bruisers: Some Boxing Buffoonery is a parody of newsreel sports coverage and sporting shorts. Brunel shot it on 10 November 1924, completing over seventy shots on 1,700ft of film in one day; as he confessed to Balcon, 'This is not the contemplative method of the masters of comedy [but] think of the money we save!' (14 November 1924, ABSC 2/111).

Sporting shorts were occasionally shown as part of the Film Society programmes and especially highly regarded was John Betts' series *Sporting Life and What Not to Do But How to Do It* (1924), which became *Sport & Interest in a Fresh Light* in 1926. These one-reel 'interest' films adopted a scientific approach to their subject, using slow motion to demonstrate boxing tactics or the movement of a hurdler's muscles.

Brunel, however, was more interested in boxing as an opportunity to indulge in national stereotyping. Boxer-cum-bullfighter 'Mañana Carambo The Tantalising Toreador of Toledo' uses a cape to confuse his opponent, in a sequence containing footage of audiences at a bullring (almost certainly from *Moors and Minarets*). A French and Italian boxer are depicted as coy and effeminate as they skip delicately round the ring, punching feebly and engaging in clinches until they end up dancing. The tiny gong to mark the end of the round is struck delicately by a hand with its little finger cocked and during the break the two boxers sip cups of tea. Their seconds are beautiful young men wearing lipstick who almost swoon when the hitherto decorous fight descends into viciousness.

The final bout is prefaced by a long sequence of shots purporting to be of Moscow and Petrograd and edited in the style of Russian formalism. As Jamie Sexton notes, this section apes the Soviet montage seen in films such as *Kino-Eye* (Dziga Vertov, 1924) and *Battleship Potemkin* (Sergei Eisenstein, 1925), though, as he points out, neither film was seen in the UK until after this burlesque was first released (2008: 60). He thus suggests that this sequence was added to the film at a later date, and the fact that *Battling Bruisers* is more than 300 feet longer than the other burlesques supports his theory. Sexton observes that the close-ups of faces reacting to the events in the boxing ring are similar to those in the Odessa Steps sequence in *Battleship Potemkin*; however, there are also similarities to Dziga Vertov's 1929 film *Man With a Movie Camera*. A dark, blurred image shows Brunel looking into the viewfinder of a camera, followed by some of the stylistic devices Vertov employs: fast cutting, Dutch tilts and titles in Cyrillic script. A montage sequence includes images of minarets, tractors and a Communist rally in Hyde Park, along with railway tracks shot from a speeding train, interiors of train carriages and feet walking in a park.

The similarities between this sequence and Vertov's film suggest it was added after *Man With a Movie Camera* was shown by the Film Society on 11 January 1931. Sexton notes that *Battling Bruisers* was screened by the Nottingham and District Workers' Film Society on 29 November 1931 and, given Brunel's habit of re-editing his work, it is possible that he cut in the Russian sequence especially for that screening. He later wrote that 'editors sometimes amuse themselves with a spot of Russian *montage*', but 'such experiments should be kept for the private amusement of technicians' (1936: 39).

These first two Gainsborough burlesques were released to coincide with particular features in order to try and boost sales. *So This is Jollygood* was trade shown the same week as *So This is Hollywood* (aka *In Hollywood with Potash and Perlmutter*, Alfred E. Green), an American feature spoofing filmmaking. W. and F. was producing a series of shorts called *The Flying Fists* starring American boxer Benny Leonard, so Brunel presumably hoped exhibitors would take advantage of a tie-in with *Battling Bruisers*.

Cut It Out

Cut It Out; A Day in the Life of a Censor was another direct comment on the British film industry and highlights some of the restrictions imposed by the British Board of Film Censors at the time. In it, a film director has his shoot constantly interrupted by Harper Sunbeam (Edwin Greenwood), 'Chairman of the Society for Detecting Evil in Others', armed with his list of 'Banned Subjects'. The film within a film is a hackneyed melodrama in which an Earl plots to kidnap a governess who rejects his advances. The finale sees her tied to a railway track by the Earl and his criminal sidekick, but she is rescued just in time by Major Cowley, played by Brunel.

Throughout the film, Sunbeam halts filming, brandishing his rules and demanding that the director 'cut out' the offending shots. As the governess climbs over a stile, he leaps into view with a tape measure to show she is revealing too much leg; the Earl and his henchman downing beer is forbidden as a 'Drinking scene carried to excess', so the sequence is run in reverse and the glasses fill up again. A scene of Cowley fighting in the trenches is curtailed for its depiction of the 'realistic horrors of warfare', while an argument between the Earl and his accomplice is halted due to its portrayal of 'relations of Capital and Labour'. As Cowley and the governess kiss, the censor takes out his stopwatch, telling them when to stop. Finally, the infuriating Sunbeam is obliterated by a speeding train and all that remain are his hat, umbrella and book.

A Typical Budget

A Typical Budget returns to Gledhill's 'chop-logic mode of discursivity' (2008: 21), aping British newsreel *Topical Budget* to get further mileage out of the format. The opening title mocks the pretentious pronouncements of newsreels, assuring that 'We guarantee that everything in this film is absolutely fictitious and totally inaccurate'. Shots from *Sheer Trickery* are reused, showing traffic in Piccadilly Circus travelling backwards to illustrate the perils of putting your clock back too early, while a chef makes a 'Cheap pie' using caviar, oysters and 1812 brandy.

The sections of the film vary in length, some just a few shots while others present a more involved narrative. In 'The Art of Self Protection', a man has his bag stolen by a robber (played by Brunel). The victim goes to 'Professor Ogo-Pogo, the Ju-Jitsu expert of the University of Mah-Yongg' to learn the art of self-defence, which consists of an elaborate series of physical manoeuvres. When next set upon by the robber, the man guides him to a patch of grass and begins to put the moves into practice. While he's doing this, the robber surreptitiously steals his watch, pushes him over, picks up his bag and runs away. This skit was inspired by the phenomenon of former boxer Johnny Coulon, who took Paris by storm in 1920 with his mystifying stage act. He had developed a 'magic grip', the finger of one hand on the ear of his opponent, the other hand holding their wrist, which, when applied, rendered them powerless; a contemporary report stated that 'one man has been robbed of £400 by an ingenious pickpocket while in the act of showing how it is done' (*Manchester Guardian*, 22 December 1920). While not really topical by 1925, the sequence is a very accomplished comic interlude and its inclusion of popular pseudo-scientific beliefs harks back to the phrenology references in *The Bump*.

The title announcing the sports section highlights the lack of immediacy of newsreels: 'Owing to films not appearing till they are out-of-date, and in order to suit all tastes, we have combined our Sports into one section.' This sequence is worthy of *Monty Python's Flying Circus* (BBC TV, 1969–74), as three men wearing mismatched sporting gear (fencing mask with cricket pads, cricket whites with riding boots) run round a field hitting rugby balls with hockey sticks and tackling each other, a title labelling their antics as 'cutting it up rough and doing other things to keep fit'. Brunel later described the making of this sequence: 'My colleagues and I all dressed up in fantastic hybrid sporting costumes, and drove out to a quiet field where we filmed our crazy sportsmanship' (1936: 91).

As a collection of unconnected skits, the newsreel burlesque is hit and miss. However, since the jokes come thick and fast and in so many different forms (visual, textual, silly, topical) and the pacing of the shots and sequences varies, it proved to be a format with potential and flexibility, which is presumably why Brunel recycled it in the second group of burlesques.

As well as mocking the content of the newsreel, Brunel points up some of the techniques it employed. In a section entitled 'Sago Making in North Borneo', he uses an 'in camera' effect, opening the iris at the start of each new shot so the image appears inside a small circle which gradually gets larger until the image fills the screen. He draws attention to this with a title which reads 'Sorry to keep on opening and closing the picture like this, but they do it in all the best topicals.'[5]

The final sequence, 'Paris Fashions for Men', returns to the homosexual stereotyping of *Battling Bruisers*. Brunel plays a male model who reclines on a chaise longue, cigarette in hand, before modelling several outré outfits for different occasions, including a game of tennis and refereeing a football match. Titles describe a 'chic little sash of multi-coloured curtain-binding "The Rudolph"', which adorns a sheik costume in the style of Rudolph Valentino, and the 'apache scarf' or 'Novello', a reference to Ivor Novello's role in *The Rat*. The review in *The Bioscope* of *The Pathetic Gazette* describes 'a display of Paris fashions for men by a male mannequin' so Brunel either reshot or reused the same sequence, presumably reasoning that no one was likely to notice given the limited release of the earlier film.

A Typical Budget premiered at the inaugural performance of the Film Society on 25 October 1925, more than a year after Brunel's commission by Balcon. Sandwiched between Walter Ruttman's 'Absolute Films' and Paul Leni's *The Waxworks* (1924), it was perhaps not the ideal outing for his rather uneven comedy and *Kinematograph Weekly* drily speculated that

---

[5] Interestingly, among the material Brunel deposited with the BFI National Archive, there is a can of fragments from *Moors and Minarets* that just contains such iris shots. It appears he cut them all out of the finished film, presumably deciding they were too repetitive and formulaic.

it 'will undoubtedly be seen in a less rarefied atmosphere' (29 October 1925: 48). Most considered it an unworthy inclusion in the programme; 'the only English film . . . was a dismal failure' wrote *Saturday Review*, *The Nation and the Athenaeum* described it as 'crude and thin', while the *Times* critic wished he 'had been better amused by it' (burlesque reviews, ABSC 5/56).

The Blunderland of Big Game

The Blunderland of Big Game is the only one of the Gainsborough burlesques that has not survived. A spoof of *The Wonderland of Big Game* (1923), Brunel's film follows the expedition of intrepid woman explorer Mrs Forseater Ford (played by a man), who embarks on the ascent of Mount Eversharp. It featured Brunel's stock company playing all the parts, the perpetuation of racial stereotypes (J. O. C. Orton blacked up as a native guide) and, no doubt, further footage from Brunel's cutting room. Alfred Hitchcock refers to the film in a letter he wrote to Brunel from Munich, asking, 'How did the Blunderland picture turn out?' He was in Germany directing his first feature, *The Pleasure Garden*, and his letter reveals how close the two men were during this period, at least in terms of their respective work for Gainsborough (n.d., ABSC 1/112).

Distribution of the Burlesques

Rachael Low attributed the burlesques' lack of exhibition potential to the fact that they 'appealed especially to those in the film trade' (1971: 149). Gainsborough certainly made little effort to promote and distribute them and only *So This is Jollygood* appears to have been screened to the press. This was understandably a source of great distress to Brunel, not least because, having worked without payment while making them, he was relying on a cut of the profits. Towards the end of 1925, a two-page advert promoting the burlesques appeared in *Kinematograph Weekly*, although it is not clear who commissioned and paid for this publicity. Balcon may have felt obliged to help out, or perhaps Brunel commissioned it himself. It depicts Brunel in his 'British Burlesque Factory' churning out comedy films on a production line, an ironic representation given the difficulties he had making them. This attempt to 'brand' his work as a product which could be sold on his name is typical of his approach to self-promotion.

Brunel approached C. & M. Productions, the distributors of Gainsborough's films, about the company's failure to push the burlesques,

Figure 4.2 Trade promotion for Brunel's Gainsborough burlesques.
Source: *Kinematograph Weekly*, 12 November 1925, pp. 10–11.

penning a letter to the company's General Manager, Jeffrey Bernerd. Bernerd had apparently written them off as 'terrible', and Brunel was incensed both by this assessment and Bernerd's lack of effort in trying to sell them, which had led to bookings of a meagre £580 (27 February 1926, ABSC 1/111). *So This is Jollygood* was shown at the Film Society on 11 April 1926, presumably in a last-ditch attempt by Brunel to secure distribution; the programme notes optimistically state that the film was 'shortly to be released' (Amberg 1972: 7th performance). Brunel then took his complaint to C. M. Woolf and the distributor made his own feelings on the films known:

> As regards the general booking value of them, I am afraid that despite the fact that of their kind they are very good Comedies, they are too subtle and clever for the average exhibitor, and it is to be regretted that even with the small amount we have done in several instances where exhibitors have booked these films unseen they have tried to get out of their contracts . . . I am afraid that I cannot hold out any hope to you that we shall even get anything like our money back on them. (27 April 1926, ABSC 1/111)

He suggested Brunel could take on the sale of the films himself, though they would have been impossible to sell so long after completion.

Woolf's assessment of the films as 'too subtle and clever' seems to reinforce the industry's view of Brunel as a highbrow and suggests an evaluation of the burlesques as appealing to a more educated audience. However, the humour is more silly than intellectual and while *Crossing the Great Sagrada* and *Sheer Trickery* have an air of spontaneity, born out of a spirit of experimentation and desire to create something new, the Gainsborough burlesques lack the same spark of originality. Brunel undoubtedly found that the pressures of his other assignments for the studio and the need to repay Woolf's loan hindered the creative process. While the first three burlesques were made as much for fun as for profit, they apparently provided Novello-Atlas with a good income, Brunel wistfully observing, 'If I had only received my share from the bookings I would have made about 900 per cent profit' (1949: 108). Yet once burlesque production became a job and his livelihood was at stake, inspiration was more difficult to find. Brunel was keen to make himself useful to Balcon and found himself re-editing Gainsborough productions and retitling foreign films being distributed by W. and F. Consequently, by the time he had completed the burlesques, the success of *Crossing the Great Sagrada* was long forgotten. An 'abbreviated edition' of *Sagrada* was shown at the Film Society on 10 April 1927 but by then Brunel had long conceded that he would never profit from his work.

Recycling and Reimagining

However, this did not stop him revisiting the films when he next found himself in financial difficulty, and the burlesques are prime examples of Brunel's efforts to maximise return for his investment, especially of his time and ideas. Thus, not only did the early films repurpose material which was a waste product from the editing process, but Brunel continued to try and exploit the concept and humour for several years to come. In 1931, he scripted sound versions of the two travel burlesques, entitled 'Recrossing Sagrada' and 'So This is Africa'. The latter script, a reworking of *The Blunderland of Big Game*, gives an indication of what the earlier film contained, and Brunel's notes reveal that the title was superimposed on a map of India and followed by the subtitle 'An Unnatural History Film' (reusing the title of Hughes' film). His plan was to recut the originals with a soundtrack over the top, which could have had some comic potential, since the juxtaposition of sound and image would be more immediate. Neither film was completed but it is possible that *Blunderland* has not survived because Brunel began cutting together this sound version.

Around the same time, Brunel wrote a series of articles for *The Era* recycling the humour of the films. One was entitled 'Trade Shows Revued' and contained spoof film reviews for titles like '"Baby's Irisch Nose" by Lowe-Brau Picture Corp' (30 December 1931: 4). Another was a comic guide for would-be screenwriters, beginning, 'Can you write? That is to say do you know how to formulate the letters of the alphabet? Yes? Then you can write film scenarios' (30 December 1932: 24).

His advice to the amateur also took a more positive and paternal direction and he wrote about his methods in order to help budding filmmakers with their own efforts. His first reflection, in *Close Up* magazine (1928), appropriately focused on the experimental aspect of the burlesques. But in his books on filmmaking, aimed at the amateur, he recommended this recycling as 'the cheapest form of film-making and in many ways the easiest' (1936: 92) and, since it did not 'rely on the usual forms of continuity, such as one requires in a story-film, you can cut out incidents bodily and boldly if they do not come up to the standard you set yourself' (1936: 24).

Conclusion: Too Subtle or Too Crude?

Brunel's burlesques have been considered part of a group of loosely defined avant-garde works made on the fringes of the mainstream. Although their humorous approach and commercial aims suggest otherwise, there are ways to accommodate them within the canon of such works. *Crossing the Great Sagrada* in particular stands out as an experimental effort which brought a genuinely original approach to filmmaking and gained Brunel attention from the industry. His first three burlesques sprang from the burgeoning home movie trend and a desire to test his theories of how manipulating and recontextualising images in different ways could produce new interpretations of the material. These films were another attempt by Brunel to exercise creative expression in a commercially viable format, yet when he tried to turn the technique into a lucrative franchise, the freshness and originality was impossible to sustain. They were deemed 'too subtle and clever' for mainstream cinemas yet too 'crude and thin' for the more 'rarefied' exhibition environment of the Film Society screenings.

The burlesques are of particular interest for Brunel's observations on the film industry and generic conventions, highlighting its lack of originality and pointing up 'aesthetic dead ends'. Brunel's burlesques are best categorised as affectionate exposés of established film forms which he felt had become hackneyed; a gentle dig at an industry failing to innovate sufficiently.

While the films facilitated Brunel's tentative entry into the studio system, this move also brought him into direct confrontation with the conservatism of those running it. Having attempted to bring originality to British cinema from a position of relative freedom on the fringes of the industry, the next phase of his career saw him struggling to innovate from within.

CHAPTER 5

'A war film with a difference': *Blighty* and Brunel's Negotiation of the British Studio System

While the burlesques brought Brunel to the attention of the industry, they failed to secure him the position he hoped for. In fact, his reputation for making successful films on a tiny budget was a disadvantage, and he effectively devalued his work by undertaking non-directorial jobs for Gainsborough. It took two years of campaigning before he was permitted to direct a feature for the studio, during which time he was kept afloat by sheer determination and a versatility that was both a boon and a hindrance. Busy with editing and other tasks, his directing career was on hold.

Thus far, Brunel had been able to make films with relative freedom and had demonstrated his potential for creativity when external interference was limited. These experiences did not prepare him for directing a feature under the watchful eye of a major studio entirely concerned with profit margins. His attachment to Gainsborough may have led him to believe that he had finally gained a position from which he could influence mainstream filmmaking, backed by financial resources and with access to a distribution set-up that would ensure his films reached an audience. However, his first feature for the studio, *Blighty*, was a stark introduction to the politics of studio production, requiring him to engage in complex negotiations in his attempts to maintain a level of creative control over the project. The various versions of the story and script of *Blighty* in Brunel's and Ivor Montagu's paper collections illustrate the decisions and compromises made to balance the intentions of the filmmakers with the commercial imperatives of the studio. *Blighty* was an example of one of the most popular genres of the 1920s, the war film, the generally conservative nature of which threw up both challenges and opportunities for Brunel in his endeavours to imbue British film with the originality he felt it lacked.

Brunel and Gainsborough

Brunel was convinced that his lack of directing opportunities at Gainsborough was due to a conspiracy by two of its dominant powers: C. M. Woolf and star director Graham Cutts. Ivor Montagu's assessment corroborates this view, recording that 'intrigues kept him ever from the floor' (1970: 275). Brunel spent more than two years engaged in post-production on other people's films, including the two Cutts films *The Prude's Fall* (1924) and *The Blackguard* (1925). He took on these tasks to convince Balcon of his value to the company; his eagerness to please was driven largely by his ongoing financial instability and a desire to be accepted by the industry. However, his willingness to work on minor projects without a contract meant that he was regarded by the studio heads as an 'odd-job man' sustained by vague promises of a feature of his own to direct.

Brunel was also fulfilling commissions outside Gainsborough, including editing and retitling foreign films for the Film Society. This was done through his editing firm, which now had two assistants, Lionel Rich and J. O. C. Orton, who he felt obliged to support financially. Although Brunel was not under contract, Gainsborough scrutinised how he spent his time and took a dim view of his association with the anti-commercial activities of the Film Society. Consequently, at the end

Figure 5.1 Cartoon of C. M. Woolf, *Kinematograph Weekly*, 10 January 1924, p. 54.

of 1925, he resigned from the board of the Society, although he continued to retitle its foreign films.

Brunel was becoming increasingly discouraged and, by the spring of 1926, approaching thirty-seven and with only one feature to his name, desperation began to set in. His profile at Gainsborough had never been high and, as time went on, his prospects of re-establishing himself both within the studio and the wider industry were looking increasingly remote. His letters to Balcon ranged from wounded and pleading to petulant and threatening. In one particularly bitter missive, he reminded Balcon of his promise that he would be 'working on a production by the beginning of last January [1926]', continuing: 'That date had to be postponed, I know, but in the meantime I find George Cooper installed before me and you are now talking about stars for Hitch's . . . picture' (n.d., ABSC 5/111). His sense of betrayal extended to other collaborators: 'Ivor Novello's hope that I would not be directing "The Rat" is the sort of thing that has done me no good. Stannard, Emelka, Freedman and others have had their fling at me' (ibid.). Clearly dismayed by the studio's perception of him, he wrote, 'I have carried on with the work, much of which you have been instrumental in getting me and for which I am very grateful; but the result has been in certain minds "Brunel is very happy – he won't mind waiting"' (ibid.). The letter inevitably comes round to the issue constantly driving his correspondence: 'I am hopelessly in debt and must again borrow a considerable sum this month' (ibid.). Later that year he reminded Balcon of the services he had provided and the assurance that his work on *The Prude's Fall* had 'improved the film "a thousand per cent"' (18 May 1926, ABSC 1/111).

Cutts was a powerful figure at Gainsborough and Brunel petitioned him several times to try and secure a commission. In January 1925 Cutts promised to take up Brunel's cause with Gainsborough's new board member, Charles Lapworth. Despite this, Brunel was convinced that Cutts mistrusted and disparaged him: 'I . . . saw how Cutt's [sic] propaganda about my being "high-brow" had so undermined me and my own restraint had made me seem so unimportant, that I could be treated anyhow' (n.d., ABSC 1/112). In the same letter he threatened to resign from the company on hearing 'from several sources that Cutts had said that he was never going to let me direct for Gainsborough if he could prevent it'. Yet he continued to pin hope on his friendship with Balcon, writing, 'When I read your reply, I realised how foolishly trusting I had been . . . You were my friend, but I thought also that you had confidence in me' and he appealed to Balcon to use his influence with Gainsborough's directors. However, Balcon may not have had such leverage, since he himself was under enormous pressure to ensure that his films returned a profit on the investment made by Woolf, sole financier of his productions since *Woman to Woman* in 1923. Woolf was a shrewd businessman with 'the capacity to reduce strong men to tears' (Balcon 1972: 30) and had considerable control over Gainsborough's production schedule, including which directors got commissions. After the failure of Brunel's burlesques, what little regard Woolf had for him would have dissipated and Cutts' apparent suspicion of him would have further hampered his progression. Even if Balcon felt a sense of loyalty towards Brunel, he had to pick his battles with Woolf; he had fought to get Hitchcock a directing job and then struggled to get the films released. Balcon's faith in Hitchcock was eventually justified after the success of *The Lodger: A Story of the London Fog* (1926), which also boosted the profile of Ivor Montagu who had done remedial editing work on it. Perhaps having secured Hitchcock's future, Balcon felt able to address Brunel's situation since, on 3 November 1926, he contracted him to direct a feature, although the commission was not what Brunel had hoped for.

Silent Genres: The War Film

The concept of genre during the silent period was of less concern to producers and exhibitors than other selling points, such as the proven marketability of certain stars or properties. As Simon Brown points out, 'it was the producers who spoke the language of genre and they spoke it not to audiences but to renters and showmen' (2016: 147). Films were divided into roughly two types: drama or comedy, with various nuances within these categories, such as social drama, Western drama or melodrama.

However, one genre that was ever-present on cinema screens during the 1920s was the war film, and its ubiquity was a subject that exercised commentators within and outside the trade. Perhaps due to this, and the fact that war films are seen by some as a measure of the national mood, they have enjoyed considerable academic attention in recent years.

The devastating effects of the First World War were explored in all forms of creative expression during the interwar years, as musicians, artists, poets and writers described, reflected on and tried to make sense of the destruction and tragic loss. Filmmakers were no exception and, throughout the 1920s, various perspectives on the war were presented in the form of screen entertainment in Britain, Europe and America. As collaborative works, these films rarely expressed emotional reactions to the conflict as directly as the other arts, and, as a commercial product, film was subject to the pressures within the British industry, which affected how war could be depicted.

The Art of War

After his experiences with *The Man Without Desire* three years previously, Brunel's ideas about film as an art form had progressed and developed. The expertise in editing he had acquired, both at Gainsborough and his own firm, along with the 'education' gleaned from working on the foreign films selected for Film Society screenings, no doubt fuelled his thinking on the balance between art and entertainment; just how much of the former could be included without interfering with the latter? Hammond and Williams maintain that the war film could be a valuable tool for enlightened filmmakers trying to develop 'respectability in terms of film as art' (2011: 3). However, this may have been hampered by what Napper regards as the way some British war films of the period 'struggle to accommodate a series of competing modes', resulting in works that are 'generally formally odd', a failing he relates to a 'crisis in language' affecting responses to the war (2011: 110). Neil Brand also detects this, regarding most British silent war films as 'a vivid record of the very confusion, insecurity and insularity of those we witnessed fighting the war, particularly on the home front' (2011: 139). Whereas Germany, having been defeated, was better able to 'speak eloquently from the grave of its losses, horrors and nightmares through the medium of Expressionism' (ibid.: 142), Brand asserts that Britain found it harder to reconcile the notion of victory with the devastating losses it had suffered.

British films about the war tended towards conventional narratives, such as Maurice Elvey's *Comradeship* (1919) and *Mademoiselle d'Armentières* (1926), *The General Post* (Thomas Bentley 1920) and *The Guns of Loos* (Sinclair Hill 1928). These used a melodramatic mode to tell a story of romance against the backdrop of the war, allowing for themes of parting, battlefield heroism, camaraderie and the loss of loved ones. Elements of comedy were often employed to lighten the tone; stereotypical chirpy Cockney characters, such as Shorty Bill in *Poppies of Flanders* (Arthur Maude 1927), reflected the humour that had been so crucial to keeping up the spirits of the soldiers in the trenches. Andrew Kelly, in his study of the war films made in the 1920s and 1930s, detected 'a depressing uniformity' in their unquestioningly patriotic approach (1997: 58), while Michael Balcon recalled that '[h]ardly a film of the period reflects the agony of those times' (quoted in Barr 1998: 13).

The non-controversial view of the war presented in these films is unsurprising if you accept that their aim was to 'honour the memory of those who die in war without celebrating war itself' (Sargeant 2011: 80), a negotiation which may have compromised the ambitions of some filmmakers. Public feelings about the war were far from straightforward during this period and accommodating the subject within familiar narrative structures was perhaps a way of attempting to impose some kind of order onto the turmoil of emotions. A letter in *The Motion Picture Studio* supports this view: '[t]he public mind is still quivering in uncertainty, unrest and doubt, as the result of many years of most ghastly and cruel warfare, and unconsciously seeks every opportunity afforded to recapture that pre-war stability, sanity and equanimity' (11 November 1922: 7).

Another popular approach to the war film taken by British producers was the reconstruction of major battles, with director Walter Summers bringing to the screen *Ypres* (1925), *Mons* (1926) and *The Battles of the Coronel and Falkland Islands* (1927). These were combinations of dramatic re-enactment with actuality footage, and aimed to bring to life battles which, for those who had not participated in them, must have been impossible to imagine. But while generally well received – C. A. Lejeune describing *The Battles of the Coronel and Falkland Islands* as 'without question the best motion picture that a British director has ever made' (quoted in Dixon 2011: 20) – these amalgams of documentary and drama tended to be rather episodic and lacked character identification. Contemporary reports suggest that their audiences were primarily male: 'That young England is taking trouble to acquaint itself with the history of the war is the conviction of a number of cinema managers . . . *Havoc*, *Ypres*, *Zeebrugge* attract audiences almost all male and 50% postwar' (quoted in Gledhill 2011: 105). This was not the audience demographic the producers were expecting, if the publicity for *Ypres* is anything to go by: 'it is estimated that there are over three million survivors who fought in that inferno during the Great War, every one of whom will be anxious to live over again at a distance those dark yet glorious days' (*The Bioscope*, 17 September 1926: 47). There was undoubtedly a sense that war films were continuing to attract audiences and offered a fairly safe box office proposition, as long as they portrayed a certain view of the conflict.

According to Kelly, the conservatism of the British film industry not only accounted for a lack of variety and imagination in the presentation of the subject of war, but also precluded the production of any films which could be described as truly anti-war (1997: 58). Conversely, Bamford implies that anti-war sentiment was common in films of the time, singling out *Mumsie* (Herbert Wilcox 1927) as an unusual example which 'ran against the anti-war theme of other films' (1999: 168–9). Whether or not the films truly reflect it, anti-war feeling ran high in Britain during this period. Richard Overy states that 'to be anti-war in the 1920s and 1930s was to acquire membership in a broad church . . . there existed a profusion of anti-war organisations . . . taken together their active members and supporters certainly numbered millions' (2009: 221). So while the subject of war was attractive to producers, it was perhaps less so to audiences. In 1927, one Member of Parliament lamented the fact that 'so much of the production . . . which goes on should only be in the direction of war films' (quoted in Bamford 1999: 129). If politicians were bemoaning the overabundance of British war films, the cinemagoing public seemed to feel the same and in Sidney Bernstein's 1927 audience questionnaire about genres, male patrons ranked the war film sixth out of the eight listed, while women placed it last (*KW*, 11 August 1927: 37).

Even before these results confirmed it, Brunel was convinced that the public had no appetite for war films, and this formed part of his objection to his first commission for Gainsborough:

> a 'war film' was about the only type of film I wouldn't direct. This was not only because nearly every war film was based upon the chivalry, bravery and sacrifice of men in the fighting forces, and inevitably pro-war propaganda, but because there had been a spate of war films and the public was sick of them. (1949: 127)

Indeed, while the genre had been a mainstay of British production schedules since 1914, it reached a peak in 1927. Under the headline 'Is War Overdone?', a contributor to *Kinematograph Weekly* observed that 'in our long list of home productions . . . about 25 per cent are war stories, and there is a risk that the public may tire of the eternal battle footage however well done' (9 June 1927: 20). Bamford suggests that the large number of war-themed films made during this year may have been due to the imminent introduction of the Cinematograph Films Bill, or Quota Act, which contained a requirement that films should be 'adequately patriotic' to register. Yet the preoccupation was not restricted to the cinema; Malcolm Bradbury points out that 'the fiction of the Twenties was . . . dominated by the war novel; by 1930, it's estimated, some seven hundred books had been written on the war' (2001: 144).

With Gainsborough insisting that he produce a war film, Brunel attempted to reconcile his own anti-war stance with the necessity of remaining patriotic and making a commercially successful entertainment film. Despite the difficulties of negotiating these elements and the politics of the studio, Brunel recalled the making of *Blighty* as 'the only time I had a free hand when I was at Gainsborough' (4 November 1935, Kent MOMI collection).

A New Pattern

According to Brunel, it was C. M. Woolf who demanded that his directorial debut for Gainsborough should be a war film, the studio's first since its major success with *Woman to Woman* in 1923. Brunel's initial reluctance was overcome through the intervention of Ivor Montagu, who convinced Balcon that a story set on the Home Front during the First World War would be more appealing to audiences than a more conventional approach. Thus, Brunel and Montagu wrote 'a British war film to a new pattern', omitting 'the grim terror' of the conflict (scrapbook of reviews, ABSC 1/85). Their story centres on an aristocratic family, Lord and Lady Villiers and their children Ann and Robin, who reside in an elegant London townhouse with a strong air of tradition in its furnishings and trappings. The opening credits list them simply as 'The Mother', 'The Father', etc., suggesting that they represent everyman/woman; 'any family from the highest to the humblest' as one critic wrote (ibid.).

The narrative traces the events that befall the family from the start of the war through to the first anniversary of the Armistice. Opening with the assassination of the Archduke Ferdinand, the film moves to the Villiers' home where the news of the event barely registers, Ann being more interested in the boxing results. Robin is studying in Germany but is forced to make a hurried return to England as the threat of war becomes real, joining up the moment he gets back, despite not yet being nineteen. The film portrays the training he undergoes and the comradeship he develops with his fellow soldiers before they are sent to France. All the action in France takes place at the Café Normand, a tavern behind the French lines; here Robin is reunited with Marshall, the Villiers' family chauffeur, now his superior in army rank. He also meets and falls in love with a French refugee; they marry and she has his baby. He is killed in action before his child is born, and it falls to Marshall to break the news to the Villiers of the new additions to their family. The arrival of Robin's wife and child in London, which coincides with Armistice Day, brings some comfort to Lord and Lady Villiers and, one year later, they prepare to welcome Marshall into the family as well, as he and Ann announce their engagement.

This transformation of the Villiers represents in microcosm the impact the war had on families all over Britain. Lord and Lady Villiers do not end up with the son- and daughter-in-law they might once have expected, yet they accept without question the choices made by their children in this new world. However, despite the deviation from tradition, the film concludes with the continuation of the family line ensured by the birth of Robin's son, albeit to a foreigner of uncertain heritage. The marriage of Ann and Marshall suggests that the First World War led to a lowering of class barriers, though there is little evidence that this actually took place, and it perhaps reflects Montagu's utopian imagination rather than a genuine societal shift. According to Virginia Nicholson, in the years after the war when young men were in short supply, gentlewomen did not contemplate marrying beneath them even if the alternative was spinsterhood. The film also highlights the phenomenon of women performing men's work for the first time and thus beginning to demand the same rights as their male counterparts; when Ann and Marshall arrive at her family home to seek permission to marry, she now drives the family car.

The Artist versus the Moneybags

Blighty was made by Piccadilly Pictures, a subsidiary of Gainsborough set up by Balcon and Charles Lapworth. With C. M. Woolf as chairman of Piccadilly, Balcon found himself completely bound to W. & F., increasing Woolf's control over the company's output. Brunel's first feature for the company was to be 'a modest, inexpensive production' (Balcon 1972: 25); Woolf presumably did not wish to invest significant sums in a film by a director in whom he had little faith, and who had shown himself willing and able to work for very little. His budget was £8,000, below the usual amount for a Gainsborough film, which averaged between £10,000 and £30,000. Due to these financial limitations, the film had to be shot entirely in the studio, the only exteriors being in the stock footage. Actor Godfrey Winn recalled the money-saving measures Brunel and the crew had to take: 'the trench-warm that I had worn in one scene had been lent to me by the young floor manager who had been "out there" himself' (1967: 226). One aspect Brunel was not prepared to scrimp on was the cast, and the fee for stage star Ellaline Terriss reportedly swallowed up such a large proportion of the budget that he was forced to employ an unknown actor, Annesley Hely, to play her husband.

The economic strictures within which Brunel was working were spelled out in the contract he signed and it was made financially beneficial to him to stick to them. His basic payment for directing the film was £350 but a £250 'bonus' was promised if he kept within budget and schedule. For each day he went over the twenty-eight-day shoot, running from 6 December 1926 to 8 January 1927, he would lose £25 of his bonus, while every extra £100 he spent would mean a £20 deduction (3 November 1926, ABSC 4/112).[1]

---

[1] Rather cannily, Brunel made the counter suggestion that if he brought the film in *under* budget, he would be paid 10 per cent of the money saved.

It was clear that Brunel was under scrutiny by Gainsborough, and not only on the studio floor. He had already resigned from the Film Society board but Balcon also expressed concern about his activities with editing firm Brunel & Montagu. Ivor Montagu was not under contract to Gainsborough and his involvement in the enterprise did not seem to be at odds with his work at the studio. In fact, his collaboration on *Blighty* undoubtedly smoothed the way for Brunel, and his idea to focus on the Home Front allowed them to draw on their own memories of the period and thus produce a more personal work. In his memoir, Brunel records that the scriptwriting process was a group effort, describing sessions taking place at his home with Eliot Stannard at the typewriter and he, and occasionally Montagu, feeding in ideas (1949: 127).[2]

Brunel was monitored by the studio to ensure he finished on time; Winn recalled set visits from the high-ups in Wardour Street and sensed the pressure the crew were under. Despite this, he recorded that Brunel maintained his composure throughout the shoot, describing him as 'an artist who achieved his best effects by never raising his voice' (1967: 226). Winn was aware of the state of the British film industry at the time and the problems Brunel faced, invoking 'the stereotyped lament in the making of all pictures . . . the artist versus the moneybags' (ibid.: 228). Brunel's self-control was tested by the foibles of his cast, particularly the temperamental nature of French actress Nadia Sibirskaïa who drove cameraman Jack Cox to distraction due to her insistence on positioning her face at a forty-five-degree angle to the camera. Ellaline Terriss had a clause in her contract to accommodate her afternoon nap, further slowing the film's progress. On 29 December 1926, Balcon wrote to Harold Boxall, Piccadilly's General Manager, concerned that Brunel would overrun his shooting schedule. The letter would have left Brunel in no doubt about his place in the studio's pecking order:

> Mr Brunel will understand that not only will the extended time affect the cost of his own production, but it will affect the cost of DOWNHILL, which is scheduled to commence on Monday 10th January and if there is any delay in this connection, it will be a very serious matter indeed owing to the director and star artist[3] being engaged at a high price for a limited period. (ABSC 2/111)

---

[2] Stannard and Montagu are credited with the script and story respectively, but Brunel does not receive a writing credit. A letter from Brunel in December 1926 mentions the involvement of playwright Charles McEvoy (ABSC 4/112) and correspondence also suggests that Balcon and George Hopton fed into script discussions.

[3] Alfred Hitchcock and Ivor Novello.

Figure 5.2 Nadia Sibirskaïa as 'The Girl' in *Blighty*. Source: BFI National Archive.

Once shooting had finished, Brunel set to work on the editing, his dual role presumably a further cost-saving measure, since his contract makes no mention of payment for his post-production work. Editing was delayed by an attack of arthritis, which had also affected him during filming, and he had to argue strenuously with Balcon against showing the film to W. & F. before it was complete. Brunel was well aware of the perils of projecting a film at an early stage of cutting and would have been extremely concerned that to do so with *Blighty* would have jeopardised his future with Piccadilly and delayed or prevented the release of the film.

Striking the Right National Note

Blighty had its initial trade show in Birmingham on 20 March 1927, followed by the London show at the Hippodrome two days later; critics focused on its national appeal and perceived realism. 'The "atmosphere" of "Blighty" stamps it as an outstanding achievement. A simple, homely story is handled so faithfully, so graphically, so convincingly . . . that it becomes real entertainment,' wrote Edith Nepean in *Picture Show*, while the *Sunday Express* critic maintained that 'to see "Blighty" after America's war films is like "going home"'.[4] References to features of Home Front life were seen as a key element of its Britishness, with Brunel and Montagu drawing on personal recollections for the period recreation. Lady Villiers scratches her head as she tries to comprehend a handful of ration cards, her husband screws up his face after sipping a cup of saccharine-sweetened tea due to sugar rationing, and a map hangs on the library wall with pins in it marking the progress of the war. Such details throw a spotlight on the way domestic life was affected by the conflict and reviewers expressed appreciation of these realistic touches:

> *Blighty* . . . is a simple, deeply touching and sincere glimpse of the home-life of very normal English people during the War, with its ration-cards, father in special constable's uniform, wounded soldiers, heart-breaking telegrams from the War Office . . . air-raids, recruiting stations and girl-widows. (*The Spectator*, 14 May 1927)

Several critics referred to the impending quota laws: 'If all the quota pictures are of the same kind . . . the British exhibitor and the British public will have no reason to complain, and they should be shown abroad as typically British' (*Liverpool Post*); 'There are a number of passages . . . in "Blighty" which . . . make it certain that in this country we have the ability to meet all that the Cinematograph Films Bill anticipates in British pictures' (*Sunday Pictorial*). The *Jersey Morning News* proclaimed *Blighty* 'the finest British picture yet made', while *The Birmingham Mail* declared it 'a fine British production which strikes the right national note'.[5]

Exaltations of British films as valuable additions to the national canon were not uncommon in the press during this period, and if they provided a contrast to American productions, so much the better. US war films, in particular, were regarded as brash, overly emotional and vulgarly jingoistic; *What Price Glory* (Raoul Walsh 1926) was described as 'lurid' while *The Big Parade* (King Vidor 1925) was deplored because 'not one mention was made of the English [sic] army' (quoted in Bamford 1999: 130). Lawrence Napper argues for a reading of British war films of the period as part of the struggle against the 'rewinding of history by Hollywood . . . that accords America centrality even in European affairs' (2011: 109). The harnessing of patriotism in efforts to further the cause of British cinema

---

[4] All reviews quoted hereafter in this chapter are from the scrapbook of reviews in ABSC 1/85, unless otherwise referenced.
[5] *Blighty* was trade shown in Birmingham before the London trade show. It was unusual for a film to have a provincial trade show first.

are an element of this struggle, and the need to combat the dominance of Hollywood was a constant theme in the British trade press during the postwar period and beyond. 'British' traits such as restraint and subtlety were regarded as antidotes to American films; significantly, the reviews of *Blighty* abound with words such as 'sincere', 'sensitive', 'intimate' and 'simple hearted'. Brunel's desire to avoid a conventional approach to the genre certainly informed the making of *Blighty* and the press was receptive to this. *The Star* reported the following incident at its trade show:

> At the Marble Arch Pavilion on Monday night . . . a woman came down the centre aisle and in a disgusted voice told her companion that it was 'another of those rotten war films' . . . I hope this severe critic later acknowledged 'Blighty' to be a war film with a difference and that she appreciated the touches of beautiful sentiment it contained.

On the surface, *Blighty* seems to display a similar conservatism to other contemporaneous war films, particularly since it recycles the common themes of loss and romance, albeit romance that transcends both class and nationality. Yet perhaps, as already suggested, this familiar narrative structure was a necessary frame within which Brunel was attempting to explore less typical ideas. By avoiding battle scenes and depicting the war almost exclusively on the Home Front, *Blighty* examines the effects of the conflict, both positive and negative, while avoiding the 'commonplace flagwagging or flamboyant heroics' (*The Pioneer*) of which many critics had expressed a weariness.

Reviewers also responded to aesthetic aspects of the film: '[t]he photography . . . has that touch of genuine artistry which one associates with the work of Jack Cox,' wrote the *Sunday Express*, while the *Glasgow Sunday Mail* felt that the film 'manages to be a little bit different from the war films that have preceded it, and gives the producer a fresh opportunity for impressionism'. Its loose narrative structure was remarked on, not always positively: 'it is at times a little disconnected and jumps too frequently from one subject to another . . . the status of the characters [is] not very clearly defined' (*The Bioscope*, 24 March 1927: 57). Monica Ewer, writing in the *Cork Weekly Examiner*, suspected this may have been deliberate: 'Perhaps Mr. Adrian Brunel was really bent on being very subtle. Can we trace here the influence of the expressionist school of drama? Are these composite portraits? Are these negative personalities of deliberate achievement?'

Ewer was unusual in perceiving a genuinely artistic intent on the part of the filmmakers, yet the various versions of the script held in the BFI's Special Collections reveal that in the early stages of preparation there were plans for more extensive visual flourishes. The Ivor Montagu collection contains a second draft of the 'film story' (IMSC 20), while an original film story (ABSC 163) and 'skeleton synopsis' (ABSC 5e/56) are also preserved. All three documents differ substantially from the finished film and testify to the compromises made.

The evolution of *Blighty*

The action of *Blighty* spans a period of five years and the second draft film story ponders the problem of 'how to effect the time lapse' between scenes. One suggestion made was to periodically insert a model shot, like that 'used in *Fridericus Rex* [Arzén von Cserépy 1923] of a valley somewhere in France ... gradually the little crosses increase in number, till the whole valley is filled with crosses', marking the progression of the war as measured by the growing numbers of dead. But Brunel and Montagu instead opted to use what they refer to as 'the panorama idea' to indicate the passing of time. Shots of recruitment posters are shown pasted to a wall, with no spatial or diegetic relation to the rest of the action, showing how the government message changed at different stages of the war. There is a grim irony in these posters on which Brunel fixes his camera, as they proclaim the jingoistic exhortations which enticed men to their deaths. Declarations such as 'We Must Have More Men' invoke thoughts of the huge number cut down on the front line, while the notion that the soldiers in the trenches were as 'Happy and Satisfied' as the Tommy smiling out from the poster is hard to credit. These posters appear at intervals in the narrative, their potent images and incitements to patriotism sometimes referencing the events just seen, at other times prefacing the action that follows. Before the scenes in the recruiting office, posters proclaim 'England Expects Every Man to Do His Duty' and 'Join the Army TO-DAY', while orders to 'Fall In' and go 'FORWARD!' lead into the departure of Robin and his detachment for France. Brunel's use of propaganda in this way has a particular resonance given his role in the production of official films during the First World War. He later recorded that while at the MoI he commissioned films that were diverting rather than didactic, urging producers to 'look after the entertainment quality of their product, and the propaganda would look after itself' (1949: 40), a tactic which served him well in his approach to *Blighty*.

Blighty and Music

From early in the development of the film story, music was a key element of *Blighty*'s evocation of wartime and, as well as visual reminders, the film triggers aural ones. Montagu's original title for the film, 'Après la guerre', was a phrase with several connotations. It became a euphemism for 'never', reflecting the seemingly endless nature of the conflict, but its main point of reference was a song popular with British soldiers in France during the war, 'Après la guerre fini', sung to the popular pre-war tune 'Sous les ponts de Paris'. Onto this melody, the soldiers grafted the following blend of French and English:

> Après la guerre fini
> Anglais soldats parti
> Mademoiselle in the family way
> Après la guerre fini

The song is sung in the film by British soldiers gathered in the French estaminet, a scene deliberately placed just after a shot of Robin's wife as she sits holding her baby and listens to the singing. The song is not intended to cheapen their relationship, rather the construction of the sequence creates an emotional juxtaposition. The dissonance between the poignancy of the shot of widow and baby (it is the first time that the audience sees Robin's child) and the rather callous sentiment of the song may have unsettled audiences. Only the first line of the lyrics appears on the intertitles, presumably on the understanding that viewers could fill in the missing lyrics and understand their relevance to the scene. As in the song, a French mademoiselle has fallen pregnant by a British soldier, although in *Blighty* they are married, and he is killed in action rather than deserting her. Yet the nature of the song does not sully the harmless release that carousing in the tavern offers the soldiers, and from her half-smile as she hears the singing, Robin's wife clearly does not detect any negative reference to her own situation.

Montagu's title was used until shooting began at the start of December 1926, when Brunel changed it, concerned that exhibitors may find French words difficult to pronounce. So the film became *Blighty*, an affectionate term for Britain which acquired a particular resonance for British soldiers during the First World War, symbolising a nostalgia for home. The appearance of the term in popular music-hall songs such as 'Take Me Back to Dear Old Blighty,' 'Marching Back to Blighty' and 'A Bit of a Blighty One' meant it was likely to evoke memories of the war and the affection with which the forces imagined home.

Music was clearly an important element in the presentation of the film and Montagu's second treatment makes suggestions for the accompaniment: 'What noise have we got? "Tiperary" [sic], "The Long, Long Trail" is obvious British Instructional Music.[6] We want "Who's Your Lady Friend?" and other less hackneyed of the popular airs of the time' (IMSC 20: 19). While each cinema would have arranged its own accompaniment to the film, the film's trade show at the London Hippodrome on 29 March 1927 had a special musical presentation. The musical director was a violinist called Max Hayman and *The Kinematograph* reported that his 'musical accompaniments had been selected with restraint and discrimination', although perhaps not with Montagu's specifications in mind. *The Cinema* also praised the effectiveness of Hayman's arrangement, noting that he

> made almost exclusive use of well-known war-time popular songs for his setting... although these songs have been used with every war film made, we have never noticed that they have been exploited anything like so freely... The idea of 'Blighty' was to reawaken in the mind the emotions we all experienced during the war. The popular songs of the day had more than an ordinary significance; 'Tipperary' for all its cheapness as a melody, has become a classic, it cannot be played without stimulating the mind to the active memory of those never-to-be-forgotten days.

While the musical accompaniment was an important element of the film's evocation of the wartime atmosphere, music was also employed on set to stimulate the actors during particular scenes. *Picturegoer*'s reporter visited Piccadilly Studios during the filming and related that there was a piano at the edge of the set with a group around it 'singing old wartime songs with sympathetic fervour, with the idea... of spurring on a dignified, elderly gentleman... to a big emotional crisis' (February 1927: 20–1). Godfrey Winn recalled that Ellaline Terriss also required assistance to emote: 'in the scene where she said farewell to her boy bound for the front, [she] asked for a record of "Evensong" to be played at the side of the set' (1967: 227).

Suggested Symbolism

The second draft of the story introduces a device which Brunel and Montagu had seen at a Film Society screening, although it did not survive into the film. Inspired by *Feu Mathias Pascal* (Marcel Herbier 1925), they wrote in 'a close-up of a wedding-card or newspaper cutting, showing

---

[6] A reference to that company's battle-reconstruction films.

Ann and David arm in arm, perfectly still like a photograph. They then walk towards the camera.' But the skeleton synopsis contains more radical visual concepts aimed at evoking the horrors of war. A montage was proposed to mark the outbreak of the conflict, beginning thus: 'across the surging faces of the excited youngsters there fades in the sinister Brenda mask of the War-God. This comes to concrete.' The montage was to continue with a sequence of stock military images in which the soldiers are never actually seen in full, merely as disembodied elements of the war machine: hands loading shells and legs marching as preparations get underway. The ominous mask is seen again but slowly fades into an image of a different mask on which 'the senseless features have contracted into an expression of hideous joy and relish'. This grinning mask was to reappear at pertinent moments during the film.

Blighty does contain a montage representing the outbreak of war, composed of stock footage of armies of the different nations mobilising, but the gloating mask does not feature, making the sequence less politically charged. However, the title card that announces 'WAR' has the letters scratched directly onto the celluloid, an effect that adds a rawness and potency. A later sequence was to reintroduce the model shot of a cemetery mentioned in the earlier film story, in which row upon row of graves are gradually revealed; this time, however, it was to end with a shot of white doves settling on an overturned gun. Balcon expressed doubt about the inclusion of such imagery but was not entirely dismissive: 'I do think a lot of consideration should be given to the suggested symbolism before we definitely decide on the present suggestions' (2 December 1926, ABSC 4/112). However, he was adamant about the removal of one particular shot, indicating the limits of his tolerance of the film's anti-war stance: 'I . . . do not agree with Lady Villiers taking up the Union Jack when she stands on the balcony to watch the departing troops' (ibid.).

Blighty as Art Film

Brunel's experiences in the industry had already led him to conclude that British film art was not safe in the hands of film financiers. These experiences, along with his awareness of his tenuous position at Gainsborough, may have made him more circumspect about including the lyrical shots originally envisaged for *Blighty*, curbing his instincts towards visual experimentation in favour of maintaining more control over the finished film. While the final version of *Blighty* bears relatively few traces of the proposed cinematic artistry, the impressionistic approach to the narrative was intended by the filmmakers from the outset. Montagu's original outline specifies: 'Plot slight, important thing, the war happenings, made acute by sympathetic nature of people who experience them. Compare this, and size of cast, with the Big Parade' (ABSC 163). Critics noted this, with one describing the film as 'a collection of brilliant ideas' rather than a coherent story. Montagu may have recalled an earlier British war film, George Pearson's *Reveille* (1923), which was also set largely after the war and apparently had 'no plot in the accepted sense of the word' (*The Bioscope*, 3 July 1924: 8). Or perhaps *Blighty*'s approach owes more to the avant-garde films shown by the Film Society, such as the experimental short *Ménilmontant* (Dimitri Kirsanoff 1926) with its fragmented narrative. *Blighty* certainly borrowed one major element from this film, in the form of its star Nadia Sibirskaïa, who plays the French refugee. Her pale skin, dark eyes and waif-like form are striking, and Brunel exploited her 'foreignness' to establish her as an outsider, physically and culturally far removed from the English family she marries into.

Sibirskaïa's stillness and calm presence are strikingly different to the more mannered performances of the British actors. Although reports about her uncooperative behaviour on set suggest she was unhappy moving from art cinema to the mainstream, Brunel coaxed a sensitive performance from her, and the scene in which she and Robin part for the last time is beautifully understated. With minimal gesture – she touches his hair, he gently fingers the collar of her dress – they prepare for his return to the front. After he has gone, the camera focuses on her face, glistening eyes raised to heaven as she utters a prayer for her husband's safe return. Several reviewers remarked on her expressiveness, while the *Graphic* praised the unconventional treatment of this scene.

> For one thing alone this picture should be crowned with laurels . . .: A girl sent her sweetheart off to the war *without standing at attention and saluting him.* I have waited many years for a film that had the grace to omit that embarrassing little ceremony. (Their italics)

As well as eschewing a continuous narrative progression, *Blighty* depicts no combat on screen, preferring to focus on the reactions to events by those affected. These events are reported rather than shown; Marshall is not seen sustaining the wound which brings him home, the audience learning he is injured when Lady Villiers encounters him at the military hospital. Likewise, Robin's death is revealed by telegram and we are not explicitly told that his wife is expecting their child until after the birth. This lends authenticity to the way events unfold, since the audience is often not privy to them until the family on the Home Front finds out. In this way the film unites audiences in a shared experience and provides opportunities for poignant scenes which all can identify with. The most notable of these is the arrival of the telegram communicating Robin's death, which several critics singled out for special mention. Renowned stage actress Ellaline Terriss was praised for the poise with which she played the scene, one reviewer writing: 'her slow mounting of the staircase, as though life had been bereft of everything worth having, was the work of one who knew how to make every movement count'.

The omission of scenes of conflict also allows the film to avoid any clear-cut portrayal of 'good' (British) versus 'evil' (Germans). Brunel's own retrospective assessment was that *Blighty* 'fulfilled the requirements of a popular patriotic picture, in that it showed a decent English family behaving decently' and avoided partiality towards either side (1949: 126). At the start of the film, Robin is in Heidelberg where he has formed a close friendship with fellow student Fritz. This is the only representation of 'the enemy' in the film and the positive depictions of Germans sets the tone. Other British films tended towards more negative stereotypes; in *Comradeship*, for example, a German impregnates an English girl before revealing himself as a spy and abandoning her at the outbreak of war.

Blighty's attitude towards the British army, however, is more complex. When he announces to the Villiers family that he has joined up, Marshall ventures that being a soldier will be 'more fun than driving a car', a flippant remark typical of those who went to war unaware of what awaited them. The film also points up the ease with which underage boys were accepted into the army. The Medical Officer accepts Robin's assurance that he's old enough to join up, without asking for proof of his age. Another potential recruit struggles to read the letters on the eyesight chart but his friend signals from behind the MO to help him pass. The light-hearted tone of these scenes goes some way to disguising the serious points underlying them, but their intention is clear.

Between Robin's recruitment and training, Brunel intercuts shots of soldiers marching through the night, with no clear indication of their spatial or temporal relation to the rest of the action. The soldiers are presented as rows of anonymous uniformed ranks, among which it is almost impossible to focus on an individual or register any expression. The armed forces are mainly seen in darkness, such as those operating the ack-ack guns and searchlights during the air raids; even in the wartime stock footage used to summarise events, soldiers are mainly presented in silhouette. When the new recruits are being trained, they are initially shown in civilian clothes which differentiate them in terms

Figure 5.3 Robin meets soldiers from all walks of life at the recruitment office in *Blighty*.
Source: author's own collection.

of class and walk of life. But once they are parading in their uniforms, all individuality is erased; they may be democratised but they are also robbed of any distinguishing features. Robin and Marshall are the only soldiers whose fate we follow in the film; the other men who train with Robin are seen briefly but eventually disappear with no indication of what has happened to them. We never learn the names of his two companions (a Cockney private and a tall curate) and after Robin meets the refugee they barely feature, except for a glimpse of the curate playing the piano at the estaminet when Marshall returns. The refugee herself is not referred to by name either (although she is called Marie and then Julie in early story versions) and the fate of the other refugees who arrive with her at the Café Normand is never revealed. These loose ends reflect the uncertainty of wartime liaisons and the damage that war does to relationships, robbing a man of his friend, a wife of her husband, a child of its father.

Blighty ends on a bittersweet note, the final scene representing another bridge between the past and the future. Ann and Marshall announce their desire to marry just as the two-minute silence is beginning on the first

Figure 5.4 Robin's son plays with toy soldiers in a scene missing from surviving prints of *Blighty*. Source: BFI National Archive.

anniversary of the end of the war, a time when thoughts turn to those who lost their lives. In this way, the film's conclusion allows the audience to embrace the changes and look to the future while not forgetting the dead. Lord Villiers' sad yet calm acceptance of Robin's death offers no comment on the legitimacy of the war, and this final sequence draws together the threads to end on a message of reflection and hope.[7] One particular shot at the end of the film, which is not present in the print which survives in the BFI National Archive, invited comment in the press. It shows Robin's son as a young boy playing with a fort and tin soldiers, watched by his mother and grandmother. This image (described by one reviewer as 'ironical') was an effective shorthand, linking memories of young men 'playing soldiers' with fears for the future. The war saw teenage boys like Robin joining the army in a fervour of patriotism and a spirit of adventure, oblivious to the horror which awaited them; even at the time *Blighty* was made, Britain

---

[7] The surviving print of the film in the BFI National Archive ends abruptly before Lord Villiers gives his answer to Marshall's request to marry Ann, suggesting there may be some footage missing.

was already haunted by the fear of another conflict in which the next generation would have to fight.

Quietly Anti-war

The fact that some of Brunel and Montagu's original 'artistic' intentions for *Blighty* had to be compromised to meet the demands of the studio suggests that such aspirations were not easily accommodated in British cinema of the time. Some war films did incorporate imaginative visual expression: *Poppies of Flanders* (Arthur Maude 1927), for example, uses a displacement device to indicate the mental state of ex-soldier Jim Brown, with a row of soldiers in a photo becoming a line of bottles. But this device sits rather uncomfortably within an otherwise conventional presentation of the story of a man broken by the Boer War redeemed by his love for a woman before being killed in the First World War. Another visual experiment can be found in the final shot of *Ypres*, in which the figure of Britannia appears superimposed onto a painting of a desolate battlefield with white crosses. The fear and desperation of those engaged in battle is conveyed in *The Guns of Loos* by an extreme close-up of a soldier screaming for more shells as rain streams down his face. However, while these brief shots offer an emotional engagement with the conflict, they rarely form part of a consistent artistic vision.

Brunel and Montagu regarded the British film industry as highly conservative. They were no doubt aware that a war film with metaphorical visual touches would be unlikely to find favour with Gainsborough, even though they had consciously focused on celebratory themes. However, *Blighty* was innovative in its approach to the genre and critics acknowledged it as an attempt to be different and 'not a stale rehash of film conventions or an imitation of anything'. Given that one of the aims of the Film Society was to expose British filmmakers to original ideas, it may have been expected that a collaboration between two of its founder members would demonstrate a more innovative filmmaking style. Yet Brunel and Montagu had to temper their ambitions for the finished film, as the existing versions of the synopsis testify. They claimed moderate success, however, in their aim to make a film which 'quietly' registered their views on war while acknowledging the sacrifices made by the soldiers and, indeed, by those who stayed at home.

Despite the pressures Brunel was under and the compromises he had to make, *Blighty* vindicated his promotion to director by Gainsborough. By taking a genre of which the public was expressing weariness, and expanding on their experiences to reflect on the legacy of the conflict, Brunel and Montagu produced a box office success on a relatively small budget. This was the only creative collaboration between these two key figures at work on the fringes of the mainstream during the 1920s. Brunel and Montagu used their interest in filmmaking techniques and appreciation of film as an art to build reputations within the British film industry which, briefly, allowed them the freedom to nudge the boundaries of commercial filmmaking. While even their fairly modest artistic pretensions could not be fully realised in *Blighty*, they were able to satisfy the demands of the industry while remaining true to their political convictions and avoiding yet another overtly jingoistic portrayal of war.

Conclusion

Despite the restrictions imposed by the powers that be at the studio, Brunel managed to bring something of his own vision to *Blighty*, which represents a relatively successful blend of his artistic aspirations and the commercial imperatives demanded of him. This was partly due to the relatively small investment the studio had made in the project but no doubt also because of his collaboration with Montagu, a figure who was trusted by Gainsborough at the time. While many of the more elaborate visual flourishes were excised before production, the film uses some effective devices, such as the 'panorama' shots used as a shorthand to mark the passing of time. Perhaps most importantly, Brunel was able to adhere to one of his central principles by basing *Blighty* on an original screen story, making it unusual in Gainsborough's filmography. But Brunel was not to be so fortunate with his next two commissions for the studio; these were to be adaptations of high-profile works, which complicated their progress to the screen and increased the pressure on Brunel as a director.

CHAPTER 6

Adaptation and Screen Censorship: *The Vortex*

While Brunel navigated the fraught production of *Blighty* with relative success, the film's positive reception did not improve his situation at Gainsborough. His next two films were assigned to him by the studio under conditions even less favourable than the first, since both were adaptations of valuable properties rather than original stories. The reliance of producers on existing works brought several issues that further complicated a director's struggle for control. Censorship was a problem and canny authors could wield considerable power over the adaptation and production process; these issues were to affect Brunel's two subsequent productions for Gainsborough.

Adaptation and Silent Cinema

Up to and including *Blighty*, all Brunel's directorial projects had been based on original screen stories, though this was contrary to the general trend in British silent cinema. For producers, the attraction of successful novels and plays as source material was obvious; a popular title possessed inherent marketing value as well as, hopefully, a well-crafted narrative on which to base their films. Stoll Picture Productions had so much faith in the strategy that it launched its filmmaking activities by acquiring the rights to a raft of literary works, branding its output the 'Eminent British Authors series' and promoting its films on the back of the success of the books. According to Jon Burrows, 118 of the 128 titles Stoll made between 1919 and 1928 were based on contemporary English novels, and the approach served the company well for several years (2009: 157). The Ideal Film Company, a distributor which branched out into production in 1915, had rarely strayed from tried-and-tested sources, while British & Colonial's 1923 series 'Gems of Literature' reduced works by Shakespeare, Dickens and Sheridan to one reel for easy digestion. Even a young, innovative producer like Michael Balcon failed to buck this trend:

of the twenty-two features he produced between 1923 and 1929, only six were from original screen stories.

Rachael Low complained that 'every possible or impossible play and novel, historical, classical, pot-boiling and contemporary, was wrung into service' by the film industry, only to be 'changed about and made uniform by the script department' (1971: 240–1). Producers were often more interested in such titles for their inbuilt publicity value than their intrinsic quality as material for the screen. However, Low's negative views of this policy do not tell the whole story and Andrew Higson regards 'the choice of source text, often combined with other elements of the country's heritage . . . [as] a key strategy by which producers sought to mark their product as part of a nationally-specific cinema' (quoted in Morris 2009: 190). Burrows challenges Low's condemnation of Stoll as a 'film factory without creative leadership' (1971: 125), describing some of the imaginative strategies it applied to the translation of literary works to the screen. Lawrence Napper has defended Gainsborough's preference for adaptation, citing the success of *Woman to Woman* (Graham Cutts 1923), *The Rat* (Cutts 1924), *The Lodger* (Hitchcock 1926) and *Hindle Wakes* (Maurice Elvey 1927) as evidence that the tactic could enhance a studio's reputation, providing it was discerning in its choice of title (2009: 72).

The four titles singled out by Napper were indeed successes for Balcon (although *The Rat* originated as a screenplay before being rewritten for the stage) but some of the studio's other adaptations failed at the box office. Balcon admitted that the profits from his first feature, *Woman to Woman* (based on the play by Michael Morton), were swallowed up by the losses of his second, *The White Shadow* (Cutts 1924; based on an unpublished novel by the same author). The company later filmed three of Noël Coward's plays in quick succession: *The Queen Was in the Parlour* (Cutts 1927), *The Vortex* (Brunel 1927) and *Easy Virtue* (Hitchcock 1928), banking on the playwright's reputation for controversy to bring in audiences. However, all three were financial failures, leading Balcon to conclude, 'It was no doubt wrong of us to seek to bask in the reflected glory of people like Noël Coward, we followed trends and did not try to make them' (1969: 27). However, Balcon was not entirely free to dictate Gainsborough's production slate and many of these choices were made by distributor and major stakeholder C. M. Woolf.

Merit Rewarded

In 1929, *Film Weekly* readers were asked to vote for their favourite British film of the previous year in order to give 'practical help to British producers' (11 February 1929: 6). A list of twenty-eight titles was printed, from which readers selected their top six.[1] Of these, twenty-two were adaptations[2] and three were directed by Brunel: *The Constant Nymph* at number one, *Blighty* at number eight and *The Vortex* at number twenty-three. *The Constant Nymph* was based on the successful stage version of a bestselling novel and was one of eight adaptations in the top ten. *The Vortex* was joined towards the bottom of the list by three other versions of successful stage plays: *The Arcadians* (Victor Saville 1927) at nineteen, Hitchcock's *Easy Virtue* at twenty-one and *Quinneys* (Maurice Elvey 1927) at twenty-two (*Film Weekly*, 22 April 1929: 5).

The production histories of *The Vortex* and *The Constant Nymph* illustrate the negotiations involved in bringing successful properties to the screen, and the greater obstacles Brunel faced to applying the ideas he had been cultivating to imbue his work with a personal stamp. The power and influence of authors and playwrights within the British film industry was considerable and many were engaged in testing the limits of that power through attempts to maintain control over their own intellectual property. Most notably, popular and prolific crime writer Edgar Wallace joined the board of British Lion in 1927, guaranteeing the company first option on all his books but also giving him significant control over how his work was presented, even down to directing two of the films. For Brunel, the added involvement of well-known authors further complicated his job and, despite the prestige of the subjects, had the effect of depleting his own symbolic capital rather than enhancing it.

The task of translating a literary work into a screenplay was rarely simple, often hampered by the fundamental unsuitability of the source material or interference by the author or the censor. Stricter film censorship could necessitate narrative changes, as could the screen persona of the star; Ivor Novello's casting in Hitchcock's *The Lodger: A Story of the London Fog* meant his character's innocence had to be established at the end of the film.

---

[1] Twenty-eight seems a rather small number. It is difficult to ascertain release dates from the available sources but over sixty British features were trade shown in 1928 (Gifford 2016).

[2] The six original screen stories were: *The Further Adventures of the Flag Lieutenant* (W. P. Kellino 1927); *Blighty; Carry On!* (Dinah Shurey 1927); *Confetti* (Graham Cutts 1927), *Victory* (M. A. Wetherall 1928) and *This Marriage Business* (Leslie Hiscott 1927).

Adaptation versus Original Screen Stories

The relative merits of adapted or original screenplays were the subject of considerable debate in both the trade and general press during the silent period. Many commentators felt that as a new medium and an essentially visual form, cinema was better served by specially written screen stories, since silent film could never do justice to a novel or play. While silent films used intertitles to advance plot and communicate dialogue, it was generally accepted that their overuse interrupted the narrative flow; as early as 1920, director Kenelm Foss declared that 'every sub-title is a confession of failure' (1920: 13). While some novels lent themselves more readily to visual communication, particularly those where the story contained sufficient action to allow for a cinematic approach, stage plays were generally dialogue-driven and dependent on nuance of language and vocal tone to convey character and motivation, which were difficult to articulate via text or facial expression.

Brunel's experience adapting novels and plays for British Actors' Film Company had cemented his belief that the cinema required scenarios that developed the medium as a new artistic form with its own language. This strategy also helped to keep down production costs since, while purchasing a successful property could be expensive, Brunel's collaborations with established authors like A. A. Milne and Monckton Hoffe had provided him with inventive outlines for his films at a fraction of the price. He could then apply his own skill to develop them into a scenario that would visualise the story for the screen.

Authors and Film

In September 1927, *The Bioscope* reprinted this joke from a publishing magazine:

> Publisher: 'Where did you get the plot for your second novel?'
> Author: 'From the film version of my first.' (1 September 1927: 55)

The perception that film producers had little respect for the integrity of authors or the literary works they purchased may well have been accurate, but authors themselves were not above reproach. In his 1925 Gainsborough burlesque *So This is Jollygood*, Brunel had portrayed the author as a hard-headed businessman, eager to exploit film producers. Yet some writers possessed sufficient integrity to acknowledge the limitations of adapting novels and plays to film. In 1921, popular Scottish writer and journalist

Neil Munro told *The Bioscope*: 'as a novelist myself . . . I declare to you my honest conviction that good – and even famous – novels can't make really good films . . . The film drama must be absolutely original, written from the beginning for the film and not for print' (24 March 1921: 77).

Five years later, Virginia Woolf added her voice to the campaign, albeit in a rather more poetic manner. In a 1926 article entitled 'The Cinema', she expressed her views about the development of the new medium:

> All the famous novels of the world, with their well-known characters and their famous scenes, only asked, it seemed, to be put on the films . . . The cinema fell upon its prey with immense rapacity, and to the moment largely subsists upon the body of its unfortunate victim. But the results are disastrous to both. (1981: 168)

While there was little danger of Woolf's brand of highbrow literature appearing on screen, her views were echoed the following year by Andrew Soutar, who had been widely adapted for the cinema both in Britain and America. In a leading article in *The Bioscope* he asserted that

> the original story written by one who possesses an exact knowledge of the screen's possibilities and impossibilities is vastly superior to ninety per cent of novels or plays . . . The novel, the stage and the screen are three distinct mediums of expression, each demanding a technique of their own. (18 August 1927: 32)

His article prompted the following letter to the journal:

> Authors hold the film industry in the palms of their hands and I believe that they will continue to do so, so long as film producers cannot be brought to realise that a novel worth £10,000 to a publisher may not be worth twopence as material for a film . . . we will continue to have bad pictures, and plenty of them, so long as the film companies refuse to put the original scenario-writer in his proper place instead of making him a literary batman to the successful novelist and playwright.
>
> But when is the budding author going to concentrate from the first on the screen itself as a medium? Not so long as film companies prefer the established novelist and playwright and treat the scenario-writer as a mere 'hack'. (25 August 1927: 35)

In 1928 *Picturegoer* canvassed the views of bestselling authors as to whether screen adaptation was preferable to original stories and asked if they were being 'encouraged to write specially for the film producer' (December 1928: 28). Several of the authors defended their profession, insisting that only an experienced writer had the skill and dedication to properly craft a narrative, while the untrained and hurried work of the 'hack' scenario writer could never attain an equal literary standard. Novelist and playwright W. B. Maxwell went further, expressing the view that 'the art of the screen should be illustrative or interpretative, and not inventive or creative'. Joan Sutherland condemned original screen stories as 'thin, weak in characterisation and somewhat lacking in plot', perhaps a rather disingenuous view considering she was a prolific writer of romantic fiction for Mills & Boon. She clearly had an axe to grind with the film industry and took the opportunity to complain that

> it seems the hardest thing in the world to sell books to film producers and novels once so posted or delivered vanish into the blue . . . not even a printed note comes to the unfortunate fondly hoping author, and, as for the aforesaid copies, heaven and the studio's office char-woman alone can know what becomes of them.

Sutherland's view provides an interesting contrast to that of Virginia Woolf; the two authors resided at opposite ends of the literary spectrum, neither of which held much appeal for film producers. As Lawrence Napper has illustrated, studios in the 1920s turned largely to middlebrow writing for their source material. Popular author Boyd Cable fell into this category and his 1923 short story 'The Rolling Road' had been filmed by Gainsborough in 1927. Despite his relationship with the cinema, Cable told *Picturegoer* that 'the adaptation . . . does not make as good a picture as the story written directly for the screen . . . because the method of telling the story is so entirely different that one loses by being wrenched to the method of another' (ibid.: 28). He regarded it as 'a weakness of the screen that it so commonly seeks its material in successful books or plays, merely because they have been successful', insisting further that

> the strongest (if unconscious) supporters of my belief are the producers themselves, because they are admitting a novel or play is not suitable for the screen when they turn it upside down and inside out and round about in the effort to turn it into a screen play. (Ibid.: 28–9)

This over-reliance on proven titles undoubtedly contributed to a stifling of originality in British cinema and held back the development and recognition of screenwriting as a creative art. Some properties did make a successful transition to the screen, usually where producers made a judicious choice of title and screenwriters adopted an imaginative approach. One writer who could be relied on to do this was Eliot Stannard. He had been in the business since 1914, had extensive experience of adapting literary works and wrote all of Hitchcock's screenplays for Gainsborough, as well as many others for the studio, including *Blighty* and *The Vortex* for Brunel. Stannard had developed the skill of teasing out the cinematic elements of a narrative and introducing visual devices that would convey theme and characterisation in an original way. However, like Brunel,

Stannard was subject to the forces that held sway at the studio and due to his freelance status had to tread carefully. While he could have been a valuable ally, Brunel failed to form a relationship with his screenwriter, as Hitchcock clearly had, instead allowing his insecurity to make him suspicious of Stannard's loyalties. In a letter to Brunel written after they had worked on *The Vortex* in 1927, Stannard sought to reassure him: 'You must believe me when I tell you I am incapable of hurting a man behind his back, of sneaking, of putting up my opinion against his where it does not directly concern me; or of crawling or flattering' (n.d., ABSC 5/112). In the same letter he also alluded to the difficulties of reconciling his position as a creative writer with the commercial demands of the industry, claiming, 'I am outspoken, impatient . . . and lost jobs through rightly or wrongly taking a certain artistic stand.' Their collaboration on *The Vortex* tested their relationship, the tensions no doubt exacerbated by Brunel's own anxiety about his position at the studio. They did not work together again.

Coward's First Hit

After *Blighty*, Brunel had hoped to direct Noël Coward's *Easy Virtue*, but that assignment was given to Hitchcock and it was announced in *The Bioscope* on 21 April 1927 that Brunel was to bring to the screen another Coward hit, *The Vortex*. Like *Blighty* it was concerned with the effects of the First World War on a well-to-do family, but the similarities ended there. While *Blighty* dealt with general societal changes relating to gender and class, *The Vortex* took a more psychological approach in its examination of contemporary family life. Announced as a 'tale of postwar youth', Coward's play hinted at the selfishness and moral confusion of the decadent years following the conflict, exploring the theme via a mother/son relationship threatened by behaviour on both sides which betrays and undermines the traditional family roles.

Coward's play had been a huge success and had brought him celebrity as both playwright and actor. However, its controversial subject matter (infidelity and drug-taking) meant it was beset by censorship issues and Coward had to appeal to the Lord Chamberlain in person to get permission to stage it, apparently managing to convince him that it was a 'moral tract' (Morley 1975: 94). His intention had been to write 'a good play with a whacking good part in it for myself' (1934: xv) to further his acting career, but West End theatrical managers would not finance it without a star name attached. So he produced and directed it himself at Hampstead's Everyman Theatre in November 1924, where it was so popular that its two-week run was immediately followed by six months in the West End.

The play focuses on the Lancasters, an upper-class English family. Florence Lancaster refuses to conform to the behaviour that society expects from a middle-aged wife and mother, preferring to leave her 'pre-war' husband, David, in his country retreat while she enjoys the company of younger men in town. In Act One, her son Nicky, a composer, brings his fiancée Bunty home to meet his mother but she finds it difficult to accept the concept of her son marrying, especially when it emerges that Bunty was once engaged to Tom Veryan, Florence's current companion. Act Two takes place at a weekend party in the Lancaster's country home, where it emerges that Nicky takes drugs, and the tensions present between him, Florence, Bunty and Tom erupt. Bunty breaks off her engagement to Nicky and Florence then finds her in the arms of Tom, causing her to have a hysterical outburst. Act Three shows the fallout from the party; Nicky goes to his mother's room to try and make her understand the effect her behaviour is having on him and their relationship. They are reconciled but it is too late for Nicky's relationship with Bunty to be saved.

If the play had proved difficult to bring to the stage, the film version was to encounter even greater obstacles and Brunel was unhappy with the assignment, knowing that major liberties would have to be taken with the plot to appease the censors. Nicky could not be portrayed as a drug-user, while Florence's dalliance with Tom Veryan would be confined to outings to the theatre and dances. Brunel and Stannard thus embarked on the challenging job of translating Coward's play to the screen.

On watching *The Vortex*, one may well concur with William K. Everson's description of it as 'a curiously flat version of the Coward play' (1973). The film sticks closely to the structure of the play, Act One mostly taking place in Florence's London home (plus some establishing scenes at Nicky's studio), while Acts Two and Three relate events during the weekend gathering at David Lancaster's country home, with a few exteriors of the garden added. Most of Brunel's set-ups exhibit little creativity or variety and consist mainly of long-shots intercut with medium shots, with almost no close-ups. In fact, during preparation Brunel expressed his dislike of 'half-meaningless close-ups', preferring to use them sparingly for greater effect (Initial Continuity, ABSC 4/43). He only brings the camera in close during emotional climaxes, when rapid cutting between the faces of the characters brings their reactions to the fore and conveys the intensity of the scene. The film's somewhat conventional construction is occasionally enlivened by devices such as a jerky panning shot around Florence's living room as Nicky takes in her 'strenuous' decor and a shot in which Nicky spies the dancer Yvette reflected in a mirror, surreptitiously taking drugs.³

Of course, presentation contributes a great deal to the effect of viewing a silent film; the copy of *The Vortex* available from the BFI National Archive lacks the tinting that the original would have had and *The Bioscope* reported that 'Gainsborough are devoting special care to the preparation of the musical score, as in "The Vortex" music plays a big part' (23 June 1927: 39), which would also have enhanced the audience's enjoyment. Everson also suggested that the dialogue was lifted from the play but in fact almost no lines are directly transposed. However, there is certainly an attempt to imbue the titles with something approaching Coward's wit; one announces that 'Florence Lancaster's townhouse was her own; her complexion was not; but both were entirely renovated at regular intervals'.

Coward on Screen

Coward himself had no input into the adaptations of his three plays by Gainsborough and at the time professed to having no interest in writing for the screen: 'I want to write words not stage directions . . . it doesn't appeal to me' (*KW*, 30 June 1927: 45). In production at around the same time as *The Vortex* was Hitchcock's version of Coward's *Easy Virtue*. Another Stannard adaptation, it takes enormous liberties with the play and includes a lengthy sequence shot on the Riviera. On stage, the action takes place at the home of the Whittakers, a staid and conservative family whose son John arrives home with Larita, a divorcée several years his senior whom he met and married in Paris. Stannard relegated the events of the play to the final third of the film, opening with a lengthy courtroom scene interspersed with flashbacks detailing Larita's unhappy first marriage and infidelity. The film's editing, especially in this first act, displays considerable ingenuity, with a variety of shot distance and a greater sense of movement within shots. Several of the flashbacks are introduced through imaginative intercutting, for example a close-up of the judge's monocle swinging becomes the pendulum of a clock. The courtroom scene is made more dynamic by the use of cutaways, for example to a shot of a reporter's notebook in which a précis of the case is being written, thus reducing the use of static titles to convey dialogue. Following the court case, Larita

---

³ Brunel had used a similar device in *The Man Without Desire* when Count Almoro spies the maid poisoning his wine.

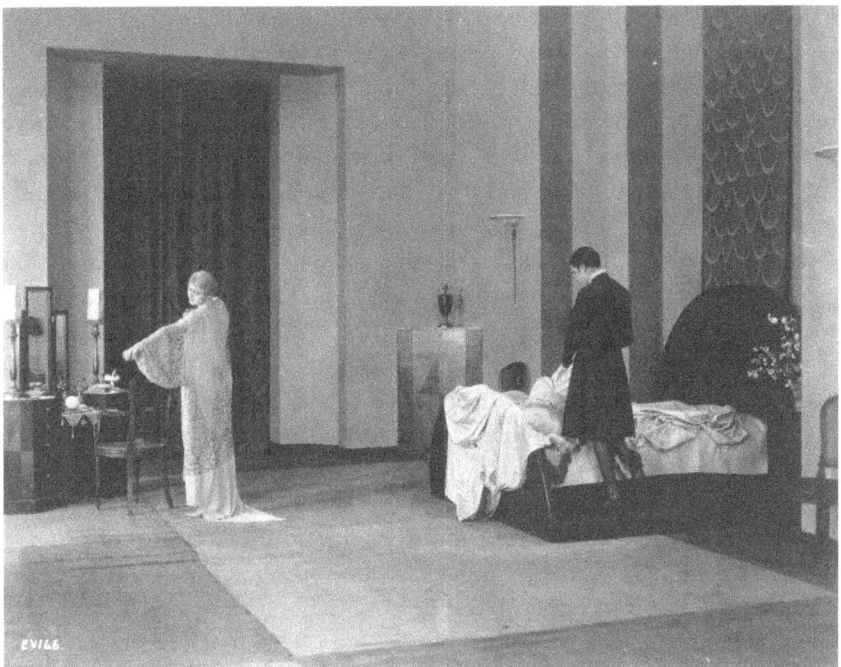

Figure 6.1 Scene still from *Easy Virtue*. Source: BFI National Archive.

travels to the Riviera, as did Hitchcock and his cast and crew to film her romance with John Whittaker.

Coward's opinion of Stannard and Hitchcock's drastic transformation of *Easy Virtue* does not appear to be on record but he did express his appreciation of the performances: 'I think Isabel Jeans and Franklin Dyall ... are both marvellous in "Easy Virtue", which I have just seen run through,' he told *Kinematograph Weekly* in an interview about his thoughts on the cinema (30 June 1927: 45). However, his tone seems to convey a slight impatience with the screen's obsession with the stage: 'pandering is a mistake ... let British film makers be honest with themselves and do their best without reference to what the public are wrongly supposed to demand.'

The contrast between the production values of these two Coward adaptations is a stark indication of the relative standing of Brunel and Hitchcock at Gainsborough at the time. The luxury of a European location shoot was denied Brunel and sequences requiring extras (a rehearsal and a party scene) were dropped from *The Vortex*, while Hitchcock's courtroom scene contains a whole gallery of observers that appears in two or three brief shots. The sets for both films were designed by Clifford Pember and in *The Vortex* they illustrate well the contrasting personalities and lifestyles of Florence and her husband. While her airy modern townhouse has high windows and rounded art deco furniture, the country residence favoured by David Lancaster is all dark wood and tapestries. *Easy Virtue* has more than twice as many sets as Brunel's film, including a lavish dining room at the Whittaker's house adorned with floor-to-ceiling murals, which is only glimpsed in two scenes.

But it was not only the budget of the two films that dictated their relative merits. Hitchcock was apparently entrusted with greater control over the direction of *Easy Virtue* and permitted the inclusion of imaginative visuals akin to those he had used in *The Lodger: A Story of the London Fog* the previous year, and which had earned praise from critics. In contrast, the ideas developed by Stannard and Brunel to make *The Vortex* more cinematic and communicate the themes of the play did not make it to the screen, although they are present in the versions of the script in the Brunel collection. As with *Blighty*, attempts to incorporate a modest expressionist mode were not supported by the studio, and the creative elements of the screenplay fell victim either to the lack of budget or Balcon's nervousness about permitting 'experimentation'.

Adapting *The Vortex*

The Brunel collection contains Stannard's film treatment and his Initial Continuity; there are also notes and letters containing thoughts and ideas from Brunel, his mother Adey and Angus MacPhail. One of Brunel's concerns was that the average viewer might not know what a vortex was and he suggested finding a way to 'illustrate the meaning of the word cinematically in the manner of [Walther] Ruttmann or [Dudley] Murphy (cf. "Metropolis" [1924] and "The Love of Sunya" [1927])' (n.d., ABSC 3/158). Following this, he advocated an opening montage

> devised from symbolic representations of Modern Society, Neuroticism, the affectations of Art with a capital A, the popularly supposed moral freedom of Paris, etc. Such a series of conglomerated shots could be made to end up with shots of Nicky's hands alternately playing the piano and writing the musical score he is engaged upon . . . I have a fondness for such shots as these last two as an introduction to our character. (Ibid.)

For later scenes, he proposed that 'the stages of Nicky's disillusionment might be marked by photographic symbolism, if we have any brain waves on the subject'. An audience that struggles with the meaning of 'vortex' may not have welcomed 'symbolic representations of . . . Neuroticism' and Brunel's montage never materialised. Stannard had his own ideas for establishing the themes of the film, imagining

> a symbolic tableau explaining the meaning of The Vortex . . . I would suggest characters in Brenda masks showing a wonderfully dressed woman in youthful mask talking to a man in evening dress with the mask head of a hog and Nicky young and happy and expressionless. His face changes to spiritual and physical horror as the masks fade off the other two characters revealing an old woman and a young man. (Initial Continuity, ABSC 1/161)

This nightmarish sequence was to be followed by scenes establishing the two main characters: Florence about to undergo a facelift, revealing her vanity, and Nicky in Paris, a successful composer leading a bohemian lifestyle. Stannard's treatment describes a party at Nicky's studio attended by 'slightly eccentric, rich Paris poseurs . . . exquisites and dandies . . . [t]he women are glorious dolls with a smattering of women who defy fashion' (ABSC 4/158). Stannard also wrote into this treatment two sequences of rehearsals for Nicky's revue: the first showed the dancers in rehearsal clothes, while the second mirrored the action of the first but was 'aided by gorgeous costumes and skilful lighting [so] the scene becomes a riot of colour and life' (ibid.). Act Two was also to gain some interesting visuals, Stannard suggesting superimposing 'phantom hands' playing the piano over shots of Bunty running upstairs, to bring some variation to an otherwise flat sequence (Initial Continuity, ABSC 1/161). More ambitiously, Stannard followed a shot of Nicky criticising Florence's taste in clothes with a cutaway of

> a mannequin parade between two biting titles showing that Florence has bought for herself dresses displayed by girls of eighteen . . . a splash of movement and colour in the midst of a very intimate sequence, which without break or relief might be somewhat monotonous on the screen (for this act relies greatly on the spoken word and inflection of voice). (Suggested film treatment, ABSC 4/158)[4]

None of these elements found their way into the finished film and, apart from the opening scenes in Nicky's studio, an introductory shot showing Florence undergoing beauty treatments, some exteriors of the Lancasters' garden and the final reconciliation scene, the film adheres fairly closely to the structure of the play.

---

[4] This sequence was shot but not used since Balcon felt that the quality of the dresses in it would 'invite unfortunate comparisons with American films' (17 June 1927, ABSC 5/112).

In his analysis of the various versions of *The Vortex* in Brunel's collection, Ian W. MacDonald regards the correspondence between Brunel and Stannard as evidence of the director's increasing power over the construction of the film, leaving the writer struggling to 'find a way past their focus on performance allied to plot selection and pace, towards an understanding of the camera as the instrument which provides power and emphasis in film narrative' (2011: 61). While MacDonald correctly highlights the lack of value placed on the work of the screenwriter within the British industry, he greatly overestimates Brunel's power as a director at Gainsborough. While an examination of the relationship between Stannard and Hitchcock may reveal a different power balance, a viewing of *The Vortex* reveals that the debates that took place between Brunel and Stannard were ultimately fruitless and the greater struggle was between them, as creative personalities within the studio, and those who controlled production and finance.

Characters and Casting

Above and beyond any artistic ambitions, Stannard's main task was to overcome the censorship issues and render the play's somewhat unsavoury events more palatable to audiences. He felt that 'the failings of both mother and son are very ticklish to handle in view of [the] healthy-mindedness of the provinces' and suggested taking a humorous approach since 'the provinces love laughing at the vanities of Mayfair' (suggested film treatment, ABSC 4/158). Characterisation and the casting of the major roles thus became key. Ivor Novello had already been selected to play Nicky and, given his status as a matinee idol, the character had to be portrayed as an upstanding young man untainted by any suggestion of degeneracy. The scenes Stannard wrote in to illustrate his bohemian existence were excised and the closest Nicky gets to debauchery is being acquainted with a dancer who takes drugs, a discovery he reacts to with horror, calling her a 'little rotter'. Novello wrote expressing his views on the character of Nicky: 'He must'nt [sic] be cynical or disillusioned at all. He must have complete and absolute faith in his mother . . . It should be his lost illusion in her that should start Nicky's gradual loss of character' (26 April 1927, ABSC 5/112).

As the star of the film, Novello was paid £100 a day (compared to Willette Kershaw's £100 per week) and thus his wishes had traction with the studio. On the film's release, however, one reviewer observed: 'There is not one of the characters in the story for whom it is easy to develop the slightest grain of sympathy' (n.d., ABSC 4(1)/112) and Nicky, devoid of the complexities he possesses in the play, becomes insipid.

The character of Florence is therefore the sole source of the 'vortex of beastliness' at the heart of the film, yet is permitted only the merest hint of infidelity. With the hard-hitting themes of Coward's controversial play removed, Stannard was aware that what remained was a rather tame and moralistic family melodrama:

> By making his mother frivolous without being physically immoral we should show that when a woman neglects her husband and son and completely ignores her responsibilities as wife and mother, then the home ceases to exist and loneliness and unhappiness are the lot of the two men in question. (Suggested film treatment, ABSC 4/158)

Florence's relegation to a narrative device made her casting very difficult and Brunel apparently saw thirty-nine actresses before choosing American stage star Willette Kershaw for the part. He was equally indecisive with the other roles and forty actresses were considered for Bunty, while Tom Veryan and David Lancaster also proved vexing to cast. This prevarication at so early a stage in the production, along with the lengthy discussions over the screenplay, may have given Balcon doubts about Brunel's ability to control the production.

Happy Ending

In the play, Nicky and Bunty are far too unconventional to bother with an engagement ring, but in the film the ring becomes an important prop when she breaks off their engagement. It is also a symbol of their reconciliation, the 'happy ending' that Brunel knew would be deemed necessary for the film version. In fact, all the contributors to the adaptation process agreed that a more solid resolution was required than that of the play, which ended on a tableau of Florence and Nicky comforting each other after promising to reform. Stannard's treatment viewed Nicky's split from Bunty as irrevocable but he added an epilogue in which Florence is 'dressed according to her age and with grey hair but happy, walking happily through the farm' (which hitherto she has loathed) (suggested treatment, ABSC 4/158). There, she and David see Nicky flirting with a young woman and look forward to welcoming her into the bosom of their now contented family. But Brunel insisted to Balcon that Nicky and Bunty should get back together, 'not because exhibitors will demand this but because audiences will' (n.d., ABSC 3/158), and the film concludes with Florence and Nicky intercepting Bunty the morning after the party and convincing her to stay. Thus one of the few aspects of the film over which Brunel was able to exert control merely cemented its conventionality and no doubt fuelled Coward's violent reaction to the results: 'he was speechless for a moment, and then let out a torrent of criticism that even the telephone couldn't stop' (Brunel 1949: 131).

When filming began on 1 June 1927 it soon became clear that Brunel was again to be under the scrutiny of the studio. George Hopton instructed him 'to exercise great care when scheduling the day's work to see that the artist is used to the best advantage on that day, particularly Novello' (10 June 1927, ABSC 5/112). Brunel's problems were compounded by the limitations of Willette Kershaw. While she had a long stage career behind her, this was her first starring role on film and she was apparently extremely difficult to direct due to a reliance on some kind of pep pills which meant she could only sustain a performance for short periods before flagging.

Brunel finished shooting *The Vortex* around the third week of July and was eager to start editing. As usual, he had planned the shoot carefully and knew exactly which takes he was going to use, especially important since he had had to work around the limitations of the actors. But he was put to work on his next film, *The Constant Nymph*, almost immediately, and on 4 August 1927 *The Bioscope* announced the imminent departure of the cast and crew to Europe. Much to Brunel's annoyance, his protégé Lionel Rich was brought in to edit *The Vortex*, which was completed by the beginning of September. Brunel did not see the finished film until mid-November and he was extremely unhappy with it, petitioning Gainsborough strenuously to allow him to recut. 'Even without re-takes I could make this a good film,' he declared to Balcon, 'and I am prepared to do anything to put this film as I intended it. I am getting on with The Constant Nymph as fast as possible so that I can have time for The Vortex before it goes to W&F' (16 November 1927, ABSC 5/112).

Brunel was no doubt keen to reinstate the 'cute shots' he had filmed: 'little twists . . . intriguing camera angles, some effective close-ups, some unexpected shots' to 'divert the attention of the critics' (Brunel 1949: 133). But the film was released without his input and for years afterwards Brunel maintained that he could have made it a success: 'It was a tragedy for all concerned that, after delaying the premiere until the trade was suspicious, . . . we didn't fool them by having me put it right' (n.d., ABSC 7/112).

The Reception of *The Vortex*

The trade show of *The Vortex* was originally scheduled for 20 September 1927 but was postponed, ostensibly because Novello was out of the country

Figure 6.2 Noël Coward visits the set of *The Vortex*. L to R: Coward, Ivor Novello, Alan Hollis, Willette Kershaw, Adrian Brunel, Frances Doble.
Source: author's own collection.

filming *The Constant Nymph*. After a delay of six months, it finally took place in March 1928, a month after *The Constant Nymph* was released; there was clearly concern about the quality of the film and reviews were mixed. 'Brilliant direction adds action and sustains interest throughout ... very good booking for discriminating patrons' was *Kinematograph Weekly*'s summary, though *The Bioscope*'s reviewer regarded it as 'another proof that the most successful of stage plays is not necessarily suitable for the screen' (cuttings, ABSC 1/122).

The film was released on 23 April and was a flop. George Hopton wrote to Brunel:

> Re: 'The Vortex'. I think that the less said about this production the better. You are no doubt aware that same has been released and the results to the exhibitor have been disastrous. I am afraid it will be some time before we hear the last about this production. (13 June 1928, ABSC 2/111)

By this stage, Brunel's protests throughout the production had been forgotten and he now felt that he was being held entirely responsible for the film's failure. He later wrote bitterly: 'Although I was not the father of

Figure 6.3 Advertisement for the cancelled trade show of *The Vortex*, *The Bioscope*, 1 September 1927, p. 26.

"The Vortex" you have tried to palm a paternity order on to me in regard to this bastard' (n.d., ABSC 1/112).

Whether the 'cute shots' that remained in the can would have succeeded in raising the film to something more than conventional can never be known, but *The Vortex* bears little trace of the creative endeavours of Brunel, Stannard and MacPhail to enliven it. It is thus difficult to assess its merits as 'an Adrian Brunel film', and he was eager to point out that it should not be considered as such. Three years after its release, his frustration was still evident in a letter to Noël Coward:

> I was not responsible for the treatment or the script (I protested against both), nor the take-choosing, the editing or the titling; nor for the fact that three of the principals had never been on the screen before and one of them was an invalid. There are many whys yet you could fire at me – and I hope you will one day, for my answers will help you to understand what's still wrong with British pictures – but there is one thing sadder than all the rest that I will reveal, and that is, I could have saved the picture even after it had all been shot if they had let me. (31 October 1931, ABSC C/170)

Brunel's position within the studio was somewhat ambiguous; although he was assigned to direct what must have been a valuable property to Gainsborough, he was not given sufficient budget or control to do what he felt was required for it to be a success. His protests to Coward were futile, since the playwright had had no involvement with the adaptation process and appeared to be indifferent to the final results, at least publicly. But Brunel's next project was an even more high-profile adaptation, and this time the authors were determined to have much greater control over the production.

CHAPTER 7

Adaptation and the Power of the Author: *The Constant Nymph*

Despite Coward's lack of input to the film, Brunel undoubtedly felt his spectre hovering over the production of *The Vortex*. However, the very solid presence of two writers exerted a much more potent influence over his next film. Margaret Kennedy's *The Constant Nymph* was the bestselling novel of 1924 and had been adapted very successfully for the stage, so the news that it was to appear on screen was received with great anticipation. *The Bioscope* expressed the view of many in the business: 'The purchase of the film rights of Margaret Kennedy's enormously successful novel and play by Gainsborough can be regarded as a triumph for British production and for Michael Balcon' (3 March 1927: 30). Balcon was therefore under pressure to produce a film that lived up to the expectations of audiences and, with so much at stake, took on some of the pre-production work himself. Like *The Vortex*, *The Constant Nymph* dealt with a controversial subject, this time a love affair between a man and a young girl, though British censors were apparently appeased when they learned that Mabel Poulton, the actress playing the teenage lead, was actually in her twenties. A much more delicate negotiation for Balcon was with the authors of the play, Kennedy and Basil Dean (also director of the stage version), both powerful figures who had to be handled carefully if the production was to have a smooth passage to the screen.

Kennedy and Dean were newcomers to film but insisted on writing the scenario themselves; while their status as novice screenwriters may have given Balcon some concern, it was certainly beneficial to have their names attached to the project on a creative level. Although their screen treatment does not appear to have survived, Brunel's collection contains the Initial Continuity, which presumably stuck to it quite closely. This was written by Alma Reville, Alfred Hitchcock's wife, who had established herself as a talented screenwriter with an excellent eye for cinematic composition and a sympathy for narratives with strong female characters. Reville's draft was passed to Angus MacPhail to embellish and his scenario is also preserved in the Brunel collection. However, there are important differences between these and the finished film which illustrate that, once again, creative compromises were made.

Brunel and Dean

Dean was an accomplished theatre director eager to make the move into film, and persuaded Balcon to let him direct *The Constant Nymph*.[1] Putting the direction of 'his company's costliest production to date, upon which the future of Gainsborough Pictures might well depend' (Dean 1973: 8) into the hands of someone with no experience was undoubtedly a risk but Dean's involvement would also be a selling point and the trade press eagerly printed regular updates on the project. Early in 1927, *The Bioscope* trumpeted Dean's directorial debut in three separate announcements and reported that he had just returned from 'studying production methods' in Berlin (17 February 1927: 55), indicating how seriously he was taking his prospective career change.

Despite the assertion in *The Bioscope* on 24 March 1927 that *The Constant Nymph* 'will go into production almost immediately', the start date was pushed back through the spring and early summer. In April, it emerged that Dean would work with an assistant director, to be named shortly after, yet this announcement was also long delayed, as was the confirmation of the casting of the lead actors. In June it was revealed, again prematurely, that filming was to begin the following month. Brunel had just started filming *The Vortex* and had not yet been mentioned in connection with *The Constant Nymph*.[2] Mid-June saw Balcon and Dean travel to the continent to scout for locations in the Tyrol and by early July, Dean had secured an agreement with composer Eugene Goossens, who had written the song 'When I Am Dead' for the stage play, to produce a new score for the film.

Ivor Novello's casting as the film's hero, Lewis Dodd, was announced three weeks later, followed swiftly by news that Brunel was 'to co-operate with Basil Dean in the direction of the film . . . the technical part of the production will be in his charge' (*The Bioscope*, 4 August 1927: 23). Here it also emerged that the coveted role of Tessa had been given to young but experienced British film actress Mabel Poulton, a casting decision

---

[1] Dean is somewhat coy in his autobiography, claiming that he merely suggested to Balcon that he should 'take part in the actual production' (1973: 7). However, it is likely that he insisted on having a role in directing the film, given his ambitions in that direction.

[2] Notes in the Brunel collection reveal that his screen tests for *The Vortex* were also being used to scout for actors for *The Constant Nymph* (24 May 1927, ABSC 5/112).

made by Brunel against the instincts of Ivor Montagu, who wrote that he 'retched at the idea' (3 August 1927, ABSC 5/111).

The constant delays indicate the amount of prevarication there was on the part of the studio, presumably over the nature of Dean's involvement and how best to manage his demands. Although Rachael Low regarded Brunel's appointment to the film as an 'attempt to promote ... [him] as a leading director' (1971: 169), this is clearly far from the truth. A week before *The Bioscope* announcement of his attachment to the film, Brunel had signed an agreement with Dean which stipulated their billing should read: 'DIRECTED BY ADRIAN BRUNEL UNDER THE PERSONAL SUPERVISION OF BASIL DEAN' (27 July 1927, ABSC 5/112). Dean insisted that he should be

> at liberty to attend as much or as little of the actual taking of the film as I see fit; that I see the takes daily if required; that Mr Brunel agrees to confer with me daily, or as often as I see fit, upon the actual shots; that retakes are to be made if required by me; that the existing agreed scenario is not departed from without my prior consent; that I may personally take part in the actual direction of any particular scenes, where I feel I can be of material assistance (ibid.).

Brunel had little choice but to agree, given his tenuous position at Gainsborough, and was probably the only director there who would have submitted to such an arrangement. Montagu wrote an impassioned letter, imploring him not to accept a job which 'no one else of your standing could even be asked to do, to get ... [Balcon] out of a hole that he's got into through sheer pigheaded ignoring of my ... advice' (3 August 1927, ABSC 5/112). Brunel would have been well aware of the damage that taking on this role would do to his status at the studio yet he ignored Montagu's advice, whether out of loyalty to Balcon, due to his own financial situation or perhaps in the hope that having his name attached to such a high-profile project would benefit his reputation.

The Plot

The film's story begins on a train approaching a lake in the Austrian Tyrol. On the train are Lewis Dodd and Kiril Trigorin, both on their way to visit the composer Albert Sanger at Karindehütte, his mountain chalet. They then board a boat and, on disembarking, are met by two of Sanger's daughters. At the chalet, they are greeted not by Sanger but by his wife Linda, and Trigorin (and the audience) is then introduced to the rest of the household: Sanger's five daughters (Kate, Paulina, Toni, Tessa and Susan), Roberto the manservant and Ike, a rich benefactor. Sanger, however, does not join the family group, remaining up in his room in front of his piano, with his dog and a bottle of wine for company.

When Sanger dies suddenly, the family falls into disarray. The position of the widowed Linda is now uncomfortable and she leaves with Trigorin, with whom she has been flirting since his arrival. Toni marries Ike but the future of the other girls is uncertain so Lewis, assuming responsibility, contacts their Uncle Charles, a Cambridge don. He arrives with his daughter Florence and she and Lewis quickly fall in love and decide to marry. Tessa is devastated, as she has long been in love with Lewis herself. She and Paulina are sent to boarding school in England but are very unhappy and run away, returning to the Chiswick home of Lewis and Florence. Florence is not pleased, especially when the deep affinity between Lewis and Tessa becomes apparent. After Lewis's performance of his new symphony, he and Tessa run away to Brussels, where she dies of a weak heart.

The Film's Reputation

The Constant Nymph was considered a lost film for many years and, as often happens with such titles, acquired the aura of a missing masterpiece. When it was eventually rediscovered, it did not entirely disappoint. One of the first academics to study the film was Lawrence Napper, who devotes a chapter of his book on middlebrow film culture in the interwar years to the relationship between the novel, the play and the film, with particular attention to the emerging development at the time of new means of presenting and propagating works of art. His premise is that not only was the text of *The Constant Nymph* subject to this trend, having been published, performed on stage and made into a film, but also that the narrative itself has that theme at its heart. He regards both Brunel and Kennedy as examples of artists who negotiated the twin aims of producing something culturally significant which also appealed to the mass market. However, as already illustrated, Brunel's artistic input to *The Constant Nymph* was limited by his late attachment to the project and the fact that he was not in full directorial control. Thus, Napper's claims for the film as an example of Brunel's ability to balance art and commerce need investigation.

Several forces were pulling the project in different directions, as the documents in the Brunel collection show. As with *Blighty* and *The Vortex*, the original script was filleted of most of its authors' attempts at poetic imagery. In the case of *The Constant Nymph*, these elements were largely the work of Dean and Kennedy, which made the negotiation process more complex than on Brunel's previous productions. Brunel found himself caught between a studio with little faith in his abilities and a strong-minded co-author and supervisory director, all of whom had a great deal at stake.

The two scripts in the Brunel collection credit Kennedy and Dean as authors of the 'scenario'; the first is Alma Reville's Initial Continuity, with a second Revised Continuity by Angus MacPhail. Neither is dated and the second is incomplete, consisting of MacPhail's revisions to Reville's version up to the end of Act One. This appears to be the copy of the scenario which was used during the location shoot in Austria, since it bears handwritten notes by both Brunel and Dean, suggesting that creative decisions were taken during filming. These scripts give an indication of how much more ambitious and 'expressionist' the film was originally intended to be.

Genesis of the Screenplay

Reville's continuity includes stylistic flourishes devised by Dean and Kennedy, including what they termed 'visions': imaginary scenes to be executed in the form of superimposition. On Dodd's arrival at Karindehütte, a brief sequence was to show the inspiration he found in the surroundings:

> a rough manuscript of music, this dissolve into little music notes, these dissolve into little birds flying about, then to a beautiful scene in the Tyrol, then to a forest, then the forest trees change into the bars of a cage, and the birds are fluttering their little wings against them, this dissolves into the actual room, the small hut and Lewis is busy scribbling. (ABSC 5/55)

A note underneath stipulates: 'the scene should never take on definite hard lines – merely impressionistic drawings – melting from one to another – with the same smoothness a symphony has'. After the death of Sanger, a more elaborate 'vision' was inserted to represent Lewis's relationship to Tessa:

> The mountain gradually takes the form of a terrific rock, a fairy castle slowly appears way up on the very top, this is dissolved into a forest, tall tree trunks, which appear to envelop the castle, a tiny figure, resembling a will-o'-the-wisp light floats in and out of the trunks. Lewis's own figure appears, very tiny and starts to chase the little light, he loses it, he is distraught, the trunks swirl and bend and again take the lines of the castle on the rock, the little light figure runs up and up the rocky mountain, Lewis's tiny one after it, the little light reaches the top, Lewis after it, as he just nears it, it vanishes, and he is left alone, a tiny weak figure. (Ibid.)

During Lewis's concert at the Queen's Hall a similar interlude was envisaged. Again, Lewis is shown in the mountains chasing a 'will-o'-the-wisp' but this time the vision was to occupy only the top half of the screen, with Lewis and the orchestra at the bottom of the frame. This superimposition is brief and, as it fades,

> the orchestra comes again sharp and clear, Lewis is urging them on, almost lashing with his baton, slowly over them again appears the shadow of Sanger – grim and horrible, as if he is dying, the instruments work up with another flourish, the figure fades away quickly, and they finish with a big crash. (Ibid.)

The technique was also to be used to illustrate Tessa's fragile health and state of mind. In a scene in which Florence accuses Tessa of being Lewis's lover, Tessa cowers before her and Florence's face was to transmogrify into that of Linda, Sanger's last wife. Additionally, the sequence depicting the journey to Belgium was considerably longer. At one point, Tessa was to be shown sitting on a tram opposite a man and woman. Gradually their faces were to transform into those of Florence and Sanger, regarding her in a stern and disapproving way. Dropping her gaze to the legs of the two people, Tessa sees the woman's umbrella turn into a hockey stick and their legs become a confusion of girls' legs as they play hockey. This final act was originally written as a parallel-cut sequence, with shots of Lewis and Tessa travelling to Brussels intercut with Florence and Charles setting off after them, Florence entering the room just in time to see Tessa lying dead in Lewis's arms. In the finished film, Florence and Charles do not feature in this final act.

A Touch of Poetry

Dean's autobiography provides clues to the inclusion and subsequent excision of these 'visions', which were apparently the idea of the First World War poet Robert Nichols:

> He wrote me long, barely legible letters . . . making various imaginative suggestions. One was that while Lewis Dodd was conducting his 'Symphony in Three Keys' at Queen's Hall, the scene should 'dissolve' into panoramic views of the mountains in the Tyrol, sunshine alternating with shade according to the mood of the music: a suggestion that would have caused the film distributors of those days to faint from shock. (1973: 8)

On viewing the finished film, Kennedy expressed delight at how it had turned out, yet voiced her preference for 'our original ending, i.e. dissolving images of the old Tyrol life mixed up with the death scene – I think it would give this scene just the touch of poetry it now lacks' (5 February 1928, ABSC 6/111). Balcon's response confirms that this had actually been shot: '[w]e have tried the dissolving scenes out and it was the general opinion of those who saw them that they rather interrupted the death scene, and was quite a shock to see them' (7 February 1928, ABSC 6/111).

'Those who saw them' would almost certainly have included C. M. Woolf, corroborating Dean's implication that it was he who took exception to the 'visions'; thus, even writers with the selling power of Dean and Kennedy did not have the clout to overrule the views of Gainsborough's major stakeholder. Woolf's likely objections to Kennedy's 'poetry' and insistence on the removal of shots which obstructed the narrative may well have reminded Brunel of his run-ins with H. J. Boam of Phillips Film Co. during his time with British Actors' Film Company. As Tom Ryall suggests, 'depicting the interior life of the mind . . . marked out the French avant-garde film makers of the day' but apparently was not part of the repertoire of British producers (1996: 25). While this project had seemed to offer the possibility of exploring these avenues in a mainstream feature, the poetry sought by Margaret Kennedy was deemed incompatible with commercial filmmaking.

The quote from Dean above shows that, in hindsight, he put his advocacy for such poetics down to his own naivety about the workings of the film industry. But what of Brunel? Such imagery was surely the kind of lyrical illustration of a film's themes that he himself had tried to bring to the screen in the hope of pleasing the critics. His views on Kennedy and Dean's visual ideas are not recorded but he would undoubtedly have been interested to see if they would survive Woolf's scrutiny. Under Dean's orders he filmed the 'visions' but was presumably not surprised when they ended up on his cutting-room floor.

The Constant Nymph as Art Film

Since Brunel had not been involved in the writing process, he was presumably less personally affected by the removal of the fantastic elements of the screenplay. His creative input came into play once he was on location, and he injected some of his own ideas into the film during the shooting and editing stages, over which he managed to exert some control. He had considerable experience of location shooting and was adept at making decisions on the spot. He wrote to Balcon:

> When I saw the local trains I realised that they were so delightfully typical that we should not lose them if we could possibly get them, for the carriages are open and the

engine is a sight to behold. You know that you can rely on me to get the most valuable shots. (19 August 1927, ABSC 5/112)

Elsewhere he described 'a short love scene I have played between [Trigorin and Linda], into which I had driven some pigs into the background. As a symbolical touch I am quite pleased with it' (letter to W. O'Bryen, 25 August 1927, ABSC 5/112).

Despite having some flexibility, Brunel was all too aware of where the power resided between himself and Dean, and he found the shoot a trying experience. Dean's role appeared to be to communicate 'what Miss Kennedy had in mind' (Brunel 1949: 138), yet his obvious lack of experience enabled Brunel fairly rapidly to establish control over the filming process and he was greatly encouraged by this validation of his own abilities. 'I found that I had to step in more and more from a purely technical position and assist in the psychological interpretation of the characters,' he wrote to Balcon, '. . . it makes me realise that I am every bit as capable as the great man of the theatre in this department of the work . . . I am something

Figure 7.1 *The Constant Nymph*: the tryst between Trigorin and Linda, with pigs.
Source: BFI National Archive.

more than a mere "technician'" (19 August 1927, ABSC 5/112). While Brunel maintained a reasonably civil relationship with Dean, American cameraman Dave Gobbett made no attempt to disguise his impatience with the novice director, an antagonism referred to both in Brunel's correspondence and Dean's autobiography. Brunel communicated his frustration with Dean to Balcon, calling him 'objectionable' and 'antagonistic', but managing to hide this on set served him well. As the shoot progressed, he found Dean 'much more amenable and reasonable' (ibid.), even acknowledging the value of Dean's work with the actors to enhance their understanding of the characters. Dean, aware of his limitations on the technical side, took to observing the process and later acknowledged his debt to Brunel:

> His choice was a wise move on Balcon's part, for I doubt whether any other English director would have put up with my fumbling attempts to maintain the integrity of the story, while knowing nothing of the mysterious ways of the film camera. (1973: 9)

Dean left Austria before the shoot was over, rejoining the crew in Munich where the interiors were to be filmed at Emelka Studios. It appears that the tension did not dissipate during the next stage of filming, as Phyllis Bottome, novelist and friend of Novello, recalled in her memoirs.

> It was, as all good films are, a difficult production . . . Several of the most attractive girls were in love with Ivor; and not in full harmony with each other. The producer . . . was in an unspeakable temper [and] had retired to his room where his meals were carried to him on a tray. Nobody knew German, yet all the mechanics in a Bavarian studio could only speak German. (1944: 54)

With both Brunel and Dean present at Emelka, it is open to conjecture which 'producer' she was referring to. When the interiors of Karindehütte were complete, the cast and crew returned to London to film the Chiswick interiors at the Gainsborough Studio in Islington, as well as the symphony scene at London's Queen's Hall.

Brunel spent three months on the post-production of the film and this unusually generous amount of time enabled him to achieve some of his best work. The editing is highly effective; although not employing the kind of ingenious intercutting seen in Hitchcock's *Easy Virtue*, it has what the *Observer* critic described as 'a very unusual briskness' in which 'every moment has lively interest' (BFIRL cuttings). As Napper observes,

> the Sanger meal, particularly, is handled with extraordinary sophistication, even by the standards of Hollywood film in the mature silent period. Several conversations are occurring at once, some at cross purposes, and some in secret, and yet Brunel's cutting and intertitling remain both unobtrusive and extremely 'readable'. (2009: 77)

Figure 7.2 *The Constant Nymph*: the Sanger family around the dinner table at Karindehütte. Source: BFI National Archive.

The film is built around such key scenes, or set pieces, in which revelations are brought to light and relationships defined and developed.

The family meal described above is the first time that the inhabitants of Karindehütte come together and tensions and rivalries surface. Sanger does not join them at the table and his absence is highlighted when the diners take up a chant for him to come down and eat. The jovial mood of the meal, celebrating the arrival of the girls' beloved Lewis, is destroyed by Linda's cross-examination of Toni about the new earrings she is sporting, reducing her to tears and breaking up the party. The scene is echoed after Sanger's death, this time with a much more subdued mealtime gathering, Lewis now at the head of the table having assumed the patriarchal position. With Sanger now permanently absent, the tensions between the family members surface in a more bitter and harmful way, and his daughters turn against Linda and her pampered daughter.

The film contains two contrasting scenes of performance, the more ambitious of which shows Lewis Dodd conducting his symphony at the Queen's Hall. *The Bioscope* reported that 'fifty-four scenes were shot there . . . claimed to be a record for a day's work' (3 November 1927: 32); Brunel later claimed to have shot seventy (1949: 142). The intercutting of these shots provides the viewer with a variety of perspectives, interspersing views of the audience with shots of the main characters. Thus Lewis is seen conducting, with his back turned, completely absorbed by the music; Tessa appears nervous after sneaking out to see the performance; Florence is tense and unhappy, knowing that Lewis plans to leave her as soon as the show ends.

An earlier performance in the film marks an equally pivotal moment, in a scene praised by one critic as 'a gem of comedy' (BFIRL cuttings). Florence has organised a musical evening at their Chiswick home to 'launch' Lewis into polite society, and her guests perform rather twee party pieces. Unimpressed by the recital, and by Florence's attempts to civilise him, Lewis persuades Tessa, Paulina and Toni to sneak out of the drawing room and go downstairs with him, where they stage their own concert in the kitchen. Florence is furious to discover them dancing round the table playing the comb and paper and various kitchen utensils, and orders Lewis back upstairs to play the piano. He humiliates her with a defiant performance of a song called 'Silver Sty', beginning 'There was a lady loved a swine . . .', a clear dig at her cultural pretensions. Embarrassed by Lewis's behaviour, the guests file uncomfortably out of the room while he thumps out what looks to be Chopin's Funeral March on the piano.

Characterisation

The shot set-ups, framing and editing used in the film are important to the characterisation, with performance and mise en scène also playing a key part. Albert Sanger is a central character in Kennedy's novel but in the film, as in the play, he becomes a shadowy figure who never emerges from the upstairs room where he sits, composing and drinking. This suggests his self-isolation, both from his family and society in general. In his few appearances in the film, he is shot entirely from behind, reinforcing the portrait of a man who has turned his back on the world. He is not seen full face until just before he dies, when he rises from his piano, unbolts the door of his room then turns and falls to the floor out of frame left. When the family discovers him, his face is illuminated by a pool of light.

Lewis Dodd is first seen behind a book, which he lowers slowly to reveal a bespectacled face smoking a pipe.[3] Later in the film, Florence is

---

[3] Brunel also used this device in both *Blighty* and *The Vortex*.

introduced in a similar way, lowering her newspaper at the breakfast table when she and her father learn of Sanger's death. Although the method of their introduction establishes a connection between Lewis and Florence, it also highlights a difference; while he has his nose buried in a book, demonstrating his affinity to literature and the arts, Florence is more interested in current affairs and gossip. We get an inkling of her rather superficial nature when the arrival of a card from 'the famous composer' Lewis Dodd causes her great excitement.

The use of locations in the film and the characters' relationship to them is crucial to its narrative development and changes in mood. While Sanger is never seen enjoying the open space he fled to from the stifling atmosphere of England, his brood of barefoot daughters are at one with it. Dressed in little more than rags they roam the countryside, with no formal education, but an innate feel for music and an appreciation of nature. Particularly in tune with her surroundings is Tessa Sanger. She is first seen standing alone near a mountain top, feeling the wind on her face as she awaits Lewis's arrival. She is often placed high up, looking down, suggesting that she occupies a high moral plane. When she sees the boat bringing Lewis, she runs headlong down the slope and finds her sister Paulina reclining in the grass opposite a row of religious effigies. This establishes a connection between the spiritual and the natural which is embodied by the Sanger girls. The association is reinforced later, when Tessa is shown leaning against a figure of Christ on the cross, once again looking down the mountainside. From her vantage point she can see her stepmother, Linda, canoodling with Trigorin and, troubled by the scene, seeks solace in nature and the divine. Seeing Lewis nearby, she goes to him for comfort but is driven to tears by his light-hearted rejection of her, establishing her sensitive nature. The relationship between Tessa and Lewis is entirely pure and never consummated; much later, Tessa is horrified by Florence's suggestion that they are lovers. Lewis tells Florence that if he tried his 'fascinating ways on [Tessa], she'd give me a black eye', a stinging remark since Florence clearly succumbed to them. The idea of Tessa's innocence and saintliness comes to a climax in the final scene, as she stands silhouetted in front of a window, arms outstretched, in a pose suggestive of Christ on the cross.

Light to Darkness

The progression through the film from light to darkness and from freedom to containment reinforces the gradual descent of Tessa and Lewis from hope into despair. The first image is on board a train through the mountains where Lewis Dodd sits, one elbow out of the window of the open-sided carriage. From the train he and Trigorin board a steamboat across a lake, the whole journey redolent of fresh air and open space. During the first act, Dodd and the Sanger girls are frequently shown outdoors and are clearly most at home among nature.

The locations elicited a great deal of positive comment in contemporary reviews and, for British critics, beautiful landscapes were a definite selling point for a film. While the English countryside could symbolise nostalgia for a pre-industrial society and an evocation of 'home', the Tyrolean landscape in *The Constant Nymph* creates a very different atmosphere. The novel reveals that Sanger left Britain due to his disillusionment with the cosseted, protected existence where genius is encouraged to produce art for the masses rather than art for art's sake. The dramatic mountainous locations symbolise the freedom and escape from these restrictions sought by both Sanger and Dodd; their musical compositions make manifest their refusal to conform to the demands of the English cultural milieu. Sanger's music, we are told, was neglected during his lifetime, while the Sanger children tease Lewis about his disdain for melody. The mountainous setting and the simplicity of the family's chalet reflect Sanger's adopted bohemian lifestyle, his lofty ideals and disregard for convention. During the first act Brunel presents the spectacular scenery to its full advantage, employing mainly medium-long and long-shots to convey a sense of space and freedom.

After the engagement of Lewis and Florence, the mood of the film changes dramatically. In contrast to the natural spirituality connecting Lewis with Tessa, he declares his passion for Florence in a much more conventional religious site, a small village church. An intertitle has already announced, 'With the marriage of Toni and Ike, Tessa began to realise that the happy days of Sanger's "Circus" were over', and the scene now shifts to civilised London society, centred on Lewis and Florence's smart Chiswick home. As per the script, the house exhibits 'the Ideal Home attempt at Bohemian decorating' (Initial Continuity, ABSC 5/55), with thick drapes, plump cushions and knick-knacks on every surface. On arrival there after their honeymoon, Florence asks Lewis if he approves of the decor and his look of disdain is answer enough. His behaviour reinforces this lack of respect: he throws the cushions onto the floor, drops a dead match on the carpet, taps out his pipe on top of the piano and kicks the door shut with relish. His lack of interest in material objects jars with her pride in her home and it is clear that, away from the romantic setting of the Tyrol, cracks have quickly appeared in their relationship. Florence even tries to tame Roberto, the Sanger family retainer, who has been brought to London, dressed in a suit and instructed to bring the post on a silver salver.

Once they leave the Tyrol the film is completely studio-bound, adding to the feeling of enclosure. The large cast of characters of the first act, the noisy dinner table and rough and tumble of family life is gradually pared down to the three central figures. Lewis, Tessa and Florence are confined within the Chiswick house (save one or two scenes at the boarding school) until the night of Lewis's concert at the Queen's Hall. After the concert, Lewis leaves Florence to entertain the well-heeled guests gathered in his dressing room and goes to the station to take the boat train with Tessa.

In this final section of the film, it reaches its darkest and most claustrophobic. A note in the continuity script instructs, 'From now on to the end the set must be lost completely – merely impressions against a hazy background – quickly passing before the camera' (ABSC 5/55). Indeed, the shots that make up this final section, particularly those of the journey, use expressionistic lighting techniques, with certain elements in the frame picked out while the rest remains obscure. The scenes charting the journey to Brussels are each barely a few seconds long and this compression adds to the feeling of furtiveness and haste and reinforces the feeling that the pair are stepping into the unknown with no hope of return. The long-shots of the first act are replaced with medium-shots and close-ups, suggesting the surroundings are closing in on Lewis and Tessa. As they arrive at the station platform, the guard has just shut the gate but opens it to let them through and bolts it behind them as they run into the blackness beyond. A brief model shot of the city lights from the enclosed, black interior of the train (a striking contrast to the mountain train of the opening shot) is followed by the couple walking up the ship's gangplank, barely visible in the gloom. Tessa falters and slips and shadowy figures rush into the frame to assist her. The scene fades to black, then fades up on the inside of a cramped cabin; Tessa lies in bed while a nurse tends to her, the tiny porthole above offering no air or light. The scene again fades to black and passengers jostle as a customs inspector searches their luggage. Tessa is shown walking into shot under a sign which reads 'BRUXELLES NORD'; she turns and waits for Lewis to join her. An intertitle reads: 'Hurry and confusion – The stabbing beats of her heart – No wonder the night's shelter of a cheap Brussels boarding house found Tessa tired out – Exhausted.' The camera pans round the room in a rolling motion, suggesting her unsteadiness, then settles on a medium close-up of Tessa, barely visible in the darkness. The final intertitles are superimposed on a background of clouds, indicating Tessa's proximity to heaven, a notion reinforced by the shot of her silhouette, arms outstretched as if on a crucifix. As she lays dying, Lewis and the landlady stand over her, only their faces and hands visible.

The Trade Show

The film was trade shown at the Marble Arch Pavilion on 20 February 1928 and press and public alike were clamouring to attend. One reviewer noted, 'The crowd to see the first showing was so great that the doors were "rushed" and numbers of people with tickets were unable to get into the theatre at all' (BFIRL cuttings).[4] Modernist British composer Eugene Goossens had failed to deliver his eagerly anticipated score and, with little time to spare, the Pavilion's musical director Louis Levy had been brought in to provide an appropriate accompaniment. This he did by using 'When Thou Art Dead' and three other Goossens compositions linked together with musical phrases of his own composition. *The Bioscope*'s music expert praised Levy's efforts and remarked that using Goossens's 'Folk Tune' as a key theme 'had much to do with creating the right atmosphere for Lewis Dodd' (1 March 1928: vii). Dodd's symphony was composed by Vivian Ellis, a surprising choice since the twenty-four-year-old was best known as a writer of popular songs for musical comedies. The screening was apparently received with enthusiastic applause and Basil Dean addressed the audience, praising Mabel Poulton as the 'ideal' Tessa.

Second to None

The critics were virtually unanimous in their praise for *The Constant Nymph*: 'One of the most brilliant pictures yet made ... exceeds in merit and interest both the novel and the play' (cuttings, ABSC 8/56); 'There are points of beauty ... that set it just as high in this respect as anyone could possibly wish amongst the achievements of the cinema'; 'as an entertainment ... it ranks second to none' (BFIRL cuttings). Some reviews attributed its success to Brunel and some to Dean, while one or two were uncertain which of the two deserved the credit: 'It is Mr Dean's first adventure in this medium and it is not clear how he and Mr Brunel (already known as a competent director) shared their task' (ibid.). Dean summed up the collaborative nature of the film in his description of the

---

[4] The cuttings available from the BFI Reuben Library and those in Brunel's scrapbook do not always have attributions in relation to the journals or the critics. However, they have been used as they represent reactions to the film that support the key arguments being made about it, or emphasise either its popularity or artistic qualities.

ADAPTATION AND THE POWER OF THE AUTHOR 171

Figure 7.3 Cover of *Kinematograph Weekly* promoting *The Constant Nymph*, 2 February 1928.

opening night, attended by himself, Brunel and Balcon: 'All three of us were jostled by huge crowds of fans who mistook Adrian for myself and me for him,' which he concluded was, 'a fitting comment upon the mix-up of functions that had attended the somewhat painful process of making the film' (1973: 14).[5]

Novel to Play to Film

One of the few reservations the critics voiced about the film was that filmgoers who had not read the book or seen the play may not comprehend the intricacies of the plot, and some maintained that it was an unsuitable subject for the screen. The *Times* critic wrote, 'the story of Tessa and Lewis, charming and moving as it is, is frankly inadequate in the form of "silent drama"' (cuttings, ABSC 8/56). Despite its success, Balcon's regret regarding Gainsborough's reliance on literary works extended to *The Constant Nymph*, which he deemed 'demonstrably unsuitable for adaptation to a medium without the power of speech' (1969: 36). Seemingly oblivious to the debates already well underway, Dean later claimed that '*The Constant Nymph* announcement started a long argument as to whether stage plays could ever be made into successful films' (1973: 7).

The criticism of British silent cinema as 'stagey', with a tendency towards an overly theatrical representational style, has been recast by Christine Gledhill as a form of intermediality. She regards this incorporation of theatrical modes as a means by which British filmmakers tried to develop a unique national cinema. This is seen in the preference for long-shots and the treatment of the film set like a stage, but Gledhill also suggests that more complex examples of the technique demonstrate 'the metaphorical significance of the public performance as a space for playing out tensions in British culture between life and artifice, private emotion and public presentation' (2003: 15). Certain scenes in *The Constant Nymph* use this staging, perhaps not surprisingly, since the film is structured around the set pieces which constitute the play. As well as the sequences of performance already mentioned, the film deploys other 'metaphoric stages'. In one scene, Paulina and Tessa look down from the balcony at the front of Karindehütte to see Linda flirting with Trigorin on the porch, and it is from here that Florence greets the morning on her first day at the chalet, secretly observed by Lewis from the window of his hut.

---

[5] Dean asserts that this occurred at the ceremony for the *Film Weekly* award but, as stated in the Introduction, he did not attend this event.

The preference for long-shots led to a sparse use of the close-up, an aspect of *The Constant Nymph* that did not go unnoticed. Brunel's ambivalent attitude towards the device has already been mentioned, yet Sydney Carroll lamented the scarcity of close-ups in the film, insisting that they could have provided 'opportunities of revealing to us the inner secrets of Tessa's mind' (BFIRL cuttings). He felt that the use of long-shots encouraged a more theatrical presentation style and that the filmmakers 'followed the narrative at too respectful a distance, afraid to bring their cameras closely upon their people lest they should forget to be natural and should degenerate into film fantastic' (ibid.). Reville's Initial Continuity does contain instructions for a number of close shots, mostly towards the final act as the film reaches its emotional climax, and Brunel conforms to her plan, using them sparingly during dramatic scenes. Of course, Carroll was not to know that 'the inner secrets of Tessa's mind' were to have been revealed in a very concrete manner, and it is interesting to speculate how the critics would have reacted to such a 'fantastic' mode of representation in a British film.

Artistic Integrity

Lawrence Napper draws a parallel between Kennedy and Brunel in their ability to steer a course between 'art' and the market. The character of Lewis Dodd is shown to be resistant to new media, and the pressure on him to conform and adapt his work for a mass audience, brought to bear by Florence, is seen as representative of the popular cultural view of art. Unlike Dodd, Kennedy embraced the opportunity to adapt and disseminate her novel via other media, Basil Dean opining that 'she was as keen as the next person for a share of American dollars' (1973: 7). However, though she had set her sights on a Hollywood deal, Kennedy was not prepared to have her opus subjected to the constraints of the Hays Code and instead sold the rights to Gainsborough at a greatly reduced price.

The temptation for authors to increase their exposure (and income) through cinematic adaptation of their work seems to have trumped the arguments over whether literary sources should be made into films simply because they were popular. While it was assumed that their popularity would guarantee them an audience, critics invariably compared the films to their source material and often found them wanting. One reviewer wrote of *The Constant Nymph*: 'Somehow . . . the story is not on the screen quite so effective as it is on the stage' (BFIRL cuttings), while another summed up the critics' position thus: 'Since there is a marked difference between stories which can best be told in pictures and those which are expressed in words, we have grown suspicious towards film versions of plays or novels' (ibid.). Yet, as Napper points out, the film's co-writer Angus MacPhail, after analysing the results of a competition in November 1929 to nominate screen stories, concluded that people would go and see a film adaptation of a novel they have enjoyed 'no matter how unsuitable the novel may intrinsically be as screen material' (2009: 73).

Kennedy herself, when questioned by *Picturegoer*, rejected the idea that 'a screen adaptation of a novel or play can ever be entirely successful' (December 1928: 31). Perhaps due to her experiences with *The Constant Nymph*, she regarded the process of screenwriting as somewhat demeaning for a novelist, continuing: 'The screen writer must be a good story-teller, but he need have no command of language at all, and since an author's whole business is to acquire such command he is wasting his especial talent if he writes for the screen' (ibid.).[6] Dean expressed less hardline views, maintaining that the success of a film adaptation is dependent on the intrinsic merit of the story and that 'a good yarn can sometimes make a first-rate film' (ibid.: 29).

Napper's comparison between Kennedy's negotiation of the various outlets available for her work and the way that Brunel tried to reconcile his artistic impulses with the constraints of making commercial features is useful up to a point. Brunel's position as a creative was far more fragile and the struggles he had maintaining control over his films inevitably limited the power of his agency. The analogy perhaps works better when viewing his work more broadly; throughout his career, Brunel was constantly attempting to recycle his own works and ideas, both successful and unsuccessful, via different media. Thus, he reused off-cuts from his films to construct his burlesques, repurposed humour from his shorts in magazine articles, rewrote silent films as talkies, turned *Blighty* into the stage play 'Only Yesterday' and adapted his 1914 theatrical work 'Til Tomorrow' for the radio, the BBC broadcasting it in 1932 and 1948. In this way, he demonstrated his ability to adapt his work for different media and maintain his profile across different audiences, an exercise largely precipitated by his precarious economic situation.

Brunel and Adaptation

While the readers of *Film Weekly* voted *The Constant Nymph* the best British film of 1928, it did not feature in the selection of the year's highlights by

[6] Kennedy went on to become a successful screenwriter and wrote a treatise on the discipline, *The Mechanised Muse* (1942).

poet and film critic Robert Herring. In fact, his book *Films of the Year 1927–1928* lists only one British feature among the French, German and American titles he deemed worthy of inclusion: Alfred Hitchcock's *The Lodger*. This should not be a surprise, however, given that Herring was an associate of the POOL group of avant-garde filmmakers and a contributor to the highbrow film journal *Close Up*. In the book's foreword he outlines the criteria he applied to his judgements, concluding that 'in the best films . . . both theme and story unfold so that there is a weaving of the two sets of images, the apparent and the real' (1928: 2). Thus, had Kennedy's 'visions' been incorporated into *The Constant Nymph*, they may have brought the film a step closer to Herring's perception of film art. Brunel had toyed with ways to portray a character's 'inner thoughts' in earlier films, though for comic rather than lyrical effect; his idea to depict the dreams of the dog in *The Beggars' Syndicate* was perhaps a wry comment on the psychoanalytic approach of European filmmakers. While he strove towards originality and away from conventional themes and what he regarded as stale, hackneyed filmmaking techniques, he may have viewed extravagant flourishes like Kennedy's visions as incompatible with British narrative filmmaking.

Conclusion

Brunel's experiences of directing literary adaptations for a major studio brought him moments of both optimism and despair. The importance of such works to the British film industry and the value producers placed on the marketing potential of popular plays and novels ran counter to his belief that the future of a viable British national industry was based around the encouragement of original screenwriting. Yet the production histories of *The Vortex* and *The Constant Nymph* demonstrate the ways that Brunel attempted to inject originality into these films any way he could, whether through contributions to the scriptwriting process or more spontaneous interventions during shooting and editing.

The fact that Brunel was entrusted to direct high-profile adaptations would seem to indicate the studio's faith in his abilities, yet his papers suggest that it is more probable he was given assignments other directors were unlikely to have accepted. Even though *The Vortex* was low-budget and studio-bound, he was accorded very little control and his vision for the film was compromised by the studio's refusal to allow him to edit it. Their lack of faith in the film was evident from the start and Balcon may have realised that it would never translate successfully to the screen and was thus unwilling to devote too many resources to it. It is interesting to speculate whether 'the director's cut' would have had more success, though it seems doubtful given the wrangling that took place over the screenplay and the fact that the play's chief selling point – its scandalous nature – was never going to make it past the censor.

In contrast, the freedom Brunel was given to assemble *The Constant Nymph* resulted in a much more sophisticated and hugely successful film, and his decision to accept the job, against advice, was vindicated. It was a lavish production and gave him the opportunity to shoot on location and work with expert German studio technicians; the money and time Gainsborough invested in it were justified by its reception and box office success. The negotiations Brunel engaged in while making *The Vortex* and *The Constant Nymph* illustrate the difficult relationship of the director to the literary work; the role essentially involves mediating between the concept of that work in the minds of the critics and audiences, and the reality of the many limitations imposed by its cinematic rendering. Brunel managed to navigate the two reasonably effectively to produce films that preserved the essence of the authors' original theme and intent while not subverting the expectations of the average cinemagoer. However, his efforts did nothing to improve his reputation at Gainsborough, which was to deteriorate further, leading to a slow descent from mainstream feature direction, as the second part of his biography illustrates.

CHAPTER 8

Contextualised Biography of Adrian Brunel, Part II

This chapter concludes the biography of Adrian Brunel begun in Chapter 2, from his last two films for Gainsborough through to the end of his life. As sound replaced silent films, Brunel's career became even less secure and, while the problems besetting the industry changed over the following decades, the issues facing him were depressingly similar.

A Light Woman

On 26 January 1928, *The Bioscope* announced that Brunel was to direct *A Light Woman*, based on a story written by his mother, under her pen name Dale Laurence. Brunel, no doubt sensitive to accusations of nepotism, was eager to point out that the subject had been chosen from several properties by an independent selection committee at the studio. But if he was pleased at last to bring to the screen a story he had a feel for, his sense of control was not to last long. According to Brunel, the story was set in England and on the Riviera and told of a wayward daughter and the aristocratic widowed father who struggles to control her. But C. M. Woolf apparently insisted on the setting being moved to Spain and, once again, Brunel was incensed to find his work interfered with.[1] Brunel was to be under intense scrutiny: Balcon sent his brother Chandos to Spain to scout for locations and keep an eye on the production as assistant director. He also issued the following memorandum to Harold Boxall:

> I want to make it quite clear to everybody concerned that 'A LIGHT WOMAN' is to be a moderate price picture only. The figure I have in mind is £10,000. £12,000 absolute maximum . . . it must be understood by everybody concerned that if they

---

[1] Balcon flatly denied this change of location: 'Your story from the outset was set in Spain, and how you could have written a treatment and a script without having Spain in your mind I do not know . . .' (3 May 1928, ABSC 6/112).

do exceed our allocation, the entire script will have to be revised in order to meet with the limitations that are now imposed upon you. (5 March 1928, ABSC 6/112)

The letter goes on to state that the studio has estimated the cost of the script as written as being between £20,000 and £25,000 and Balcon demanded to see it himself, presumably insisting on rewrites to bring costs down.[2] A week earlier, he had written directly to Brunel, reminding him of the importance of the Continental market and requesting a European star in one of the film's main roles. In the end, Brunel cast all British actors and the director set off with them and his crew for Spain on 7 April to begin what was to be another trying experience.

Brunel's relationship with Gainsborough, and particularly with Balcon, was reaching a nadir. It was around this time that Balcon warned Brunel against continuing his involvement with his editing firm Brunel & Montagu, stating that 'any development of their activities might cause a certain amount of confusion as far as you are concerned' (5 March 1928, ABSC 6/111). Earlier in the year Brunel had fuelled his own unpopularity by complaining about the size of his name in an advert for Gainsborough in *The Bioscope*; the terse response from studio manager George Hopton leaves no doubt about his attitude towards Brunel: 'the placing of the advertisement and the drawing up of the matter took less of my time than given to the dictation of this letter' (5 January 1928, ABSC 6/112).

While the ups and downs of the Spanish shoot of *A Light Woman* are recounted light-heartedly in *Nice Work*, a very different account of events emerges from an eleven-page letter in Brunel's collection. Here he reveals that, once again, his work was heavily scrutinised at the script and preparation stage, this time by Gainsborough's Director General T. Hayes Hunter, presumably to ensure it did not exceed the allocated budget. 'I then began to realise that I had definitely lost your confidence,' wrote Brunel to Balcon (n.d., ABSC 1/112). He describes the atmosphere on location as extremely tense, partly due to the problems they encountered, but also because of the constant missives from the London office, which led to 'a growing feeling that we had to "account" for everything, and that all we said would be taken down in evidence against us' (ibid.).

Disagreements had arisen over the members of Brunel's entourage; without the studio's permission, he had taken on a Spanish advisor to assist with negotiations and location hunting and Balcon insisted that Brunel would have to pay him from his own money. Balcon also objected to the presence of the actor Beaufoy Milton, another of Brunel's acolytes,

---

[2] Brunel later recorded the eventual cost of the film as £17,000 (1949: 152).

Figure 8.1 Irene and Christopher Brunel in Spain with Benita Hume during the filming of *A Light Woman*. Source: author's own collection.

whom the studio director seemed to dislike, and he was not best pleased that Babs and Christopher were going along for the trip. Brunel was aware that much of the footage they shot in Spain was compromised, especially the mountain-climbing scenes, since the actors could not be expected to perform dangerous stunts and the crew lacked the right equipment to ascend to great heights and film on narrow ledges. The loss of a transit case containing all the shot negatives was a serious setback which, although it was eventually recovered, contributed further to making the shoot a fraught experience.

This was also an anxious time for Balcon. It was becoming clear that the days of silent film were numbered and Gainsborough was about to be taken over by Gaumont-British. The public issue of shares was announced by *The Bioscope* on 3 May and the new company, Gainsborough Pictures (1928), was to be under the directorship of Woolf, Balcon and Maurice Ostrer. The changes in directorship meant a loss of independence for Gainsborough, which now became a 'wholly-owned outpost of the Gaumont-British empire' (Kemp, 1997: 28).

By June, Brunel was back in Britain filming interiors at the studio in Islington, after which *A Light Woman* was edited by Arthur Tavares. Brunel voiced his discontent with the finished version, lamenting, as he had with *The Vortex*, the forfeiting of his personal vision, which he described as 'those pseudo-clever touches that the critics like so much' (n.d., ABSC 1/112). He refers to two scenes which were intended to echo each other, 'the former cut out and the latter truncated' (ibid.), as well as several dissolves between scenes which, he states, Tavares felt were not to the public's taste. Brunel describes how he would have approached

Figure 8.2 Brunel (seated, wearing a hat) with Benita Hume and the cast and crew of *A Light Woman* on location. Source: author's own collection.

the task of editing: 'I would have reduced the length of the titles, taken out the preliminary topical shots and so made room for that other stuff,' concluding: 'It would have been a hard job, but as they were my own ideas, I would have fought hard to have presented them as effectively and briefly as possible' (ibid.).

It is impossible to gauge the success or otherwise of Tavares' editing, since *A Light Woman* has not survived in its original release version. However, a 9.5mm Pathé Baby version is in circulation among collectors; released in 1933 under the title *Dolores*, it was heavily abridged and runs 27 minutes, a fraction of the 88-minute original cut. While much of the subplot about the father's less than respectable lifestyle has been excised, this small-gauge version preserves some of the local colour and attractive landscapes that elicited positive comment on the film's release, justifying the choice of an Iberian setting. Several critics focused on the direction, *The Stage* emphasising that 'Adrian Brunel's direction . . . maintains the great ability and artistry evident in his previous pictures', while star Benita Hume was hailed as 'a new and glorious discovery' by the *Manchester Evening News* (reviews, ABSC 1/134).

A Final Gainsborough Production

Brunel was already preparing the second feature in his three-film deal, an adaptation of stage thriller *The Crooked Billet* by popular Australian dramatist Dion Titheradge. At the end of July 1928, Brunel and Angus MacPhail went to stay at the Burlington Hotel in Eastbourne to work on the screenplay, attending a production of the play at the Brighton West Pier in August. It was entirely set in the eponymous inn and they attempted to render it more cinematic, opening it out to include a nightclub scene and a night shoot on Chelsea Embankment. This latter plan, however, was obstructed by the police, resulting in London locations being reproduced in the studio. It was to have an excellent cast: Brunel's former partner Miles Mander, Gordon Harker, Carlyle Blackwell and Madeleine Carroll, and was a good bet for success given its stage pedigree.

Yet Brunel was not happy with the project and drew up a list of 'difficulties', presumably to present to Gainsborough at a later date, including that it was 'not my story' (ABSC 1/112). Filming took place throughout October 1928 and *The Bioscope* printed several set reports, recording incidents such as Mander breaking a rib during a fight scene and Brunel felling actor Danny Green while demonstrating ju-jitsu (24 October 1928: 31). Meanwhile, Arthur Tavares was editing *A Light Woman*, which had its trade show on 3 December.

In September 1928 Brunel had sought clarification about his contractual situation at the studio, drafting a letter requesting confirmation of the 'terminating date of my twelve months agreement with the Company' (22 September 1928, ABSC 6/112). It was approaching a year since he had finished *The Constant Nymph*, from which point his three-picture deal was to commence. He had signed a one-year contract with Gainsborough under which he was to make a minimum of three films for a payment of £3,000, with a vague promise of a 'selected bonus scheme' (29 June 1927, ABSC 5/111). He suggested that the year be calculated from 24 December 1927, since, after completing the first cut of the *The Constant Nymph* earlier in the month, he had spent two weeks making the short sound on disc film *In a Monastery Garden* under a separate contract.

Over the year he had completed *A Light Woman* and was due to start *The Crooked Billet* but, as he pointed out, this only allowed thirteen weeks to make two films, with the third title not even selected. It soon became clear to Brunel that Gainsborough did not intend him to direct a third film and he embarked on what was to become a lengthy battle with the studio that ended up in court.

The announcement in *Film Weekly* of Brunel's upcoming film version of *The Crooked Billet* appeared alongside news that *The Jazz Singer* was ending its long run at the Piccadilly Theatre. The juxtaposition of these two pieces of information is significant; while Brunel shot *The Crooked Billet* entirely silent, Gainsborough, along with other production companies, was becoming nervous about releasing silents into a rapidly changing market and the film was never seen in this form. The following summer, in the middle of Brunel's legal battle with the company, Gainsborough approached him to reshoot it as a sound film. He reluctantly declined, writing to a friend that although

> I hate to think of anyone else touching 'The Crooked Billet' . . . it would weaken my position very much if I went back to Gainsborough to direct the talking version without being paid what I claim, because the obvious interpretation would be, 'They couldn't have treated him so badly if he goes back to work for them.' (26 July 1929, ABSC 1/111)

Angus MacPhail tried to persuade him to take the commission, to which he must have responded positively since a letter arrived from Harold Boxall suggesting they meet to discuss the possibility, though clearly to no avail. It must have been incredibly difficult for Brunel to turn down the chance to make his first talking feature but he stuck to his guns and it was reshot by Robert Atkins, a theatre actor and producer with very little film experience. It was eventually released in March 1930 as a 'part-talkie', with the whole of the first and a section of the final reel silent. But critics were more interested in the film's sound sections: the dialogue was 'clearly delivered and recorded' according *Kinematograph Weekly*, while *To-day's Cinema* expressed the view that 'the recording is yet another tribute to the excellence of the RCA process' (reviews, ABSC 5g/56). Although most of the footage shot by Brunel was jettisoned, his name was still attached to it; presumably the success of *The Constant Nymph* meant that it may still have carried some weight. At least one print of the film survives on 16mm in a private collection but none is currently available to view.

Early in 1930, Brunel's case against Gainsborough was settled by an out of court payment, with Gainsborough agreeing to assign him one last film to direct. However, this never materialised, the official reason being a major fire at Islington Studios in January 1930 that interrupted the company's production schedule. Brunel had spent nearly three years directing films for Gainsborough and this period had marked his most intense battle to maintain creative control over his work. The scrutiny he was under led to a difficult working situation that he sometimes lacked the diplomacy to deal with. Having established his ability to make films for a pittance, and having shown a willingness to salvage the work of others, he was unlikely to rise up the ranks of the company, particularly since his occasionally arrogant self-belief meant he was too eager to speak his mind.

Talking Pictures

At first, Brunel's prospects looked reasonably good. He was busy throughout 1929 with Brunel & Montagu, although the company had abandoned its Dansey Yard offices for rooms at 80–82 Wardour Street. He continued to retitle foreign films for British release, earning praise for his work from the likes of Ufa's director Erich Pommer. However, as silent films gradually dwindled and eventually disappeared from cinema screens altogether, this work dried up, and Brunel and his colleagues shot a short film that summer satirising the company's imminent demise. Filmed on the roof of their building, *Brunel & Montagu* (1929) shows 'the staff . . . once gay and debonair' (Brunel, Ivor Montagu, Ian Dalrymple and Lionel Rich) throwing themselves over the edge as their careers appear to be doomed. However, Brunel continued to run the firm for several more years, until at least 1931.

Brunel still had some useful allies in the business, including Walter Mycroft, Film Society stalwart and ex-film critic of the *Evening Standard*, now a scenario editor at British International Pictures (BIP). Mycroft was instrumental in getting Brunel a commission from studio head John Maxwell and, towards the end of 1929, Brunel began work on his first sound feature. *Elstree Calling* combined music-hall acts, musical numbers

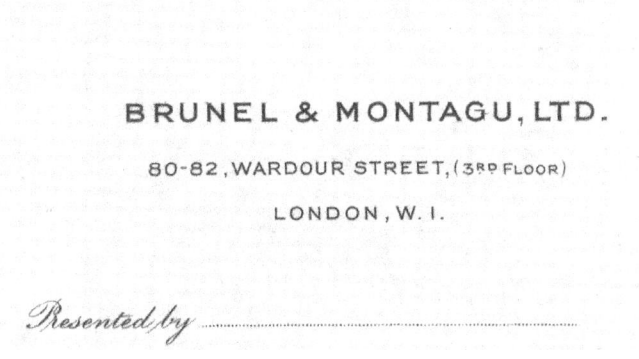

Figure 8.3 Brunel & Montagu business card. Source: author's own collection.

from Jack Hulbert's current West End stage revue *The House that Jack Built* and some original sketches, all to be shot at BIP's Elstree Studio. Approaching the project with enthusiasm, Brunel set about planning ways to enliven the stage-bound subject. As with *The Vortex*, he shot with the editing process very much in mind, filming the acts from several different angles so that, when assembled, the film would not simply be a static presentation but rather, as he told Mycroft, 'something really new and arresting in the way of film revue' (15 April 1930, ABSC 5/153). He claims to have chosen the film's title, and with it the idea of foregrounding the studio itself, conveying the atmosphere with behind-the-scenes shots. He wrote comic sequences between the acts that aimed at sending up filmmaking conventions and featured himself as 'the director' with three megaphone-bearing 'yes men'. He suggested a montage of various activities around the studio, again with his vision of the finished effect built in:

> Shot of carpenters' shop, overlapping with a shot of floor with the sets prominent, large sun arc, make-up man making up a girl, a director directing a scene, crowds outside Casting office, and other interesting studio scenes. Each separate picture of these lap dissolves is a travelling shot so we get the continual movement and rhythm. (First skeleton scenario of *Elstree Calling*, 8 December 1929, ABSC 2/161)

His script also proposed shots of other BIP figures, including directors Alfred Hitchcock and Monty Banks, the film's cameraman Claude Friese-Greene and using film and radio stars such as Donald Calthrop, Anna May Wong and Tommy Handley.

Figure 8.4 Brunel with Donald Calthrop on the set of *Elstree Calling*.
Source: BFI National Archive.

The production did not run smoothly. Brunel had drawn up a detailed plan of when each artiste was available to shoot their act, with the cast of Hulbert's revue travelling out to the studio after their nightly performances, often filming until the early hours. The original shooting schedule of three weeks in December 1929 kept expanding, and it appears that around the middle of January BIP's patience with Brunel ran out. They were presumably keen for the film to come out while *The House that Jack Built* was still on in the West End and so the decision was made to bring in another director to do essential retakes and get the film finished as quickly as possible. Thus it was that Alfred Hitchcock, Brunel's former associate at Gainsborough, was brought onto the film to undertake the kind of remedial work that Brunel himself used to do at that studio. Unsurprisingly, Brunel was extremely upset when he eventually found out, regarding Hitchcock's involvement as 'a contravention of my original terms' (16 February 1930, ABSC 5/153).

Hitchcock's precise contribution to *Elstree Calling* has been mulled over by various scholars, Kerzoncuf and Barr tempering James Vest's rather exaggerated assessment of his involvement. They attribute three sections of the finished film to Hitchcock: Donald Calthrop's comic interludes in which he attempts to perform Shakespeare, the 'Home sequences', in which Gordon Harker tries to fix his television set, and the short sketch 'The Wrong Flat'. It is certainly true that the first two of these three 'interpolations' did require partial reshoots due to problems with the sound-recording equipment, as made clear in a letter from Brunel to Mycroft on 9 January 1930 (ABSC 5/153).

'The Wrong Flat' sketch had been rewritten and expanded by Brunel in his various revised scripts. The version of the script dated 30 December 1929 contains a plan for it to be filmed in four different styles: a 'West End stage' version set in a middle-class milieu, followed by three cinematic versions to demonstrate the contrast between theatre and screen. The first of these was in the style of an Alfred Hitchcock thriller and set on a tenement landing, the second to be played along the lines of a D. W. Griffith Western and the third as an Al Jolson musical. This idea also accommodates Brunel's desire to foreground cinematic technique, as well as his love of aping different generic styles, but it is unlikely that these variations were ever shot. The version of the sketch that appears in the film is firmly set among the middle classes but is tightly edited and uses some effective close-ups.

Most of Brunel's ideas for engaging with cinematic tropes were dropped or compromised, and his own appearances as director were written out. The elaborate montage of the studio had to be curtailed, since there was little activity over the festive period, although the thirty seconds or so of studio shots that do appear early in the film are very dynamic and make dramatic use of shadows and silhouettes. Despite the detailed notes Brunel passed to Emile de Ruelle, BIP's supervising editor, and his assistant A. C. Hammond, the elaborate editing plans were largely ignored, sacrificed to the speedy assemblage demanded by the studio. Between 20 January and early February, Brunel was waiting to be summoned to Elstree to view and comment on the edit; yet the next thing he knew, the trade show had been announced and he was not even invited (though BIP claimed this was an oversight rather than a deliberate snub). News of Hitchcock's involvement reached Brunel at the same time, and he was particularly upset about the review of the film in *The Cinema*, which suggested that he had been under the younger director's supervision.

Kerzoncuf and Barr assert that Brunel 'plainly and understandably saw this as an act of betrayal by an old associate' (93), but he may well have filed it under his general rejection by the industry and he seems to have maintained reasonably cordial, if distant, relations with Hitchcock during the 1930s. In fact, Brunel put the blame for his ill treatment firmly onto BIP's general manager, J. A. Thorpe, and wrote a long letter to studio head John Maxwell on 16 February 1930 outlining his grievances and concluding: 'the result of Mr Thorpe's action has not only been damaging to the film but damaging to myself, to say nothing of its discourtesy' (ABSC 5/153). In his interview for the British Entertainment History Project, Sidney Gilliat asserts that Thorpe was disliked by many at the studio for his philistinism, though interestingly he also asserts that Thorpe had been instrumental in getting Hitchcock a job at BIP.

Thorpe appears to be yet another 'vulgar' trade figure of the type that Brunel had come up against throughout his career, and the bitter experience he had over *Elstree Calling* continued to rankle. In a letter to theatrical agent Dan Fish on 26 October 1931, Brunel described the film as 'that classic sacrifice at the altar of the great god Thorpe' and confessed he had never seen it, since 'the editor warned me that it would break my heart to see what they did with it!' (ABSC F/170). Had Brunel shot *Elstree Calling* simply and cheaply, he may have found himself a niche at BIP but he was still eager to prove himself an innovative and creative director. The studio conceived of *Elstree Calling* as a straightforward revue, perhaps feeling that the novelty of sound and the striking stencil-coloured musical sequences were innovation enough. If Brunel had had his way, the film could have been an interesting experiment in intermediality, bringing theatrical performances to cinema audiences and exploring the notion of television and radio delivering entertainment into the home in an original and creative way. However, despite a few glimpses of Brunel's artistic vision, such as the studio shots and the eye-catching presentation of the Three Eddies number ''Tain't No Sin (To Dance Around in Your Bones)', it serves as little more than a record of popular musical theatre stars and another symbol of his declining status.

Brunel's letters indicate his growing dissatisfaction with the British industry: 'I still hanker after Hollywood and am more convinced than ever that the best day's work I shall ever do is when I pack up and shake off the grime of Wardour Street,' he wrote to a friend (11 March 1931, ABSC C/170). Thus he entered the 1930s under a larger cloud than the one hanging over him for much of the previous decade. Severely in debt and with few in the industry willing to employ him, his correspondence took on a more desperate quality. He wrote to Harold Boxall:

> Having been out of work for so long, all the time eating my heart out with jealousies and bitterness, getting more desperately hard up each day and never knowing where my next week's money was coming from and often not getting it, my nervous system is in need of fresh air. (26 April 1931, ABSC 9/112)

As he had done in the bleak period after *The Man Without Desire*, he reached out to former colleagues, keeping up a regular correspondence with Balcon and others at Gainsborough throughout 1931, reminding them of his past successes and conjecturing about his failures. He turned down quota productions in favour of better opportunities, none of which materialised. He agreed to take on a project that came via Gainsborough to make a promotional film for omnibuses, conceding: 'I am not keen to do commercial films but I would rather do them than cheap Quota junk' (ibid.). Yet again, this assignment fell through.

Though Gainsborough had little sympathy after his legal action, he continued to petition for directing work, until an encounter with Simon Rowson near the end of 1931. Brunel recorded that Rowson summed up the company's refusal to employ him with the judgement that: 'I was not fit to make pictures . . . I hadn't the temperament' (2 November 1931, ABSC 9/112). Brunel was incensed by this damning indictment of his talents but realised that his career at the studio was over. Angus MacPhail, one of his Dansey Yard trainees, worked in the scenario department at Gainsborough and helped Brunel when he could, reading his story submissions and passing him bits of writing work. In early 1932, he took a cast of British actors to Rome to dub Italian film *La Wally* (Guido Brignone) into English. But these disparate assignments were not enough to sustain him and he had little choice but to go where the work was, in quota production.

Quota Quickies

Quota quickies were low-budget features made to fill the quota of British films that cinemas were obliged to show by the Cinematograph Films Act of 1927. What had begun as a genuine attempt to encourage British film production had become an excuse for producers to fund cheap, quickly made films which were guaranteed a release with little need for promotion. While Steve Chibnall (2007) has done much to rehabilitate their reputation, Brunel's view of the quickie is clear from his choice of the title 'Slumming It' for the chapter in *Nice Work* that covers this period of his career. His resolve not to make cheap pictures crumbled under economic necessity but he threw himself into the task with his usual fervour, despite feeling dejected at the degree to which his career had declined. Quota production was a section of the industry in which several young filmmakers learned their craft (most notably Michael Powell) but was also where many established directors worked out their last years. Chibnall's list of the 'jobbing directors' at Elstree reads like a *Who's Who* of pioneers and innovators of the silent period: Adrian Brunel, George Pearson, George Cooper, Henry Edwards and Sidney Morgan (2007: 68). However, Brunel still had supporters in the trade press and an article about him in *To-Day's Cinema* suggested that quota production would be enhanced by his participation: 'Just look at some of the appalling hooptedoodle we turn out and call "quota productions" and ask yourself if Brunel could not help doing better than that!' (28 May 1931, ABSC 1/164). It certainly kept him busy throughout the decade and his sparse and varied credits during the 1920s were transformed into an impressively robust, if insalubrious, filmography.

His first assignment came in 1933 making quota quickies for George Smith Enterprises. He directed six in just over a year: *A Taxi to Paradise*, *I'm an Explosive*, *Follow the Lady*, *Little Napoleon*, *The Laughter of Fools*, *Two Wives for Henry* (all 1933) and *Important People* (1934), none of which survives. Having had experience of making films on a shoestring, he proved to be quick and efficient, turning out films within budget and on time. Chibnall describes him as 'among the fastest directors working in British quickie production . . . Brunel . . . pursued a picture's completion like a guided missile' (2007: 36). It must have been some compensation to have a relatively free hand on these productions, a privilege rarely afforded him while directing for Gainsborough. Although Smith was often in the studio during shooting, he was there to assist rather than scrutinise and Brunel's association with him was mutually satisfying.

After seven productions for Smith, Brunel moved to British and Dominions (B&D) where he filmed *Badger's Green* (1934), from a play by R. C. Sherriff, author of *Journey's End*. By all accounts it was a huge success, costing £6,000 to make and taking £60,000 in bookings. A play by a distinguished writer was quite unusual in quota production, yet the success of this film actually put Brunel under greater strain. He expressed his annoyance to Sheriff over the 'appalling stupidity of the people who think that one just waves a wand and on the ... basis of an inane farce one can repeat another Badger's Green' (n.d., ABSC 2/158). Brunel went on to make two more films for B&D, *Cross Currents* (1935) and *Love At Sea* (1936), finishing the second on time despite a fire destroying the studio.

By the end of this period, Brunel felt he had established himself as a 'quickie king ... evolving a technique that showed what could be done when facing fearful odds' (1949: 171) and earning the nickname 'One-shot Brunel' (*Evening Telegraph*, 10 June 1933: 200). Yet he was never reconciled to the comedown of making cheap pictures and finding himself among the kind of uncultured figures he had clashed with during the 1920s, men with 'no judgment or critical faculty, no ability to assess or analyse', as he lamented to Sheriff (n.d., ABSC 2/158).

Figure 8.5 David Horne, Frank Moore and Sebastian Smith in a scene from *Badger's Green*. Source: author's own collection.

Budgets Increase

Brunel next went on to direct some slightly bigger-budget films and was paid £750 by Norman Loudon at Sound City to write a treatment for and direct *Menace* (1934). The sensational plot revolves around an explosives expert so traumatised by shelling during the First World War that excessive noise compels him to blow up trains. This melodramatic premise obviously gave the film an appeal to foreign markets as it was released in America under the title *Without Warning* and in Mexico as *El Rayo Demoledor*. Brunel was then contracted to a co-production by Argyle Talking Pictures and Butcher's, being paid £650 for his services, which included 'scenario, dialogue, preparation, direction and supervision of editing' (3 December 1934, ABSC 3.4/160). Initially entitled *Pageant of Variety* it was released as *Variety* and contrasted historic theatrical acts with modern ones in its story of a family of music-hall proprietors. While the film has not survived, sections of it were used in a later Butcher's release, *Cavalcade of Variety* (1940), which incorporated acts from three different films. While this was a lower-budget production than *Elstree Calling*, Brunel's level of control was greater and his sections of *Cavalcade of Variety* stand out as exhibiting a range of set-ups and some imaginative techniques, such as showing dancers silhouetted in the foreground.

Producer Paul Soskin brought him in to salvage *While Parents Sleep* (1935), a light comedy based on a successful play which had been started by Austrian émigré Frederick Zelnick. Despite having to rewrite and recast the film as he went along, Brunel managed to turn it into a fairly entertaining drawing-room piece. It is one of his few surviving quota films and, although its low budget is apparent, it earned some good reviews, such as the one in *Film Pictorial*: 'To those filmgoers who are constantly moaning about the "sameness" of British comedies, this film will be something of an eye-opener. The story starts off with plenty of laughter and will keep you chuckling most of the way' (15 February 1936, ABSC 177).

Spiegel and Keaton

In September 1934 Brunel was taken on by Sam Spiegel to make *The Invader*, designed to revive the flagging career of silent comedy star Buster Keaton. As Brunel later wrote to the producer, the shoot was 'a nightmare neither of us will ever forget' (30 July 1952, ABSC Spiegel/207) but worse was to follow. After Brunel and his editor Daniel Birt presented their cut, Spiegel wrote to say 'the film has not lived up to my expectations' (10 January 1935, ABSC Spiegel/207). His distribution deal with

Figure 8.6 Mexican lobby card for *Menace*. Source: author's own collection.

Gaumont demanded the film should be a six-reeler but Brunel was adamant the script could only support 5,200 feet. Spiegel brought in another editor to put back much of what had been deliberately left out and Brunel was so disgusted with the result that he wrote to MGM in January 1936 demanding that his name be removed from the credits. While having his work interfered with in this way was extremely vexing, in addition he was not paid his entire fee for the job, as Spiegel's company went into liquidation soon after. He threatened to take legal action against Spiegel but was urged by a friend not to 'brood over The Invader . . . [it] will be forgotten before your many good jobs of direction' (15 January 1936, ABSC 6/153). However, brooding was something Brunel had ample time for and in 1952 he approached Spiegel yet again to try and recoup the money owed to him.

Butcher's and Korda

By mid-February 1935, Brunel had signed another contract with Butcher's, to direct *The City of Beautiful Nonsense*, a deal brokered by his former colleague Wilfred Noy who was co-producing the film. This time his fee was only £500, presumably because the script had already been written, and the result was deemed 'an altogether pleasing film' (*MFB*, June 1935: 68), though Brunel privately described it to Sherriff as 'certainly nonsense and a far from beautiful treatment' (n.d., ABSC 2/158).

1936 was a quiet year for direction, although several of Brunel's films were released. The Keaton title finally reached the screen, along with another production for George Smith, *Prison Breaker*, based on an Edgar Wallace story and starring James Mason. The comedies *Vanity* and *Love at Sea* also came out. Early in 1937 he began working for producer Alexander Korda. He was commissioned to co-write the script for *The Return of the Scarlet Pimpernel* (Hanns Schwarz 1937) with Korda regular Arthur Wimperis. He was also appointed associate producer on the film but his experience on the floor was frustrating, given that the role involved 'tactfully trying to guide the most inelastic director it has been my lot to encounter' (Brunel 1949: 181). His visits to Denham Studios from January 1937 onwards offered some respite from despondency, though they were interspersed with assignments that he found less edifying, such as addressing Ilford Cine Society, as they distracted from his main focus of securing his industry position.

The payment for his work at London Films would not sustain him for long and he was still bent on directing, even if quota quickies were the only projects available to him. He confided to his diary: 'Perhaps on the whole, since my plans have gone wrong, it is better to be despised for making quickies and to have money, than to have none and be worried as I am' (Diary 1937, Private collection). He continued to pursue various options: Graham Cutts tried to broker him a deal with American producer Joe Rock to make a Billy Bunter film that failed to materialise, while he lost out to Manning Haynes on a George Smith quota comedy, both of which further deepened his gloom. Despite his financial difficulties he continued to frequent venues like The Ivy and the Savoy Grill, where he would encounter industry figures like producer Harry Cohen and directors Hitchcock and Lothar Mendes. This vital networking sometimes led to opportunities, but was just as likely to bring dispiriting revelations, such as writer Charles Bennett's boast of the Hollywood contract he had signed for £200 a week.

In 1938 Mabel Poulton, star of *The Constant Nymph*, wrote to tell Brunel that she had been 'practically engaged to play Liza Doolittle in Shaw's Pygmalion' (1 June 1938, ABSC OP/170) and hoped to secure the role of director for him, but she lost the part to Wendy Hiller. In the meantime, Brunel had been asked by Korda to rescue an abandoned production, a request that must have revived unhappy memories of his two years of toil at Gainsborough. Based on Gogol's short story 'Taras Bulba', the film had been shot in French and English versions, both starring French actor Harry Baur, but neither had reached the screen. Brunel's job was to try and integrate the original footage into a rewritten script and reshoot parts with different actors, including Roger Livesey and newcomer Patricia Roc. Unsurprisingly, the film, entitled *The Rebel Son* (1939), ended up a 'curious and hybrid production' (*MFB*, April 1939: 74) and was neither a critical nor a box office success.

Daniel Birt

His demoralising experience on *The Rebel Son* contributed to 1938 being a year of great despondency for Brunel and he again petitioned Balcon, now at Ealing Studios, for employment. Balcon responded positively, saying 'there is no reason why there should not be writing assignments for you' (3 November 1938, ABSC 4/153), and Brunel replied in a typically mournful tone: 'It's time something good happened to me, for the last six weeks have been the most desperately disappointing in my whole life' (22 November 1938, ABSC 170).

No work for Balcon materialised, but the following year Brunel was approached by Daniel Birt, his editor on *Variety* and *The Invader*, who was now establishing himself as a producer in collaboration with his wife Louise. They had picked up the rights to a play called 'The Young

Person in Pink' and were producing it under the auspices of Butcher's Film Service. Brunel was contracted on 15 June 1939 to work with Louise Birt on the script and direct the film for a fee of £500. Working with a former colleague and a cast that comprised such acting talent as Elizabeth Allan, Enid Stamp Taylor and Basil Radford led Brunel to describe this as 'almost my happiest picture' (1949: 183). Unfortunately, by the time *The Girl Who Forgot* (as it was eventually titled) was ready to trade show in mid-September, the Second World War had broken out and cinemas had closed. Although this was only a brief interruption to film exhibition, its timing was such that it severely affected the film's release.

Brunel had spent the 1930s churning out relatively cheap talkies or salvaging unmarketable productions, and on the surface his career appeared to have taken a nosedive, given the aspirations he harboured at the end of the 1920s. Most of his fellow directors from Gainsborough found themselves in similar circumstances and Hitchcock was the only contemporary whose career had progressed. By the mid-1930s, his former colleagues Michael Balcon and Basil Dean were two of the most powerful men in British cinema, Balcon having cemented his reputation as a canny producer and Dean becoming successful in both producing and directing. Yet neither came to Brunel's assistance, and the conclusion that both agreed with Rowson's assessment that he was 'not fit to make pictures', or at least regarded him as too difficult a personality to employ, cannot be avoided.

Amateur Film

Brunel wrote two books during the decade: *Filmcraft: The Art of Picture Production* in 1933 and *Film Production* in 1936, which earned him a following among amateur filmmakers, a popular hobby by this time. He also wrote occasional articles for the journals *Home Movies and Home Talkies* and *Amateur Cine World*, attended events and gave talks to gatherings of the Institute of Amateur Cinematographers. Acknowledging his contribution, Wimbledon Cine Club named one of their annual awards 'The Brunel Cup' in the 1940s. When compiling advice for amateurs he drew on his own filmmaking experiences, in particular the techniques used for the burlesques, and emphasised the importance of editing. He had also produced his own home movies: *J.C.B./1920*, which recorded the development of his son Christopher from birth to the age of fourteen, and the previously mentioned travel film *The Boy Goes to Biskra*. Apart from some off-cuts held in the BFI National Archive, neither film has survived, but Brunel recalled *J.C.B./1920* as 'not unlike those "Secrets

Figure 8.7 Adrian Brunel awards the Brunel Cup to an amateur filmmaker. Source: author's own collection.

of Nature" films, where you see a plant growing and flowering before your eyes' (1949: 104).

War Again

On 4 September 1939, just after the outbreak of the Second World War, Brunel turned fifty. While his enthusiasm for filmmaking had not waned, he no longer had youth on his side. However, the advent of a second major conflict led Brunel into another phase of his career. Korda had been quick to exploit the threat of war and a feature-length propaganda film about Britain's air force, *The Lion Has Wings*, was already underway. To speed up production, three directors were appointed: Michael Powell, Brian Desmond Hurst and Brunel. Brunel moved out of London, both to be near Pinewood and to escape the bombing, though with little to do on the film he occupied himself with tightening up the script.

Once again, war had interrupted Brunel's career on several fronts. His stage play *Only Yesterday* (based on *Blighty*), which was being performed at London's Intimate Theatre, closed and tour plans were cancelled; further directing work for the Birts was put aside, as was a lecture tour of America. Brunel saw an opportunity to share the expertise in propaganda production he had acquired during the First World War but his letters to the government received polite, dismissive replies. He at last got a brief spell at Michael Balcon's Ealing Studios assisting the company's war efforts by writing and directing two propaganda shorts in the form of fictional narratives: *Food for Thought* and *Salvage with a Smile* (both 1940). A great believer that propaganda was better put over as entertainment, Brunel undoubtedly relished the opportunity to put his talents towards the cause and concocted two neat six-minute films.

Finding himself unemployed, Brunel was compelled to turn to the Cinematograph Trade Benevolent Fund for financial assistance, which helped tide him over until Balcon took him on to work on *Yellow Caesar* (Alberto Cavalcanti 1941), a satirical short presenting the life story of Benito Mussolini. Brunel is credited with 'Additional scenes' and 'Dialogue', although in *Nice Work* he claims to have been 'part-director, part-scriptwriter, part-historian, part-editor, part-dubber' (1949: 189). It has been described as 'probably the most striking of the 30-odd propaganda shorts released by Ealing Studios during WWII' due to its 'creative play with archive footage' (Duguid 2009), which, with its echoes of his own burlesques, strongly suggests Brunel's contribution. Throughout the war, Brunel wrote and submitted various scripts and ideas for propaganda films and, after the conflict, continued to petition for a permanent government film department.

In 1942 Leslie Howard reappeared in Brunel's life. Howard had spent much of the 1930s in Hollywood but returned to Britain to assist with the war effort and was living near Brunel at Beaconsfield. He had recently begun a directing career and offered Brunel the position of Production Consultant on *The First of the Few* (1942), which brought Brunel back into contact with C. M. Woolf, who was involved (uncredited) on the production side. Brunel was to manage the second unit, one of his main contributions being a montage of aircraft manufacture edited to music. He put considerable time and thought into the project, only to find his editing plans ignored once again and the sequence drastically cut. Memos from the production suggest Brunel's appointment to the project may have been somewhat begrudging and that Howard anticipated conflict. 'I was warned not to be assertive or argumentative,' Brunel wrote to production manager Phil C. Samuel: 'I have therefore scrupulously refrained from pressing any suggestions of mine' (BFIRL cuttings).

Following this, Derrick de Marney, one of the stars of *The First of the Few*, invited Brunel to direct *The Gentle Sex* (1943), a film about the ATS, backed by Filippo del Giudice. In a demoralising turn of events, Brunel was asked to resign from the film and Howard took over, with Brunel relegated once again to Production Consultant. His hopes of continuing the collaboration with Howard were dashed when Howard's plane was shot down by the Nazis on the way home from Lisbon in June 1943.

The same year, the BBC commissioned Brunel to write a radio play about Thomas Paine, a figure he had a long-standing interest in, but the project never saw the light of day.[3] While the episode is accorded only a passing mention in *Nice Work*, it was clearly an important project to Brunel and he argued with his close friend at the Corporation, Walter Rilla, over the decision to shelve it. Further indignity ensued when Gabriel Pascal asked him to act as a stand-in for Claude Rains during the final shooting on *Caesar and Cleopatra* (1945). Brunel swallowed his pride and took the job, but drew the line when asked to travel to Egypt to complete location filming.

Throughout this period he kept up a correspondence with George Elvin, General Secretary of the Association of Cine-Technicians (ACT), regarding his membership of the Feature Directors and Associate Producers Committee. His campaign to remain a member, despite not having directed a feature since 1939, lasted three years, Elvin gamely continuing to engage in the debate long past the point that most would have given up. Brunel rather wryly explained why he had not directed for so long, writing: 'Although I might have been well enough . . . to undertake the pleasant and comparatively unarduous task of directing, I was in no condition to undertake the unpleasant and strenuous task of getting a job as Director' (7 June 1945, ABSC 7/153). Elvin was respectful yet firm, dismissing Brunel's suspicions of a conspiracy:

> no-one in A.C.T., or indeed the British Film Industry, would want to do anything to discredit the magnificent contribution you have made to British films. I can assure you the decision is merely an operation of rule and is in no way a get together to exclude you, as an individual, from the section. (12 May 1947, ABSC 7/153)

Postwar Enterprises

Throughout the late 1940s and early 1950s, Brunel continued to generate ideas. In 1946 he and Christopher started up a company called Pocket Cinemas Ltd to 'promote and operate 16mm cinemas, mobile and/or static' (7 January 1950, ABSC 9/56). They also considered the production of educational films, putting forward the idea for a series called 'The Children's Magazine', described as 'special one-reelers of value

---

[3] Brunel accumulated the largest collection in Europe of books and pamphlets on Paine, which is now housed at the Working Class Movement Library in Salford.

in entertainment and education' (13 March 1950, ABSC 'shadowettes' folder/172). During the early 1950s, Brunel corresponded with Mary Field, Executive Officer of The Children's Film Foundation, regarding a revival of the 'living shadowettes' that Atlas-Biocraft had released in 1923. Once again, Brunel attempted to recycle past successes and reintroduce them via new media; he pitched the shadowettes yet again, this time for television through Overland, a company he had set up with Anthony Bartley, husband of Deborah Kerr. In 1951 he directed a television pilot called *Jack Sterling – White Hunter* for Overland but it was never shown.

Despite the lack of film projects, Brunel kept busy. His play *Waifs that Stray* was staged at the New Lindsey Theatre in April 1947. The critics were not kind to it but it apparently did reasonable box office. His collection is crammed with notebooks and letters from this period proposing ideas for film productions, articles and stories, inviting him to address conferences and discussing a variety of pursuits. Brunel's final credit to see the light of day was a BBC radio broadcast of his 1914 play *Till Tomorrow* on 22 September 1948. He became a regular radio contributor, appearing in the BBC series *Film Time* hosted by Peter Noble, as well as *Woman's Hour* and *Town and Country*. He also published a series of 'broadsheets', decorative printed educational posters covering a wide range of subjects from English monarchs to salad ingredients.

Endings

Adrian Brunel died on 18 February 1958 at his home in Gerrards Cross at the age of sixty-eight. Irene Brunel outlived her husband by nearly thirty years, dying aged ninety-five in March 1987. Christopher died two years later, on 27 April 1989 at sixty-eight, and *The Independent* marked his passing with a tribute by Peter Cotes, brother of Roy and John Boulting and a close friend of the Brunel family. Cotes devoted much of the obituary to his memories of Adrian Brunel, writing that, during the difficult period for the British film industry between the two wars, 'many bad practices were combated, some even swept away [which] was in no small measure due to such people as Adrian Brunel and Ivor Montagu' (Cotes 1989).

Conclusion

The two biographical chapters of this book have provided a perspective on Brunel and his career which fills many gaps in his own autobiography and gives a more comprehensive view of his work and career. They illustrate the multifaceted nature of his pursuits; while his filmmaking career was the main focus of his energy, it was only one of many outlets through which he fulfilled his creative impulses, and his paper collection is full of stories, articles and ideas in various stages of development. To some degree, this ability to diversify, both within the film industry and beyond, was necessary for his survival in the uncertain environment of British cinema and applies to many of his contemporaries. As he observed in the preface to his memoirs, his 'varied experiences in filmland . . . may have reflected an outline history of British film production during the last thirty years' (1949). His career reveals that the limitations and vagaries of the British film industry of the 1920s continued into subsequent decades, and the lack of vision that he deplored among producers persisted. By the time the industry began to pick up and British cinema hit on successful formulae such as the music-hall comedies and Alexander Korda's historical dramas, it was too late for Brunel to resume mainstream directing work.

The curtailment of his career must be partly attributed to the way he conducted his relationships and the biography gives an insight into his personality; while Geoff Brown's 'satirical jester' is undoubtedly in there, it is only one element of a complex character. Robert Murphy's description of Brunel's career contains much of the vocabulary often associated with it: 'disappointment', 'setbacks', 'resilience' and 'resourcefulness' sum up the main themes of his working life as depicted in his autobiography. However, his correspondence reveals a different side of his character, and one could add 'bitterness', 'frustration', 'desperation' and 'paranoia' to the list.

This biographical summary is not exhaustive but provides both a backdrop and a complement to the detailed study of Brunel's filmmaking activities during the silent period undertaken in this book, pointing up the interests, preoccupations, ambitions and personal traits that influenced the choices he made. It highlights some of the threads running through his career: his pursuit of originality in all his projects, regardless of budget or scale; his recycling, reinventing and reimagining of ideas and techniques; and his enduring interest and participation in debates about film in its many forms. In both his filmmaking and other arenas, his humour is ever-present, while his fascination with representing the social, industrial or technological aspects of cinema through his work is also evident.

As a chronological record of his many pursuits, interspersed with his personal ups and downs, it is hoped that it will contribute to a better understanding of his career and the legacy he leaves behind.

CONCLUSION

Brunel's Legacy

On 8 February 1957, Adrian Brunel attended a screening of his 1923 film *The Man Without Desire* at the British Film Institute's National Film Theatre, as part of its celebration of sixty years of cinema. It was the only British film among the programme of postwar silent titles, which included works by Film Society favourites Marcel l'Herbier, Carl Dreyer, Victor Sjöström and Fritz Lang. In fact, the accompanying blurb asserts that Brunel's film 'stands comparison with the remarkable contemporary decors of the German cinema' (National Film Theatre brochure, November 1956–February 1957: 23), suggesting that silent film should be appreciated above all for its European art credentials. The print shown had been restored especially for the event by the technical team at the National Film Archive under Brunel's personal supervision. The evening was reportedly a great success; Brunel had many requests for his autograph and independent distributor Contemporary Films expressed an interest in acquiring the theatrical rights to the feature.

Brunel was now sixty-seven years old and had just over a year of life left. It was twenty-eight years since he had received the *Film Weekly* award for *The Constant Nymph* and he had not directed another successful A-picture in that time. Whether the attention he received at the BFI that evening brought him comfort in the knowledge that his work was still appreciated, or dejection at the thought of the years he had spent in the wilderness, is impossible to know.

Past Faults

At the beginning of the sound period, Brunel had spent a great deal of time reflecting on the reasons for his rejection by the major British studios. By 1931, with his health suffering, he lamented that 'every possible symptom of a nervous breakdown is afflicting me' (22 July 1931, ABSC 9/112). He tried to pinpoint where his career had gone wrong. 'I've been trying to

Figure C.1 Adrian Brunel towards the end of his life.
Source: author's own collection.

discover my past faults,' he wrote to Balcon, 'so that I might correct any bad impressions I may have left with Gainsborough' (23 February 1931, ABSC 9/112). His legal action against the studio was undoubtedly one of these 'faults' and he later conceded that it was 'the greatest mistake in my life' (1949: 154). Simon Rowson's damning verdict that Brunel's temperament made him unfit to be a film director sealed his fate and it was clear from Balcon's replies that certain figures in the company did not want him anywhere near the studio floor.

The industry remained largely uninterested in Brunel's ideas about filmmaking and he continued to detect 'a definite antagonism to the educated worker and the creative artist' (16 February 1931, ABSC 170). Indeed, he was not the only Film Society founder whose ideals had been undermined by the state of the industry. *Evening Standard* critic Walter Mycroft had taken a job at Elstree in 1927 where he 'had to suborn any loose aesthetic ideas to the practical imperatives of producing films . . . that would make a profit' (Porter 2006: xv). According to Brunel, Ivor Montagu had 'retired in disgust from our picture production business, as he regards the fight too uneven' (16 February 1931, ABSC 170). Brunel had to accept that his efforts to influence British cinema would now never succeed and he too withdrew from the fray, moving into the production of the quota quickies he so disdained. However, although his career failed, in the sense that he never secured a high-profile studio appointment where he could truly indulge his creativity, there are positive ways to assess his legacy.

Brunel and 1920s Revisionism

Christine Gledhill has analysed the ways British filmmakers adapted literary, pictorial and theatrical modes to the screen in pursuit of a national mode of cinematic expression. However, this reliance on traditional forms was something that Brunel was keen to distance himself from. He believed that British films should be developed along more original and innovative lines and his direction of travel, with one or two deviations, was away from existing cultural models, which he regarded as hampering a creative approach. He devoted his efforts to an exploration of how to utilise the attributes of the medium itself, employing the narrative power of the camera to communicate ideas through visual cues and using the potential of editing to offer new interpretations of the image. While some revisionist studies have linked Brunel to the avant-garde, he was neither truly experimental nor an 'art' director but sought to blend his conception of cinematic art with commercial entertainment.

Rachael Low described Brunel as being 'in the forefront of the movement towards film art' (1971: 170), yet expressed surprise that his films did not exhibit more overt signs of this interest in artistic developments. She clearly considered European art films as the natural source of inspiration for a British director attempting to raise his work above the level of 'good little pictures' and Brunel's involvement with the Film Society naturally fuels the perception that his aesthetic interests lay in that direction. Yet Brunel also absorbed ideas from his collaborators and from other British directors, in particular George Pearson. Ivor Montagu named Pearson as 'the climax, the last example of films that were very "English" and had a feeling' (Wollen, Lovell and Rohdie 1972: 80). Brunel's use of pictorialism in *The Man Without Desire* and his debt to Pearson's narrative approach both in that film and in *Blighty* indicate that his work brought together what he saw as the best of American, European and British cinema, while also injecting his own humour and original ideas.

During the early 1920s, the vocabulary to describe the way Brunel was thinking about film did not yet exist. Vincent Porter suggests its gradual development in Britain may well have sprung from the gatherings of the Film Society founders, quoting Mycroft's use of the word 'filmatics' in 1926 as an example of a term which may well have been generated by their discussions (2002: 76). This soon evolved into the word 'cinematic', which, according to the *Oxford English Dictionary*, first appeared in print in Britain in 1927. By the end of the decade it was being used regularly in magazines such as *Film Weekly* and helped describe the kind of approach Brunel had been advocating and practising for some time. Roy Perkins and Martin Stollery also credit Brunel with being one of the first to introduce into his industry writings the distinction between 'cutting' film as an artisanal practice and 'editing' as a creative intervention.

The correspondence contained in the Adrian Brunel Special Collection at the BFI provides an alternative perspective on his career to the one presented in his autobiography and offers a clearer picture of the reasons for its ultimate failure. It tempers Gledhill's depiction of Brunel as part of a 'group of free-wheeling film-makers' having fun on the fringes of the industry (2003: 170) and reveals that he was subject to frequent bouts of depression and ill health brought on by his precarious economic situation. 'The life of a director . . .' he told *Motion Picture Studio*, 'is a long succession of homeopathic doses of lunacy' (14 October 1922: 7), a restorative which presumably helped him endure the trying times in between, but did not eliminate their effects. While Sexton's exploration of Brunel's burlesques offers valuable insights into Britain's alternative film culture, his claims for him as a purveyor of scathing attacks on the British film industry are surely overstated. While the earlier examples were a way of testing out his theories of editing, the later burlesques are affectionate satires which offered 'homeopathy' of a different kind, allowing Brunel to air his frustrations with the business he was addicted to.

Reappraisal of Brunel's work had actually begun long before Low's book on the 1920s was published in 1971. At the time of the BFI screening of *The Man Without Desire*, Brunel's burlesque *Crossing the Great Sagrada* was widely available in the form of 16mm prints hired through the film society circuit, inspiring a glowing review in *The Film User* which dubbed it the 'reductio ad absurdum of the travel film' (June 1953: 323). While Sexton suggests that Brunel's burlesques had previously been omitted from the critical appraisal of alternative film culture, they were considered experimental as early as 1949, when *Crossing the Great Sagrada* was exhibited as part of a festival of avant-garde work, while in the 1960s it was described as 'abstract' in the Contemporary Films catalogue.

Brunel himself was undoubtedly responsible for generating some of the interest his films received later in his life; he had contacts in many spheres and was constantly engaged in promoting his own work and proposing ideas for projects. Rachael Low recounted that he was a frequent visitor when she was writing her survey of British cinema, petitioning her in order to ensure his own inclusion (author's correspondence with Christine Gledhill, 21 July 2021). However, interest in his work did not abate after his death. On 8 August 1962, the BFI resurrected *Blighty* as part of a season of films about the First World War. Speeches were given by Ivor Montagu, Sir Michael Balcon and Godfrey Winn, who later reflected that 'the picture was so sensitively directed by Adrian Brunel that it has withstood to a remarkable degree the erosion of Time and changing tastes' (1967: 226). In the 1980s, the discovery of a print of *The Constant Nymph*, long believed lost, led to another BFI screening, this time with Mabel Poulton in attendance. The screening prompted Kevin Brownlow (who had brought the film back to light) to moderate his previously damning view of British silent films, conceding that it was 'quite absorbing' (Brownlow's private collection, 15 May 1985).

Brunel and his Collaborators

While acknowledging Brunel's creative vision, it is also important to recognise the collaborative nature of his filmmaking. The degree to which he can be credited with the 'authorship' of his films varies considerably, and the contributions of other figures are key to their effect. *The Man Without Desire* benefited from the creative input of three unconventional personalities in the shape of designer Hugo Rumbold, writer Monckton Hoffe and actor Ivor Novello, as well as the work of the German studio technicians, all co-ordinated by Brunel to make a highly unusual and original film. Yet the production was also made under the watchful eye of the financier, who stepped in at certain points to curb some of the excesses of these characters.

By the time he made the burlesques, Brunel had gathered round him a group of co-workers more in tune with his own irreverent, light-hearted approach and, although he claimed credit for writing, directing and editing the films, his 'trainees' undoubtedly lent much to the creative process. In contrast, his third Gainsborough feature, *The Constant Nymph*, saw Brunel forced into a working relationship with theatrical director Basil Dean. Despite the tension between them, the result was the film in Brunel's filmography that came closest to achieving his twin aims of popularity and aesthetic value. His subsequent productions for the studio found him in a much less favourable position and, without the support of sympathetic, like-minded co-creators, he struggled to achieve the same results.

Perhaps Brunel's most important collaborator, and one who received virtually no credit for their contribution to his work, was his wife Irene. She was an actress in her own right and as well as appearing in at least two of her husband's films, *The Cost of a Kiss* and *The Man Without Desire*, she had a career outside his work. According to her obituary in the *Telegraph* (written by family friend Peter Cotes), she 'played a key role as an assistant at Minerva Films . . . and the Film Society . . . [and] would display the vision and energy of a highly efficient secretary' (BFIRL cuttings). On top of that, she must have possessed an enormous amount of patience and resilience to keep the family afloat through frequent periods of difficulty and debt, as well as dealing with her husband's regular descents into depression and ill health. In fact, Brunel dedicates his memoirs to 'Babs . . . who has had more than her share of the work and less than her share of the fun'.

Their son Christopher was another staunch supporter and occasional partner in Brunel's enterprises. He followed his father into the film

Figure C.2 Adrian and Irene Brunel. Source: author's own collection.

business, joining the Army Kinematograph Unit during the Second World War, where he became an accomplished editor. After demobilisation, he and his father set up a company to distribute 16mm films for educational purposes, an endeavour that seems to have had little success. Christopher then got an editing job at National Screen Service (NSS), the principal company responsible for making trailers and other promotional material for distributors in Britain. In the 1960s he worked in the company's 'Special Production Department', where he deployed his father's tactic of drumming up business through profuse letter writing. On occasion, these letters were addressed to figures who had benefited from Adrian Brunel's patronage, yet their indebtedness to his father did not seem to make them more receptive to Christopher's approaches. The collection held by the Kent Museum of the Moving Image contains missives from him to Leigh Aman (Brunel's assistant director on *The Invader*) at Woodfall and Ian Dalrymple at Wessex Film Distributors, both of which received polite rejections. He remained with NSS until the mid-1980s, when he was made redundant, and he then did occasional film production work in the few years before his death.

Christopher also inherited his father's firm left-wing views, if anything becoming more militant than Adrian had been. In 1958 he was involved in a campaign led by jazz musician Johnnie Dankworth against the race riots, drumming up support for the cause from friends and colleagues. He was a committed member of technicians' union the Association of Cinematograph, Television and Allied Technicians (ACTT, formerly ACT) for much of his life, receiving a special award in 1989 for his work in film services and the union. He was an accomplished photographer and wrote articles on filmmaking, mainly from a technical or legislative angle.

Brunel's Industry Legacy

Brunel's informal film education programme is perhaps his major legacy to British cinema. Most of its graduates went on to play key roles in the creation of what Brunel was convinced would one day emerge: original and typically British films that found success both at home and abroad. Montagu regarded this coaching of young aspirants eager to get into the business to be his most important contribution:

> The number of young men who passed ... through this schooling, learning from Adrian Brunel not only the rudiments of their craft but his infectious love for it, to make their own mark on the film production of the thirties and forties, is

quite extraordinary: Henry Harris, Reggie Beck, Lionel Rich, 'Jock' Orton, Ivor Montagu, Angus McPhail, Sergei Nolbandov, Frank Wells, Ian Dalrymple, Michael Hankinson. (BFIRL cuttings)

Brunel's humour, inquiring mind and assiduous attention to detail were surely part of his bequest to these figures and surfaced in their contributions to British cinema in the coming decades. J. O. C. Orton went on to write screenplays for the popular comedies of Will Hay and Arthur Askey in the 1930s and 1940s, and Angus MacPhail and Sergei Nolbandov became central figures at Balcon's Ealing Studios. Ian Dalrymple built a reputation as an editor and writer, headed up the Crown Film Unit during the Second World War and became a successful producer in the 1950s. Frank Wells, son of H. G. Wells and a business partner in Brunel & Montagu, worked in art direction and production. All had come up through Brunel's cutting rooms in Dansey Yard, where they gained an excellent grounding in film assemblage that earned them entry into the industry.

Amateur versus Professional

Perhaps encouraged by this success, Brunel shared his ideas and knowledge more widely via three manuals: *Filmcraft: The Art of Picture Production* (1933), *Film Production* (1936) and *Film Script: The Technique of Writing for the Screen* (1948). Daniel Gritten's survey of British filmmaking manuals of the late 1920s and 1930s classifies Brunel's industry writings as representing the views of the 'minority film culture' of the period, offering an opposing perspective to manuals written by mainstream industry figures. Gritten asserts that Brunel 'maintained a commitment to the principles of silent cinema: a focus on movement, on montage as opposed to continuity editing, on visual storytelling, on film as art and on film as an international medium' (2008: 271).

In 1931, Brunel's passion for training led to his involvement with an unsuccessful project to establish 'The British Cinematograph Training Studios Ltd' with Sinclair Hill and Arthur Boulting (father of John and Roy Boulting and Peter Cotes). Having failed in this attempt to offer professional instruction, he aligned himself with amateur filmmakers and much of the advice in his three books was aimed at the growing community of hobbyists. He hoped, in vain, that this type of filmmaking, 'untrammelled by commercialism and unhampered by censorship' (1936: 26), would emerge as the source of genuine experimentation in the medium. Through his articles in amateur film magazines he developed close ties with local cine-clubs, where non-professionals showed their films and exchanged ideas. The instruction and encouragement he gave within this nascent area no doubt rewarded him with a level of respect and authority he had largely lost within the film industry proper.

Hard and Bitter Struggles

Despite the skill he showed at quota production, which at least meant regular employment, Brunel was never reconciled to his descent in the directing ranks and continued to ponder on his failure. In a rare moment of seriousness, he confessed:

> I have passed through periods without work – bleak patches of two years and three years, when every time I was on the point of signing a contract some mysterious force intervened and I found myself out on the street again. (*The Era*, 1 January 1936: 25)

He concluded his ruminations with the question: 'How many film workers could tell the same story of hard and bitter struggles against difficult odds?' (ibid.).

The answer is many, some of whom crossed paths, or even swords, with Brunel along the way. Among the figures whose legacy to British cinema is now forgotten or undervalued are once-celebrated directors such as Graham Cutts and Manning Haynes. Cutts was one of the most famous British directors of the 1920s but his reputation has been overshadowed by his association with Alfred Hitchcock, which has led some to ascribe the success of his films to the contribution of his protégé. Yet, as both Gledhill and Barr suggest, Hitchcock undoubtedly learned a great deal from working with Cutts, who made some thoughtful contributions to debates on British film. In 1924 he predicted the demise of the 'empty artificial creations' of the national cinema and called for films to be 'more artistic, more sincere and more allied to reality and life' (1924: 51). Haynes too was regarded as a great talent and was dubbed by *The Bioscope* an 'artist in celluloid' (18 June 1927: 99). His film *Passion Island* was deemed 'entirely novel', *The Bioscope*'s critic boldly proclaiming that his 'imposition of close-up upon long shot is an amazingly effective device which to-morrow will be adopted by the world' (2 June 1927: 21).

There are also those whose imprints have been more firmly erased, such as Harry Hughes and George A. Cooper. Hughes' collaboration with Brunel on the burlesques has been completely forgotten, but he clearly shared a similarly witty and original approach to film. He claimed to have made the first British sound-on-film short, recorded in his diary as an 'epoch-making moment' (*Film Weekly*, 13 May 1929: 7), a tantalising reference that leads the historian to wonder what other insights his journals might have provided. Cooper's 'Quality Film Plays' were praised as 'little dramatic or humorous stories in which the subtlety of detail finds expression' (*MPS*, 2 June 1923: 4) and their success led to a US sale, a rare accolade for British films at the time. Cooper, like Brunel, was taken on by Gainsborough in the mid-1920s but left after two months, frustrated by the lack of a directing project.

A study of these directors could reveal much about the struggle for a more artistic approach to British film in the silent era. Each attempted to strike out in new directions both through their filmmaking and in the ways they thought about cinema. They undoubtedly faced many of the same setbacks and frustrations as Brunel, and an investigation of their careers would no doubt reveal similar tales of 'hard and bitter struggles'.

Final Thoughts

Brunel has been marked out by various academics as a figure who, through his silent films, navigated a path between art and commerce. Laying out the production histories of these films, and the complex processes behind their creation, hopefully brings a greater understanding of how he attempted to steer a course around the obstacles that stood in the way of both his creative and economic objectives. By identifying what Brunel hoped to accomplish and measuring it against what he actually achieved it is possible to consider the degree to which his aspirations were curbed by prevailing conditions within the British film industry.

Adrian Brunel's career, which looked so promising at various points, was ultimately a failure in terms of his own ambitions and aspirations. This was partly attributable to the difficult and unstable conditions that existed within the British film industry, but also to Brunel's own reluctance to compromise his artistic ideals. This led some in the trade to regard him as a highbrow, and his views on the lack of culture of industry bosses undoubtedly did not endear him to them.

The breadth of Brunel's achievements and legacy makes him a worthy subject of study; as something of a misfit within the industry, his trajectory is erratic but that very fact tells us a great deal about the nature of the industry and the ways that figures such as Brunel navigated it. The aim of this book has been not only to shed new light on Brunel's contribution to British cinema but also to increase understanding of the film industry and, to a lesser degree, film culture during the 1920s. Brunel's films are valuable works in their own right, but acquire greater significance when looked at as products of the tussle between art and the market that was taking place in British cinema in the 1920s. Each represented a battle fought on various planes: for freedom from control, for creativity over commerce and for originality over conformity. While Brunel won minor victories over the course of the decade, the powerful producers and distributors, whose interests rarely extended beyond their profits, ultimately won the war.

Bibliography

Amberg, Dr George, *The Film Society Programmes, 1925–1939* (New York: Arno Press, 1972).
Armes, Roy, *A Critical History of British Cinema* (London: Secker & Warburg, 1978).
Baker, Bob, 'Adrian Brunel', *Film Dope*, No. 5, July 1974, p. 41.
Balcon, Michael, *Michael Balcon Presents . . . A Lifetime of Films* (London: Hutchinson & Co., 1969).
Bamford, Kenton, *Distorted Images: British National Identity and Film in the 1920s* (London and New York: I. B. Tauris, 1999).
Barr, Charles, *Ealing Studios* (Berkeley: University of California Press, 1998).
— 'Do We Love Hitchcock?', *Viewfinder*, October 2012, pp. 11–13.
Beaton, Cecil, 'Suggestions for Fancy Dress', *Vogue*, 15 December 1937, pp. 114–16.
Beaver, Frank Eugene, *Dictionary of Film Terms* (New York: Peter Lang Publishing 2007).
Bordwell, David, *The Films of Carl-Theodor Dreyer* (Berkeley and Los Angeles: University of California Press, 1981).
Bottome, Phyllis, *From the Life* (London: Faber and Faber, 1944).
Bradbury, Malcolm, *The Modern British Novel 1878–2001* (London: Penguin, 2001).
Brand, Neil, 'Hello to All This: Music, Memory and Revisiting the Great War', in Hammond, Michael and Williams, Michael (eds), *British Silent Cinema and the Great War* (Basingstoke and New York: Palgrave Macmillan, 2011), pp. 137–44.
Breen, Myles P., 'The Rhetoric of the Short Film', *The Journal of the University Film Association*, Vol. XXX, No. 3, Summer 1978, pp. 3–13.
Brown, Geoff, 'Adrian Brunel', Screenonline. Available at: www.screenonline.org.uk/people/id/446817/ (11 August 2005).
Brown, Simon, *Cecil Hepworth and the Rise of the British Film Industry 1899–1911* (Exeter: University of Exeter Press, 2016).
Brownlow, Kevin, *The Parade's Gone By . . .* (London: Abacus, 1973).
Brunel, Adrian (1920), 'How to Make Dull Films Jolly', *Pictures and Picturegoer*, 3 April 1920, p. 348.
— (1921a), "Enery' Utching Presents – An Essay in Studio Humour', *The Motion Picture Studio*, 11 June 1921, p. 11.
— (1921b), 'The Film Value of Sub-Titles', *Motion Picture Studio*, 30 July 1921.

— (1921c), 'When the Weather's Warm', *The Picturegoer*, September 1921, p. 58.
— (1921d), 'The Uneasy Chair', *The Picturegoer*, October 1921, pp. 17–20.
— (1923), 'The Internationalism of Our Art', *The Motion Picture Studio*, 24 March 1923, p. 12.
— (1924), 'Is Originality Popular?', *Motion Picture Studio*, 5 January 1924, p. 11.
— (1928), 'Experiments in Ultra-Cheap Cinematography', *Close Up*, Vol. III, No. 4, October 1928, pp. 43–6.
— (1929), 'Statement Regarding the Political Significance of the Present Position in the British Film Production Industry', 12 September 1929, Adrian Hope Brunel press cuttings, BFI Reuben Library.
— (1933), *Filmcraft* (London: George Newnes, 1933).
— (1936), *Film Production* (London: George Newnes, 1936).
— (1949), *Nice Work: Thirty Years in British Films* (London: Forbes Robertson, 1949).
Buckell, Gareth, 'Transgressing the Borders', *Filmwaves*, Issue 28 2/2005, pp. 34–9.
Burrows, Jon, *Legitimate Cinema: Theatre Stars in Silent British Films 1908–1918* (Exeter: University of Exeter Press, 2003).
— 'Big Studio Production in the Pre-Quota Years', in Murphy, Robert (ed.), *The British Cinema Book* (London: BFI/Palgrave Macmillan, 2009), pp. 155–62.
Campbell, Russell, *Codename Intelligentsia: The Life and Times of the Honourable Ivor Montagu: Filmmaker, Communist, Spy* (Stroud: The History Press, 2018).
Chibnall, Steve, *Quota Quickies: The Birth of the British 'B' Film* (London: BFI, 2007).
Clayton, Alex, 'Burlesque, Slapstick and the Avant-garde', Presentation at BFI Southbank, September 2010.
Cooper, George A., 'Faith in Ourselves', *The Motion Picture Studio*, 29 December 1923, p. 7.
— 'What George Cooper Thinks', *Kinematograph Weekly*, 10 January 1924, p. 71.
Cotes, Peter, 'Christopher Brunel', *Independent*, 27 April 1989, accessed via Christopher Brunel press cuttings, BFI Reuben Library.
Coward, Noël, *Play Parade* (London: William Heinemann, 1934).
Crew, F. Rupert, 'The Tragedy of a Short Film', *The Motion Picture Studio*, 15 April 1922, p. 8.
Cutts, Graham, 'What Does the Public Want?', *Kinematograph Weekly*, 14 February 1924, pp. 50–1.
Dean, Basil, *Mind's Eye: An Autobiography 1927–1972* (London: Hutchinson & Co., 1973).
Dixon, Bryony, *100 Silent Films* (London: BFI, 2012).
Duguid, Mark, 'Yellow Caesar', BFI Screenonline. Available at: http://www.screenonline.org.uk/film/id/1423861/index.html (12 February 2009).
Everson, William K., 'Theodore Huff Memorial screening notes', 5 November

1973. Available at: https://www.nyu.edu/projects/wke/notes/huff/imagefiles/huff_731105.pdf (accessed 3 June 2010).

Fawcett, A. W. L'Estrange, *Film: Facts and Forecasts* (London: Geoffrey Bles, 1927).

Foss, Kenelm, *The Work of the Film Producer* (London: Standard Art Book Co., 1920).

Gifford, Denis, *The British Film Catalogue 1895–1994* (London and New York: Routledge, 2016).

Gledhill, Christine, 'Wit and the Literate Image: The Adrian Brunel/A. A. Milne Collaborations', in Burton, Alan and Porter, Laraine (eds), *Pimples, Pranks and Pratfalls: British Comedy Before 1930* (Trowbridge: Flicks Books, 2000), pp. 82–8.

— *Reframing British Cinema 1918–1928: Between Passion and Restraint* (London: BFI, 2003).

— 'Play as Experiment in 1920s British Cinema', *Film History*, Vol. 20, 2008, pp. 14–34.

— 'Remembering the War in 1920s British Cinema', in Hammond, Michael and Williams, Michael (eds), *British Silent Cinema and the Great War* (Basingstoke and New York: Palgrave Macmillan, 2011), pp. 94–108.

Gliddon, John, Unpublished autobiography, n.d., BFI Special Collections.

Lord Grantley, 'Silver Spoon', *Sydney Morning Herald*, 6 January 1954, p. 11.

Graves, Robert and Hodge, Alan, *The Long Week-End* (first published 1949) (Harmondsworth: Penguin, 1971).

Gritten, Daniel, '"The Technique of the Talkie": Screenwriting Manuals and the Coming of Sound to British Cinema', *Journal of British Cinema and Television*, November 2008, pp. 262–79.

Hammond, Michael and Williams, Michael, 'Goodbye to All That or Business as Usual? History and Memory of the Great War in British Cinema', in Hammond, Michael and Williams Michael (eds), *British Silent Cinema and the Great War* (Basingstoke and New York: Palgrave Macmillan, 2011), pp. 1–16.

Herring, Robert, *Films of the Year 1927–8* (London: The Studio Limited, 1928).

Higson, Andrew, 'The Heritage Film, British Cinema, and the National Past: *Comin' Thro' The Rye*', in Higson, Andrew (ed.), *Young and Innocent: Cinema and Britain 1896–1930* (Exeter: Exeter University Press, 2002), pp. 26–97.

Hjort, Mette, 'What's So Funny? Reflections on Jokes and Short Films', *P.O.V. A Danish Journal of Film Studies*, No. 9, pp. 81–93.

Houston, Penelope, *Keepers of the Frame* (London: BFI, 1994).

Hunter, I. Q. and Porter, Laraine (eds), *British Comedy Cinema* (Abingdon: Routledge, 2012).

Hutchings, Peter, 'Authorship and British Cinema: The Case of Roy Ward Baker', in Ashby, Justin and Higson, Andrew, *British Cinema, Past and Present* (London and New York: Routledge, 2000), pp. 179–89.

James, David E., *The Most Typical Avant-garde: History and Geography of Minor Cinemas in Los Angeles* (California: University of California Press, 2005).
Kennedy, Margaret, *The Constant Nymph* (first published 1924) (London: Virago, 1990).
Kenworthy, J. M., 'What is Wrong with British Films?', *The Bioscope*, 11 June 1925, p. 16.
Kemp, Philip, 'Not for Peckham: Michael Balcon and Gainsborough's International Trajectory in the 1920s', in Cook, Pam (ed.), *Gainsborough Pictures* (London: Cassell, 1997), pp. 13–30.
Kerzoncuf, Alain and Barr, Charles, *Hitchcock Lost & Found: The Forgotten Films* (Lexington: The University Press of Kentucky, 2015).
Low, Rachael, *The History of the British Film 1906–1914* (London: Allen and Unwin, 1949).
— *The History of the British Film 1914–1918* (London: Allen and Unwin, 1950).
— *The History of the British Film 1918–1929* (London: Allen and Unwin, 1971).
MacDonald, Ian W., 'The Struggle for the Silents: The British screenwriter from 1910 to 1930', *Journal of Media Practice*, Vol. 8, No. 2, 2007, pp. 115–28.
— 'Screenwriting in Britain 1895–1929', in Nelmes, Jill (ed.), *Analysing the Screenplay* (London: Routledge, 2011), pp. 44–68.
Mannock, Patrick L., 'Our Hate Party', *Picturegoer*, October 1927, p. 18.
Marriner, Sheila, 'Cash and Concrete: Liquidity Problems in the Mass Production of "Homes for Heroes"', in Davenport-Hines, R. P. T. (ed.), *Business in the Age of Depression and War* (London: Routledge, 1990), pp. 53–90.
Mayne, Marjorie, 'The New Masters', *Pictures and Picturegoer*, January 1924, pp. 41–4.
McFarlane, Brian, *The Encyclopedia of British Film* (London: Methuen/BFI, 2003).
McKernan, Luke, 'How to make *Ben Hur* Look Like an Epic', in Burton, Alan and Porter, Laraine (eds), *Pimples, Pranks and Pratfalls: British Comedy Before 1930* (Trowbridge: Flicks Books, 2000), pp. 7–9.
Mear, Harry Fowler, 'My Introduction to the Film Industry', *The Motion Picture Studio*, 30 June 1923, p. 11.
Miller, Henry K., *Where We Came In: Minority Film Culture in Britain 1917–1940*, unpublished PhD Thesis, Birkbeck, University of London, 2013.
Montagu, Ivor, 'Adrian Brunel, 1892–1958', *Film and TV Technician*, April 1958, pp. 230–1.
— *The Youngest Son: Autobiographical Sketches* (London: Laurence and Wishart, 1970).
— 'Old Man's Mumble: Reflections on a Semi-centenary', *Sight and Sound*, Vol. 44, No. 4, Autumn 1975, pp. 220–4, 247.
Morley, Sheridan, *A Talent to Amuse: A Biography of Noël Coward* (Harmondsworth: Penguin, 1975).
Morris, Nathalie, *An Eminent British Studio: The Stoll Film Companies and British*

Cinema 1918–1928, unpublished PhD Thesis, University of East Anglia, May 2009.
Morton, H. V., *The Heart of London* (London: Methuen & Co. Ltd, 1925).
Murphy, Robert (ed.), 'Adrian Brunel', *Dictionary of National Biography*. Available at: www.oxforddnb.com/view/article/57303?docPos=1.
Mycroft, Walter C. and Porter, Vincent, *The Time of My Life: The Memoirs of a British Film Producer* (Lanham, MD and Oxford: Scarecrow Press, 2006).
Napper, Lawrence, '*Blighty* and the Continent', Paper given at 'Channel Crossings' Nottingham Silent Cinema Weekend, 8 April 2006.
—— *British Cinema and Middlebrow Culture in the Interwar Years* (Exeter: University of Exeter, 2009).
—— 'Remembrance, Re-membering and Recollection: Walter Summers and the British War Films of the 1920s', in Hammond, Michael and Williams, Michael (eds), *British Silent Cinema and the Great War* (Basingstoke and New York: Palgrave Macmillan, 2011), pp. 109–17.
—— *The Great War in Popular British Cinema of the 1920s* (Basingstoke and New York: Palgrave Macmillan, 2015).
Nicholson, Virginia, *Singled Out: How Two Million Women Survived Without Men After the First World War* (London: Penguin, 2008).
O'Pray, Michael, 'The British Avant-Garde Film in the Twenties and Thirties', pamphlet accompanying the VHS releases *History of the Avant-Garde: Britain in the Twenties* and *History of the Avant-Garde: Britain in the Thirties* (London: BFI, 2000).
Overy, Richard, *The Morbid Age: Britain and the Crisis of Civilisation, 1919–1939* (London: Penguin, 2010).
Perkins, Roy and Stollery, Martin, *British Film Editors: The Heart of the Movie* (London: BFI, 2008).
Perry, George, *The Great British Picture Show: From the Nineties to the Seventies* (St Albans: Paladin, 1975).
Porter, Laraine, 'From slapstick to satire: British Comedy Cinema Before 1930', in Hunter, I. Q. and Porter, Laraine (eds), *British Comedy Cinema* (Abingdon: Routledge, 2012), pp. 18–37.
Porter, Vincent, 'The Construction of an Anti-Hollywood Film Aesthetic: The Film Criticism of Walter Mycroft in the 1920s', in Burton, Alan and Porter, Laraine (eds), *Crossing the Pond: Anglo-American Film Relations Before 1930* (Trowbridge: Flicks Books, 2002), pp. 72–81.
Raskin, Richard, *The Art of the Short Fiction Film* (Jefferson, NC and London: McFarland & Co., 2002).
Ryall, Tom, *Alfred Hitchcock and the British Cinema* (London: Athlone, 1996).
Sargeant, Amy, *British Cinema: A Critical History* (London: BFI, 2005).
—— 'A Victory and a Defeat as Glorious as a Victory: *The Battles of the Coronel and Falklands Islands* (Walter Summers 1927)', pp. 79–93, in Hammond, Michael and Williams, Michael (eds), *British Silent Cinema and the Great War* (Basingstoke and New York: Palgrave Macmillan, 2011).

Sexton, Jamie, 'Parody on the Fringes: Adrian Brunel, Minority Film Culture and the Art of Deconstruction', in Burton, Alan and Porter, Laraine (eds), *Pimples, Pranks and Pratfalls: British Comedy Before 1930* (Trowbridge: Flicks Books, 2000), pp. 89–95.

—— *Alternative Film Culture in Inter-war Britain* (Exeter: University of Exeter Press, 2008).

Thompson, Kristin, 'Early Alternatives to the Hollywood Mode of Production: Implications for Europe's avant-gardes', in Grieveson, Lee and Krämer, Peter, *The Silent Film Reader* (London and New York: Routledge, 2004), pp. 349–67.

Tourneur, Maurice, 'Meeting the Public Demands', *Shadowland*, May 1920. Available at: http://www.silentera.com/taylorology/issues/Taylor77.txt.

—— 'Tourneur Protests – Motion Pictures Not Art', *Kinematograph Weekly*, 3 January 1924, p. 101.

Townsend, Christopher, '"The Art I Love is the Art of Cowards": Francis Picabia and René Clair's *Entr'acte* and the Politics of Death and Remembrance in France after World War One', *Science as Culture*, Vol. 18, No. 3, September 2009, pp. 281–96.

Turvey, Gerry, 'Enter the Intellectuals: Eliot Stannard, Harold Weston and the Discourse on Cinema and Art', in Burton, Alan and Porter, Laraine (eds), *Scene-Stealing: Sources for British Cinema Before 1930* (Trowbridge: Flicks Books, 2003), pp. 85–93.

Van Damm, Vivian, *Tonight and Every Night* (London: Stanley Paul, 1952).

Vest, James M., 'Alfred Hitchcock's role in *Elstree Calling*', *Hitchcock Annual 2000–2001* (New Hampshire: Hitchcock Annual Corporation, 2000).

Waring, Hubert, 'A Film "Transformation" Factory', *The Bioscope*, 13 November 1924, p. 39.

Welsh, T. A., 'Give Me Leave to Speak My Mind', *Kinematograph Weekly*, 23 June 1927, p. 31.

Wilde, Oscar, *The Picture of Dorian Gray* (first published 1891) (Harmondsworth: Penguin, 1983).

Wilson, Sandy, *Ivor* (London: Michael Joseph, 1975).

Winn, Godfrey, *The Infirm Glory* (London: Michael Joseph, 1967).

Wollen, Peter, Lovell, Alan and Rohdie, Sam, 'Interview with Ivor Montagu', *Screen*, Vol. 13, No. 3, Autumn 1972.

Woolf, Virginia, 'The Cinema' (first published 1926), in Woolf, Virginia, *The Captain's Death Bed and Other Essays* (London: The Hogarth Press, 1981).

Index

Note: *italics* indicates image; n indicates footnote

£5 *Reward* (Brunel, 1920), 54–6, 57, 60
adaptation, 138–44, 174–5, 181;
    see also *Constant Nymph, The*; *Vortex, The*
Alfred, F., 33n5
Algiers, 31, 32
Allan, Elizabeth, 194
Aman, Leigh, 206
Amateur Cine World (journal), 194
amateur filmmaking, 97–8, 194–5, 207–8
American film industry, 3–4, 11, 12, 173
    and avant-garde, 94–5
    and caricatures, 105–6
    and Minerva, 52
    and short films, 48
    and talking pictures, 5
    and Tourneur, 67
    and war films, 126–7
Anna Christie (Wray, 1923), 80
Anstey, F., 61
Arcadians, The (Saville, 1927), 140
Argyle Talking Pictures, 190
Armes, Roy, 12
art, 12, 13, 67–71, 88–9, 202
    and *Blighty*, 131–6, 137
    and *The Constant Nymph*, 159, 162–6, 168, 173–4
    and *The Man Without Desire*, 80–3
    and short films, 50–2

Askey, Arthur, 207
Asquith, Anthony, 9
Association of Cine-Technicians (ACT), 197
Association of Cinematograph, Television and Allied Technicians (ACTT), 206
Atkins, Robert, 182
Atlas-Biocraft Company, 30, 32, 71–4, 76, 88, 91, 198
Aubrey Smith, C., 27, 44, 45, 53
Auction Mart, The (McRae, 1920), 24
Austria, 157, 158, 160, 161–2, 164, 168
auteurism, 10–11
avant-garde, 11, 12, 91, 92–5, 132, 175

Badger's Green (Brunel, 1934), 188–9
Baker, Bob, 6, 12
Baker, Reginald, 38
Balcon, Sir Michael, 6, 8, 13, 33–5, 194
    and adaptations, 138–9
    and *Blighty*, 122, 123, 124, 125, 131, 204
    and 'Brewer Street Pack', 36
    and Brunel, 37, 38, 116, 117–18, 187, 201
    and burlesques, 104
    and *The Constant Nymph*, 1, 40, 156, 157, 158, 162–4, 172
    and Ealing Studios, 193, 196
    and *A Light Woman*, 177–9
    and *The Vortex*, 151

Balcon, Sir Michael (*cont.*)
    and war films, 119
    and *Woman to Woman*, 87–8
Ballet mécanique (Léger, 1924), 94, 99
Bamford, Kenton
    Distorted Images: British National Identity and Film, 6
Banks, Monty, 184
Barrie, J. M., 61
Barrymore, John, 29
Bartley, Anthony, 198
Bass, E. T., 30
Battles of the Coronel and Falkland Islands, The (Summers, 1927), 120
Battleship Potemkin (Eisenstein, 1925), 106–7
Battling Bruisers: Some Boxing Buffoonery (Brunel, 1924), 91, 106–7, 109
Baur, Harry, 193
BBC (British Broadcasting Corporation), 197, 198
Beaton, Cecil, 74
Beaverbrook, Lord, 97
Beggars' Syndicate, The (Brunel, 1921), 28, 42, 63–4, 175
Bennett, Arnold, 61
Bennett, Charles, 193
Benson, Annette, 28, 62
Bentley, Thomas, 119
Bernerd, Jeffrey, 112
Bernstein, Sidney, 121
Betts, John, 47, 106
BFI (British Film Institute), 9, 92, 200
Big Parade, The (Vidor, 1925), 126
Bioscope, The (magazine), 11, 25, 38, 40
    and adaptations, 141–2
    and burlesques, 102, 105, 109
    and *The Constant Nymph*, 156, 157, 165–6
    and Film Society, 35
    and funding, 65
    and Gainsborough, 179
    and Haynes, 208
    and *A Light Woman*, 177
    and *The Man Without Desire*, 31, 85–6
    and New Era, 47–8
    and short films, 62–3
    and Stannard, 50
    and *The Vortex*, 146, 152, 153
BIP *see* British International Pictures
Birt, Daniel, 92, 95, 190, 193–4
Birt, Louise, 193–4
Blackguard, The (Cutts, 1925), 34, 35, 116
Blackwell, Carlyle, 181
Blakeston, Oswell, 92
Blighty (Brunel, 1927), 15, 38, 39, 115, 122–8, 140
    and anti-war sentiment, 136–7
    and art, 131–6
    and BFI reissue, 204
    and Birmingham trade show, 126n5
    and evolution, 128
    and music, 129–30
    and Pearson influence, 202
    and Stannard, 143
    and symbolism, 130–1
Bluebird, The (Tourneur, 1918), 68
Bluebottles (Montagu, 1928), 92
Blunderland of Big Game, The (Brunel, 1925), 91, 110, 113
Boam, H. J., 24–5, 162
Bonzo the Dog (cartoons), 9
Bookworms (Brunel, 1920), 56, 57
Bordwell, David, 10
Bottome, Phyllis, 164
Boulting, Arthur, 207
Boxall, Harold, 124, 177–8, 182, 187
Boy Goes to Biskra, The (Brunel, 1924), 31, 194
Bradbury, Malcolm, 121
Brade, Reginald, 23
Bramlins Agency, 26, 65, 76
Brand, Neil, 119

Breen, Myles P., 43
'Brewer Street Pack', 36
British Actors' Film Company (BAFC), 22–5, 44
British and Colonial Kinematograph Company (B&C), 49–50, 138
British & Dominions (B&D), 188–9
British film industry, 2–6, 199, 208–9
    and Brunel, 72, 201–2
    and burlesques, 92–3
    and quota quickies, 188–9
    and silent film archives, 9–10
    and war films, 119–21, 126–7
British Instructional Films, 27, 47
British International Pictures (BIP), 103, 183–7
British Lion, 140
British National Pictures, 39
British Silent Film Festival, 6
Bromhead, Colonel, 76
Brown, Geoff, 6, 91, 199
Brown, Simon, 118
    Cecil Hepworth and the Rise of the British Film Industry 1899–1911, 10n1
Brownlow, Kevin, 6, 204
Brunel, Adrian, 1–3, 4, 5, 9–15, 192–3, 198–9
    and adaptations, 141, 174–5
    and art, 67, 68, 69–70, 88–9
    and Atlas-Biocraft, 71–2
    and BAFC, 22–5
    and *The Beggars' Syndicate*, 63–4
    and biographical legend, 7–8
    and Birt, 193–4
    and Bramlins, 26
    and burlesques, 32–3, 91–3, 95–7, 98–110, 112–14
    and *The Crooked Billet*, 181–2
    and early life, 16–17
    and *Elstree Calling*, 183–7
    and experimentation, 47
    and Film Society, 35–6
    and friends, 36–9
    and Gainsborough, 33–5, 116–18, 182–3
    and home movies, 194–5
    and legacy, 200–10
    and *A Light Woman*, 177–80
    and Mander, 72–4
    and Minerva, 26–8, 44–6, 52–3, 65–6
    and Mirror Films, 20–1
    and *Moors and Minarets*, 109n5
    and Moss Empire, 19–20
    and post-Second World War, 197–8
    and quota quickies, 188–9
    and revisionist studies, 6–7
    and Second World War, 195–7
    and short films, 42–4, 49, 53–61
    and Solar Films, 28–30
    and Stannard, 143–4
    and *A Temporary Lady*, 61–3, 64–5
    and war films, 121
    see also *Blighty*; *Constant Nymph, The*; *Crossing the Great Sagrada*; *Man Without Desire, The*; *Vortex, The*
Brunel, Christopher (son), 27, 179, 194, 197–8, 205–6
Brunel, Frances Lucy Adelaide (Adey) (mother), 16, 17, *18*, 20, 22
    and *A Light Woman*, 177
    and *The Vortex*, 148
Brunel, Irene ('Babs') (wife), 20, 22, 36, 198, 205
    and *A Light Woman*, 179
    and *The Man Without Desire*, 74
Brunel & Montagu (Brunel, 1929), 183
Brunel & Montagu Ltd, 36, *37*, 178
Buckell, Gareth, 93
budgets, 3, 4, 44, 65, 190
    and *Blighty*, 123, 124
    and *A Light Woman*, 177–8
Bump, The (Brunel, 1920), 53–4, 57, 59, 60

burlesques, 14, 32–3, 34, 91–3, 95–6, 113–14
  and collaborators, 204
  and distribution, 110
  and Gainsborough, 104–10, *111*
  and Hughes, 102–4
  and recycling, 113
  and *Sheer Trickery*, 98–9
  see also *Crossing the Great Sagrada*
Burrows, Jon, 20, 138, 139
Bushey Studios, 22, 53
Butcher's Film Service, 38, 190, 192–4

C. & M. Productions, 110, 112
Cabinet des Dr Caligari, Das (Wiene, 1920), 79
Caesar and Cleopatra (Pascal, 1945), 197
Calthrop, Donald, 184, 185
Cambridge University Kinema Club, 97
Cannibals of the South Seas (Brunel, 1923), 31, 88, 96
Carrodus, Bernard, 45, 57
Carroll, Madeleine, 181
Carroll, Sydney, 173
Carry On! (Shurey, 1927), 140n2
Cavalcade of Variety (Bentley, 1940), 190
Cavalcanti, Alberto, 196
Celli, Faith, *54*
censorship, 15, 107–8, 138, 140, 173
  and *The Constant Nymph*, 156
  and *The Vortex*, 145, 150
Chaplin, Charlie, 94, 99
Chibnall, Steve, 188
Children's Film Foundation, 198
Churchill, Winston, 23
Cinematograph Film Act (Quota Act) (1927), 4–5, 121, 188
Cinematograph Intelligence Bureau, 59
Cinematograph Trade Benevolent Fund, 196

City of Beautiful Nonsense, The (Brunel, 1935), 192
Clair, René, 94, 95, 99
Clarendon Film Company, 17, 22
Clarke, Frederick Charles, 27
Clarke, Sir Rupert, 31
class, 55–6, 67, 68, 122–3
  and *Blighty*, 127, 134
  and *The Vortex*, 145
Clayton, Alex, 94
Close Up (magazine), 113, 175
close-ups, 53, 98, 106–7, 185, 208
  and *The Constant Nymph*, 169, 173
  and *The Vortex*, 145–6, 152
  and war films, 136
COD A Mellow Drama (Richardson et al., 1929), 92
Cohen, Harry, 193
comedy see burlesques; Milne, A. A.
Comradeship (Elvey, 1919), 119, 133
Conan Doyle, Arthur, 105
Confetti (Cutts, 1927), 140n2
Constant Nymph, The (Brunel, 1928), 1, 13, 15, 40, 152, 176
  and adaptation, 140, 156–7, 172–3, 173–4
  and advertisement, *171*
  and art, 162–6
  and BFI screening, 204
  and characterisation, 166–7
  and light to darkness, 167–70
  and plot, 158–9
  and pre-production, 157–8
  and reception, 170, 172, 174–5
  and reputation, 159–60
  and screenplay, 160–2
Cooper, George A., 38, 50–2, 117, 188, 208, 209
Cost of a Kiss, The (Brunel/Mear, 1916), 20–2, 44, 205
Cotes, Peter, 198, 205
Coulon, Johnny, 108
Coward, Noël, 39, 139, 144–7, 151–2, *153*, 155–6

Cox, Jack, 127
Crab Tree Club, 60
Crew, F. Rupert, 47, 50–1
Crooked Billet, The (Brunel, 1929), 181
Cross Currents (Brunel, 1935), 189
Crossing the Great Sagrada (Brunel, 1923), 7–8, 32, 73, 93, 112
  and avant-garde, 92
  and experimentation, 114
  and intertitles, 59
  and making of, 96–7, 99–102
  and reappraisal, 203
  and screening, 104–5
Crown Film Unit, 207
Cserépy, Arzén von, 128
Cut it Out; A Day in the Life of a Censor (Brunel, 1924), 91, 107–8
Cutts, Graham, 8, 9, 36, 39, 87–8
  and *Confetti*, 140n2
  and *The Blackguard*, 34, 35
  and Brunel, 38, 116, 117, 193
  and Hitchcock, 208
  and *The Rat*, 30n4

Dalrymple, Ian, 183, 206, 207
Dankworth, Johnnie, 206
Darley, Bert, 42, 64
Dawe, Tommy, 75
Dean, Basil, 1, 40, 156, 157–8, 159–60, 170, 194, 204
  and adapations, 174
  and Brunel, 163–4
  and poetics, 162
Delius, Frederick, 16
Denham Studios, 192
Destiny (*Die Müde Tod*) (Lang, 1921), 80
Dickens, Charles, 50, 104, 138
distribution, 3–5, 21, 49
  and burlesques, 110, 112
  and *The Man Without Desire*, 30–1, 76
Dixon, Bryony, 47
Dolores (Brunel, 1933), 180

Dr Jekyll and Mr Hyde (Robertson, 1920), 29
Dracula (Stoker), 78
Drew, Sidney, 52, 53
Dreyer, Carl, 200
Dulac, Edmund, 60
Dulac, Germaine, 93, 95
Dyall, Franklin, 147

Ealing Studios, 35, 193, 196, 207
Easy Virtue (Hitchcock, 1928), 139, 140, 144, 146–8
Ebury Studios, 21
editing, 21, 24, 51, 107, 112–13
  and *Blighty*, 39, 125
  and Brunel, 11–12, 72, 116, 203
  and burlesques, 34–5, 36, 96, 98, 100
  and *The Constant Nymph*, 162, 164–6
  and *A Light Woman*, 179–80
  and *The Man Without Desire*, 30, 31, 81, 86
  and *The Vortex*, 146, 152, 155
  see also Brunel & Montagu Ltd
Edwards, Henry, 188
Eisenstein, Sergei, 106–7
Ellis, Vivian, 170
Elstree Calling (Brunel, 1935), 183–7
Elvey, Maurice, 69, 119
Elvin, George, 197
Embassy Theatre (Holborn), 47–8, 50
Emelka Studios, 33, 164
'Eminent British Authors series', 138
Empire Building Corporation Ltd, 26
Entr'acte (Picabia/Clair, 1924), 94, 95, 99
Evans, Fred, 104
Everson, William K., 145–6
Everyday (Richter, 1929), 92
Ewer, Monica, 127

Faculty of Arts, 69–70
Famous Players–Lasky, 61

Fawcett, Arthur Wellesley L'Estrange, 88
Feu Mathias Pascal (Herbier, 1925), 130
Field, Mary, 198
Film Production (Brunel, book), 194, 207
Film Script: The Technique of Writing for the Screen (Brunel, book), 207
Film Society, 4, 12, 35–6, 70
  and Brunel, 116–17, 202
  and burlesques, 93, 94, 109, 112
  and experimentation, 47
  and sporting films, 106
'Film Tags', 22, 43
Filmcraft: The Art of Picture Production (Brunel, book), 194, 207
First National, 39
First of the Few, The (Howard, 1942), 196
First World War, 3, 15, 23, 38–9, 67
  and Brunel, 17, 22, 43
  see also *Vortex, The*; war films
Fish, Dan, 186
Follow the Lady (Brunel, 1933), 188
Food for Thought (Brunel, 1940), 196
Foss, Kenelm, 22, 141
Fowell, Frank, 75
Fraser, Claud Lovat, 60
Fridericus Rex (Cserépy, 1923), 128
Friese-Greene, Claude, 184
Friese-Greene, William, 9
Further Adventures of the Flag Lieutenant, The (Kellino, 1927), 140n2

Gainsborough Studios, 7, 8, 11, 179
  and adaptations, 139, 143–4
  and Brunel, 33–5, 37–8, 116–18, 182–3, 187, 201
  and burlesques, 91, 104–10, *111*
  and *The Constant Nymph*, 1, 157–8, 176
  and *The Crooked Billet*, 181–2
  and Film Society, 36
  and *A Light Woman*, 177–8
  and *The Rat*, 30n4
  see also Balcon, Sir Michael; Piccadilly Pictures
Gance, Abel, 32, 79
Gaumont-British, 33, 179
'Gems of Literature' series, 49–50, 138
General Post, The (Bentley, 1920), 119
Gentle Sex, The (Howard, 1943), 196–7
George Smith Enterprises, 188
German film industry, 3, 4–5, 11, 12, 200
  and Brunel, 29–30, 33–4
  and *The Man Without Desire*, 79–80
  and war films, 119
Gilliat, Sidney, 186
Girl Who Forgot, The (Brunel, 1940), 193–4
Giudice, Filippo del, 196
Gledhill, Christine, 4, 6, 13, 65, 202, 203
  and art, 69
  and burlesques, 93, 99–100, 108
  and *The Man Without Desire*, 83
  and Milne comedies, 59
  'Play as Experiment in 1920s British Cinema', 45
  and theatricality, 172
Gliddon, John, 26
Gobbett, Dave, 164
Golem, Der (Wegener, 1915), 79
Goossens, Eugene, 157, 170
Greenidge, Terence, 97
Greenwood, Edwin, 36, 88
Griffith, D. W., 30, 31, 104, 185
Gritten, Daniel, 207
Guns of Loos, The (Hill, 1928), 119, 136

Hammond, A. C., 186
Handley, Tommy, 184
Harker, Gordon, 181, 185
Harris, Henry, 32, 36, 79, *80*
Harrow School, 17
Harrow Weald Park Estate, 23
Hay, Crispin, 28
Hay, Will, 207
Hayman, Max, 130
Haynes, Manning, 9, 193, 208
Hely, Annesley, 123
Hepworth, Cecil, 104
Herbier, Marcel l', 130, 200
Herkomer, Hubert von, 22
Herring, Robert
  Films of the Year 1927–1928, 175
Higson, Andrew, 139
Hill, Sinclair, 119, 207
Hiller, Wendy, 193
Hindle Wakes (Elvey, 1927), 139
Hitchcock, Alfred, 7, 9, 10, 36, 124n3, 194
  and Brunel, 193
  and burlesques, 110
  and Coward, 144, 146–7
  and Cutts, 208
  and *Elstree Calling*, 184, 185, 186
  and Gainsborough, 38, 39, 117, 118
  and Germany, 33, 34, 35
  and Stannard, 49, 143, 150
Hoffe, Barbara, *55*
Hoffe, Monckton, 30, 75, 79, 141, 204
Hogarth, William, 100
Holmes, Sherlock, 105
Hopton, George, 8, 152, 178
Horne, David, *189*
Howard, Leslie, 26–7, 31, 34, 65, 72
  and £5 *Reward*, 54–6
  and Minerva, 44, 45
  and Second World War, 196–7
  and USA, 61
Hughes, Harry, 8, 102–4, 208–9
Hulbert, Jack, 184, 185
Hulton, Sir Edward, 97

Hume, Benita, *179*, 180
Hunter, T. Hayes, 178
Hurst, Brian Desmond, 195
Hutchings, Peter, 11

Ideal Film Company, 26, 49, 138
I'm an Explosive (Brunel, 1933), 188
Important People (Brunel, 1934), 188
In a Monastery Garden (Brunel, 1928), 181
Ingrams, Rex, 87, 88
International Artists, 29
Invader, The (Brunel, 1936), 190, 192

J'Accuse (Gance, 1919), 79
Jack Sterling – White Hunter (television pilot), 198
Jacobs, Bertram, 26
Jacobs, W. W., 61
James, David E., 93, 94–5
Jazz Singer, The (Crosland, 1927), 182
J.C.B./1920 (Brunel home movie), 194–5
Jeans, Isabel, 147
Jenkins, Herbert, 29
John, Augustus, 60
Jolson, Al, 185

Keaton, Buster, 94, 190, 192
Kelly, Andrew, 119, 120
Kennedy, Margaret, 40, 156, 173, 174
  and screenplay, 159–60, 161–2
Kerr, Deborah, 26, 198
Kershaw, Willette, 150, 151, 152
Kine Weekly (magazine), 32, 85, 88
Kinematograph Weekly (magazine), 51, 59
  and *Blighty*, 130
  and burlesques, 109–10
  and *The Constant Nymph*, *171*
  and *The Crooked Billet*, 182
  and *A Temporary Lady*, 61–2
  and Tourneur, 67–8
  and war films, 121

Kino-Eye (Vertov, 1924), 106
Kirsanoff, Dimitri, 132
Korda, Alexander, 192, 193, 195, 199

Lady Clare, The (Noy, 1919), 23
Lanchester, Elsa, 97
Land of Hope and Glory (Knoles, 1927), 38–9
Lang, Fritz, 200
Lapworth, Charles, 117, 123
Lasky, Jesse, 61
Laughter of Fools, The (Brunel, 1933), 188
Ledoux, Jacques, 93
Léger, Fernand, 94
Leigh, Vivien, 26
Lejeune, C. A., 120
Leni, Paul, 109
Leonard, Benny, 107
Levy, Louis, 170
Leyda, Jay, 93
Life and Death of 9413 – A Hollywood Extra, The (Vorkapich, 1927), 95
Light Woman, A (Brunel, 1928), 177–80
Lion Has Wings, The (Brunel, 1939), 195
Little Damozel, The (Noy), 75n2
Little Napoleon (Brunel, 1933), 188
Livesey, Roger, 193
Lloyd, Harold, 34
Locan, Arthur T., 64
Locke, W. J., 24
Lodger: A Story of the London Fog, The (Hitchcock, 1926), 118, 139, 148, 175
Lomas, H. M., 27, 45, 57
London Independent Film Trading Company, 51
long-shots, 81, 145, 168, 169, 172, 173
Longhi, Pietro, 69, 74, 80–2
Loudon, Norman, 190
Love At Sea (Brunel, 1936), 189, 192
Love, Life and Laughter (Pearson, 1923), 69, 86
Lovers in Araby (Brunel, 1923), 31
Low, Rachael, 3, 5–6, 39, 204
  and adaptations, 139
  and art, 202
  and burlesques, 91, 103–4, 110
  and *The Constant Nymph*, 158
  and short films, 46
Lululaund, 22–3
Lye, Len, 92, 95

MacDonald, Ian W., 150
McEvoy, Charles, 124n2
McFarlane, Brian, 6
McKernan, Luke, 10n1, 91
MacPhail, Angus, 148, 155, 187, 207
  and *The Constant Nymph*, 156–7, 160, 174
  and *The Crooked Billet*, 181, 182
McRae, Duncan, 24
Mademoiselle d'Armentières (Elvey, 1926), 119
Malins, Geoffrey, 26
Malvern, Gerald, 24, 25
Man With a Movie Camera (Vertov, 1929), 107
Man Without Desire, The (Brunel, 1924), 13, 14, 30–2, 68, 74–6, 89–90
  and art, 69, 80–3, 202
  and BFI screening, 200
  and collaborators, 204
  and filming, 72
  and Hughes, 103
  and Irene Brunel, 205
  and literary sources, 77–80
  and plot, 76–7
  and release, 87–8
  and reviews, 85–6, 89
  and structure, 82–5
  and titles, 82–3
Mander, Miles, 28, 29–30, 31–2, 71–4
  and *The Crooked Billet*, 181

and *The Man Without Desire*, 75, 76, 87, 88, 89
and *A Temporary Lady*, 62
Mari, Sergio, 75
Mark of Zorro, The (Niblo, 1920), 29
Marney, Derrick de, 196–7
Mason, James, 192
Matthews, A. E., 22
Maude, Arthur, 119
Maxwell, John, 183
Maxwell, W. B., 142
Mayne, Marjorie, 69, 72
Mear, Harry Fowler, 8, 20–1
Méliès, Georges, 94
Menace (Brunel, 1934), 190, *191*
Mendes, Lothar, 193
Ménilmontant (Kirsanoff, 1926), 132
Merivale, Bernard, 23
Merson, Billy, 29
Mike Murphy as Picture Actor (Aylott, 1914), 104
Mill Wadham, 61, 63
Miller, Henry K., 29, 48, 33n5, 51
Miller, Hugh, 4, 35
Milne, A. A., 11, 42, 45, 65, 141
  and comedies, 27, 29, 52, 53–61
Milton, Beaufoy, 178–9
Minerva Films Limited, 14, 26–8, 44–6, 52–3
  and *The Beggars' Syndicate*, 62–3
  and Milne, 53–61
  and short films, 42–4, 65–6
  and *A Temporary Lady*, 61–2, 63–4
Ministry of Information (MoI), 22, 23, 43, 128
Mirror Films, 20–1
Mons (Summers, 1926), 120
Montagu, Ivor, 9, 34, 35, 36–9, 201–2, 206–7
  and avant-garde, 92, 94
  and *Blighty*, 115, 122, 124, 126, 128, 129, 130, 131–2, 133, 136–7, 204
  and Brunel & Montagu, 183
  and burlesques, 99

and *The Constant Nymph*, 158
and Film Society, 70
and Gainsborough, 116, 118
Moore, Frank, *189*
Moors and Minarets (Brunel, 1921), 28, 29, 31, 88, 96, 100–1, 109n5
Morgan, Sidney, 26, 188
Morton, Michael, 139
Moss Empires, 19–20, 59
Motion Picture Studio (magazine), 8, 26, 51, 71–2, 103
  and *The Man Without Desire*, 76, 77, 86–7
  and war films, 120
Mumsie (Wilcox, 1927), 120–1
Munro, Neil, 142
Murphy, Dudley, 94, 148
Murphy, Robert, 6–7, 10, 199
Mycroft, Walter, 183, 184, 201, 203

Napper, Lawrence, 7, 119, 126, 139, 143
  and *The Constant Nymph*, 159, 164–5, 173, 174
National Screen Service (NSS), 206
Nepean, Edith, 57–8, 125–6
Nettlefold Studios, 103
New Era Films, 47–8
newsreels, 22, 32, 48, 102, 106, 108–9
Nichols, Robert, 161
Nicholson, Virginia, 123
Noble, Peter, 198
Nolbandov, Sergei, 207
Northam, Col W. Arthur, 22
Norway, Carlo, 54n4, 59–60
Nosferatu (Murnau, 1922), 79
Novello, Ivor, 30–1, 140, 157
  and *The Man Without Desire*, 74, 79, *80*, 83–4, 85, 204
  and *The Rat*, 30n4, 88, 89, 109, 117
  and *The Vortex*, 150, 152
Novello-Atlas Renters, 76
Noy, Wilfred, 22, 23, 27, 192

Only Yesterday (Brunel, play), 195
O'Pray, Michael, 91, 92
Orton, J. O. C. (Jock), 35, 110, 116, 207
Ostrer, Maurice, 179
Overy, Richard, 121

Paine, Thomas, 197
Pascal, Gabriel, 197
Passion Island (Haynes, 1927), 208
Pathetic Gazette, The (Brunel, 1924), 32, 102, 109
Patterson, Mary, 64
Paul, Fred, 60
Payne, John Meredith ('Jack'), 23, 25–6, 28, 29, 65
Pearson, George, 5, 9, 62, 66, 202
  and *Love, Life and Laughter*, 69, 86
  and quota quickies, 188
  and *Reveille*, 132
Pember, Clifford, 147–8
Perkins, Roy, 203
Perry, George, 59
Phillips, Bertram, 104
Phillips Film Company, 24–5, 34
Piccadilly Pictures, 38, 123, 124, 125, 130
Picture of Dorian Gray, The (Wilde), 78–9
Pimple as a Cinema Actor (Evans, 1912), 104
Pimple Writes a Cinema Plot (Evans, 1913), 104
Playfair, Nigel, 27, 44, 59
Pleasure Garden, The (Hitchcock, 1925), 33, 35, 110
Polytechnic Cinema, 28
Pommer, Erich, 34, 183
Ponting, Herbert, 73
Poppies of Flanders (Maude, 1927), 119, 136
Porter, Laraine, 91, 98
Porter, Vincent, 202
Poulton, Mabel, 1, 156–7, 170, 193, 204

Powell, Michael, 188, 195
Power, Richard Fitz, 44, 64
Prison Breaker (Brunel, 1936), 192
Prude's Fall, The (Cutts, 1925), 35, 116, 117
Prunella (Tourneur, 1918), 68

Quality Film Plays, 50–2
Queen Was in the Parlour, The (Cutts, 1927), 139
Quinneys (Elvey, 1927), 140

Radford, Basil, 194
Rains, Claude, 197
Raphael, Irene *see* Brunel, Irene
Rat, The (Cutts, 1925), 30n4, 139
'Rat, The' (Novello), 88, 89, 109, 117
Rebel Son, The (Brunel, 1939), 193
Reisz, Karel, 9
Return of the Scarlet Pimpernel, The (Schwarz, 1937), 192
Reveille (Pearson, 1923), 132
Reville, Alma, 156, 160, 173
Rich, Lionel (Tod), 35, 116, 152, 183
Richter, Hans, 92
Rilla, Walter, 197
Roc, Patricia, 193
Rock, Joe, 193
Romance and Rings (Drew, 1919), 52
Rowson, Simon, 49, 187, 194, 201
Ruelle, Emile de, 186
Rumbold, Hugo, 74–5, 204
Ruttman, Walter, 109, 148
Ryall, Tom, 4, 13, 162
  Alfred Hitchcock and the British Cinema, 10

Salvage with a Smile (Brunel, 1940), 196
Sargeant, Amy, 91n1, 98
Saville, Victor, 36, 140
Scaramouche (Ingrams, 1923), 87
Scarlet Woman, The (Greenidge, 1924), 97

screenplays, 15, 20, 23, 71, 140–1, 207
    and *The Constant Nymph*, 160–2, 174, 176
    and *The Crooked Billet*, 181
    and Hitchcock, 143
    and *The Man Without Desire*, 30
    and *The Vortex*, 148, 151
Second World War, 43, 194, 195–7, 207
Sexton, Jamie, 7, 92–3, 95, 106–7, 203
Shakespeare, William, 25, 32, 50, 138
Shaw, George Bernard, 61
Sheer Trickery (Brunel, 1923), 91, 96, 98, 108, 112
Sherriff, R. C., 189, 192
short films, 14, 34, 46–7, 50–2
    and *The Beggars' Syndicate*, 63–4
    and exhibiting, 47–9
    and Milne, 53–61
    and Minerva, 42–4, 65–6
    and profit, 49–50
    and propaganda, 22
    and *A Temporary Lady*, 61–3
    see also burlesques
Sibirskaïa, Nadia, 124, *125*, 132
Sjöström, Victor, 200
Sleeper Awakes, The (Wells), 79
Smith, George, 188, 192, 193
Smith, Percy, 47, 62, 65
Smith, Sam W., 38
So This is Hollywood (In Hollywood with Potash and Perlmutter) (Green, 1924), 107
So This is Jollygood (Brunel, 1924), 91, 105–6, 107, 110, 112, 141
Solar Films, 28–30, 65, 73
Soutar, Andrew, 142
Spain, 177, 178–9, 180
Spiegel, Sam, 190, 192
Sport & Interest in a Fresh Light (Betts, 1926), 106
Sporting Life and What Not to Do But How to Do It (Betts, 1924), 106

Stannard, Eliot, 36, 49–50, 68, 88, 143–4
    and *Blighty*, 124
    and *Easy Virtue*, 147
    and *The Vortex*, 148, 149, 150, 151, 155
Stoker, Bram, 9
Stoll Picture Productions, 47, 138, 139
Stollery, Martin, 203
Summers, Walter, 9, 120
Sutro, John, 97
Sykes, Sir Percy, 28, 100

Tavares, Arthur, 179–81
Taxi to Paradise, A (Brunel, 1933), 188
Taylor, Enid Stamp, 194
Temporary Lady, A (Brunel, 1921), 27, 28, 29, 45, 61–3, 64–5
Tennyson, Alfred Lord, 23
Terriss, Ellaline, 38–9, 123, 124, 130, 133
They Forgot to Read the Directions (Beaverbrook, 1924), 97
This Marriage Business (Hiscott, 1927), 140n2
Thompson, Kristin, 11
Thorpe, J. A., 186
Till Tomorrow (Brunel, play), 198
Titheradge, Dion, 181
Tivoli Theatre (London), 73, 75, 87
To-Day's Cinema (magazine), 182, 188
Too Many Cooks (Brunel, 1921), 27, 62
Tourneur, Maurice, 67–8, 70–1, 87–8
Towler, Harry F., 44
Townsend, Chris, 99
travel films, 28–9, 31, 73, 100–1
Turvey, Gerry, 68
Tusalava (Lye, 1929), 92
Twice Two (Brunel, 1920), 56–7, 60
Two Wives for Henry (Brunel, 1933), 188
Typical Budget, A (Brunel, 1924), 91, 108–10

Ufa, 33–4, 36, 183
Unclean World, The (Hepworth, 1903), 104
Unnatural Life Studies (Hughes, 1924), 102–3
Unseen World, The (scientific series), 104
Usurper, The (McRae, 1919), 24, 25

Valentino, Rudolph, 109
Van Damm, Vivian, 36–7, 75, 87, 97, 104
Vanity (Brunel, 1936), 192
Vanna, Nina, 74, 83
Variety (Brunel, 1934), 190
Vertov, Dziga, 106, 107
Victory (Wetherall, 1928), 140n2
Vidor, King, 126
Vorkapich, Slavko, 95
Vortex, The (Brunel, 1927), 15, 39–40, 144–8, *154*
  and adaptation, 139, 139, 140, 148–50
  and Brunel, 175–6
  and characters, 150–1
  and happy ending, 151–2
  and reception, 152–3, 155
  and Stannard, 144

W. & F., 35, 36, 123, 125
Waifs that Stray (Brunel, play), 198
Wallace, Edgar, 140, 192
Wallis, Bertram, 20, 21
Wally, La (Brignone, 1932), 187
Walsh, Raoul, 126
Waring, Hubert, 96–7
Warren, Dorothy, 75
Waugh, Evelyn, 97
Waxworks, The (Leni, 1924), 109
Wells, Frank, 207

Wells, H. G., 61, 97
  The Sleeper Awakes, 79
Welsh, T. A., 5, 62
West, Rebecca, 97
Weston, Harold, 68
What Price Glory (Walsh, 1926), 126
While Parents Sleep (Brunel, 1935), 190
White, James, 30, 73, 75
White Rose, The (Griffith, 1923), 31
White Shadow, The (Cutts, 1924), 88, 139
Wilcox, Herbert, 36, 120
Wilde, Oscar, 78
Wimperis, Arthur, 192
Winn, Godfrey, 97, 123, 124, 130, 204
Woman to Woman (Cutts, 1923), 87, 118, 122, 139
Woman Who Did (Die Frau mit dem schlechten Ruf), The (Christensen, 1925), 34
Wonder Women of the World series (1923), 49
Wong, Anna May, 184
Woolf, C. M., 8, 33, 34, 116, 118, 196
  and adaptations, 139
  and *Blighty*, 122, 123
  and burlesques, 104, 112
  and *The Constant Nymph*, 162
  and *A Light Woman*, 177
Woolf, Virginia, 142, 143

$X + X = 0$ (Salt, 1936), 92

Yellow Caesar (Cavalcanti, 1941), 196
Ypres (Summers, 1925), 120, 136

Zelnick, Frederick, 190

EU representative:
Easy Access System Europe
Mustamäe tee 50, 10621 Tallinn, Estonia
Gpsr.requests@easproject.com

www.ingramcontent.com/pod-product-compliance
Lightning Source LLC
Chambersburg PA
CBHW071838230426
43671CB00012B/1994